Rights and Persons

Rights and Persons

———

A. I. MELDEN

UNIVERSITY OF CALIFORNIA PRESS
Berkeley and Los Angeles

TO
MY WIFE
AND
DAUGHTERS

———————

UNIVERSITY OF CALIFORNIA PRESS
Berkeley and Los Angeles, California

ISBN: 0-520-03839-8
Library of Congress Catalog Card Number: 77-80180
© A.I. Melden, 1977
First Paperback Printing, 1980

Printed in the United States of America

Contents

Preface

In this work I try to explain why and how it is that rights are of central importance in morals. Not infrequently, however, and especially so to those who are disadvantaged by the accidents of birth, race, social or economic position, the talk by persons about their rights appears only to serve the interests of the advantaged. Indeed, philosophical doctrines of rights have even been cited or advanced in order to defend what appears to many to be economic privilege and inequity. One of the main objectives of this work is to dispel this misconception. The appeal to moral rights, one's own or those of others, may be made with moral propriety or impropriety, depending upon circumstances. For moral rights, as I shall argue, may be enjoyed justifiably, not against, but only with humanity; the fears and suspicions of those who associate any coherent doctrine of moral rights with social inequity and injustice are altogether unfounded.

I owe much to many for the help they have given me in commenting on the ideas presented here, preeminently but not exclusively the following: those who attended the American Studies seminar I taught in Kyoto, Japan during the summer of 1974; the students in seminars I have taught at Irvine; Professor H. J. McCloskey; Mr. Michael Martin who was also helpful in preparing the index; and especially Professor D. Z. Phillips whose detailed comments and queries enabled me to avoid error and clarify my expositions and arguments.

Thanks are due also to the editor of *The Monist* for permission to incorporate into Chapter I materials from an article of mine published in that journal in October 1972, and to the Rockefeller Foundation for the residency granted me in the fall of 1975 at their Bellagio Study and Conference Center during which I completed an important phase of my work on this book.

I

Introduction

Actions which otherwise would be arbitrary or capricious may be quite reasonable when they are in fact cases in which rights are being exercised or accorded. But a reason that may be decisive in normal circumstances may not be so when, unpredictably, complicating factors intervene. Sometimes, and unavoidably so, we are forced to choose between according or exercising a right and following still another line of conduct for which there is also good supporting reason. Rights conflict with rights. Indeed, they conflict in the demands they make upon us with moral considerations to which the concept of a right does not seem to apply at all: the requirement that we help someone in need, the generosity or kindness we ought to extend to persons simply out of love and affection for them, and even the humane treatment we ought to give animals unable to fend for themselves.

It has long been fashionable to decry the view that there are any rights, even those traditionally labelled 'natural', or 'human', which are absolute in the very special sense that they cannot yield under any conceivable circumstances. To say in this sense that a right is absolute is to say that, no matter what the circumstances may be, a person possessing such a right is fully justified in demanding, asserting or exercising, and others always wrong in denying him, his right. Viewed in this way an absolute right is, morally speaking, a note that is payable on demand. It is this doctrine of the rights of human beings which Jeremy Bentham attributed to the authors of the French Assembly's 'Declaration of the Rights of Man' in 1789, and, presumably but not explicitly, to John Locke, whose *Second Treatise of Government* is the important source of the French and American concept of imprescriptable or inalienable rights. But there is in fact no warrant for supposing that Locke or any other reputable thinker ever held such a mindless doctrine of absolute rights, a doctrine that would indeed merit Bentham's scathing description 'nonsense upon stilts'. (Cf. *Anarchical Fallacies*.)[1] In any case Bentham's attack has had this important consequence: it became a long-lasting item of philosophical folklore that the concept of human or natural rights is, as Hume would have put it, more popular than philosophical, an efficacious rallying point for political causes that is, nonetheless, conceptually incoherent because it involves the irrational view that there are rights which everyone must be accorded without limitations or restraints of any sort, either of private conscience or of public good.

In recent years, however, there has been a revival of interest in the doctrine of human rights, stripped however of the absurd idea that such rights may be exercised and accorded under any and all circumstances, and without reference to any sort of rational constraints. In order to pursue this matter further, however, it is necessary to prepare the ground by discussing in this and the next several chapters, and in considerable detail, not only the manner in which rights function as grounds of action but also the place of rights in the broader scheme of moral concepts.

II

Traditionally, attention has been paid to rights almost exclusively in respect of their role in justifying conduct, so much so that thinkers representing very different philosophical traditions have been led to attempt to elucidate the concept of a right in terms of what it is right or obligatory for persons to do. Scholastics like Maritain, for example, have attempted to derive the right that a person has to his life from the duty he has to preserve and achieve the fullness of his being.[2] A more familiar kind of move of this general type is made by Ewing who identifies rights with 'powers or securities of a kind such that the individual can rightly demand of others that they should not morally interfere with them'.[3] (I ignore the equivocation in this talk about powers; but, setting this aside, the question of how rightful demands can be made remains unresolved in this account.) And a suggestion coming this time from a member of a very different tradition, and dictated by the identification of moral with institutional matters, is to be found in Bradley's essay 'My Station and Its Duties'; the claim by him that there can be no rights without duties, and no duties without rights, is simply his way of collapsing the rights of persons into their duties as defined by their stations in life. Indeed, this idea that moral talk about rights can be collapsed somehow into talk about what it is right or obligatory to do is suggested by Kant's attempt to subsume considerations involving rights, along with those that do not, under what he considers to be the morally fundamental concept of duty. Thus the duty of beneficence that does not involve the idea of a right to the help we ought to give those in need, is labelled 'an imperfect duty' on the ground that the duty turns on inclination: the desire for assistance by those in need and the consideration that those offering it are also subject to this desire. The duty of promise-keeping (a duty to others) and that of preserving one's life (a duty to oneself) would appear to involve rights and hence the duty to the promisee and to oneself, respectively, not to violate the right in question; but this distinctive feature of these duties is obscured by Kant's talk of these duties as perfect, on the ground that inclinations are morally irrelevant.[4] And the subsumption of both sorts of requirements under the general concept of duty, i.e. of what one is, by virtue of the moral law, duty-bound to do at least suggests and certainly fosters the idea, later taken up by others, that 'duty' or 'ought' talk is more fundamental than talk about rights,[5] and that it is possible to define or elucidate the concept of a right in terms of what it is that one ought, is duty-bound or is right for one, to do. At the very least what is implied is that what is of central and paramount importance in the idea of the right of a person is the notion of the duties he has to perform in the connection with them.

But if this is true, then we are back again, this time with respect to what it is that one ought to do, to the kinds of conflicts we noted in the case of rights. We ought or are duty-bound to keep our promises; but unless we hold as Kant is often supposed to have held that the obligation of promises admits of no exception, not merely because of inclination, but for any other possible reason, we shall be forced to concede that in a specific case the obligation to keep a given promise might well yield before some more pressing consideration. For surely some promises turn out, when the opportunities to keep them arise, to be far less important than they were supposed to be when they were made; and in the face of the extreme need even of a

stranger, when a choice must be made between keeping such promises and helping those in need, the duty of promise-keeping must
yield before the so-called duty of beneficence. Admittedly one ought
to keep one's promises; one would rightly suspect someone who
seriously claimed to be rejecting this precept that he simply did not
understand what he was saying. But this does not settle the question
whether, here and now, in such-and-such circumstances, one ought
or is duty-bound or, to put it another way, that it is right for one, to
keep one's promise. For it may be the better part of moral wisdom to
break one's promise in order to help a stranger in need, or, in quite
different circumstances, to turn away from someone in need in order
to keep one's word.

It is the fact that sentences, in which 'ought' occurs as in the
examples I have just cited, can be employed in two different ways,
first, in order to cite a moral consideration that needs to be weighed
in order to determine what one is required to do, and, second, in
order to state a moral conclusion concerning what it is that this,
taken together with any other relevant moral consideration, requires
one to do in a particular situation, that has led W. D. Ross, and a host
of writers who have followed him, to speak of two kinds of 'oughts'
(and so too with other deontic terms like 'duty', 'obligation', and
'right' as an adjective qualifying an action verb), one a *prima facie* and
the other an 'ought' *simpliciter* or *sans phrase*.[6] It is clear that for Ross,
'*prima facie*' is employed as a technical term; for to say as he does that
something is a *prima facie* duty is not to say that it is, *prima facie*, a
duty. That is to say, '*prima facie*' does not refer us to something
merely apparent or presumptive. For a *prima facie* duty, according to
Ross, is a genuine or objective matter, the fact that it is merely *prima
facie* implying that it may not, given other morally relevant features,
establish the action in question as the morally required act, the act
that is one's duty *tout court*. A *prima facie* duty, he tells us, is a kind of
duty, not in the sense in which the duty to keep a promise is one kind
of duty and the duty to help those in need another; it is, rather, that
feature of a genuine duty that would make the act in question one's
actual duty, i.e. one's duty *sans phrase*, were it not for the possibility
that might well be realized in a given case that there is some other
prima facie duty, which, as a no less real kind of duty and stemming
from other considerations pertinent to the given situation, would
then and there constitute the agent's duty *simpliciter* or *sans phrase*.

What precisely that feature is that serves as the attribute of duty designated by the phrase '*prima facie*', Ross appears unable to say. He first suggests the notion of a tendency; a *prima facie* duty tends to be one's duty.[7] And he even suggests that this is the notion embodied in the conception of laws of nature, the idea being that, for example, 'the law of gravitation enables us to recognize that each body tends to move in a particular direction with a particular velocity; but its actual movement depends on all the forces to which it is subject'.[8] Unfortunately, the notion of tendency is eliminable by means of a conditional clause such as the following: if no other forces operate upon a body, the law of gravitation states precisely its movement as such-and-such. And if we accept this analogy, the obligation of promises could be put in some such way as the following: that if no other obligations are present, then one is duty-bound to keep one's promises. In that case, the notion of a *prima facie* duty would be definable in terms of duties *sans phrase*. It would follow that in the event that some other obligation is more stringent in any given situation, there would be nothing in the form of an obligation to keep the promise that remains, and no regret, no compunction, that one need feel because of the more stringent obligation that prevailed which required one to break one's solemn word. But if this translation of a conditional duty signified by the expression '*prima facie* duty' is disallowed, we are confronted by other problems not the least of which is the obscure ontology suggested by the word 'tendency'. In that case the explanation of the obscurity involved in the alleged technical use of '*prima facie* duty' threatens us with unintelligibility. And this is precisely what happens on Ross's account. For he warns us that the notion of a tendency involved in the concept of a *prima facie* duty is not a causal relation, one that involves succession in time. He tells us that it is more like that which connects the attributes of a mathematical figure; but he is evidently uneasy about this matter. For in the end he seems to give up any hope of being able to offer a satisfactory explanation when he declares that 'if the word "tendency" is thought to suggest too much a causal relation, it is better to talk of certain types of acts as being *prima facie* right or wrong . . . than of their tendency to be right or wrong'.[9] But unless this is a return to the ordinary and quite non-technical use of the expression '*prima facie*' to mark something presumptive or apparent, the suggestion, coming as it does at the end of an attempted explanation of a proposed technical use of the qualifying expression, is tantamount to a confession of failure to provide any kind of explanation.

One way out of these difficulties has recently been offered by John Rawls which he bases on a suggestion made by Donald Davidson.[10] On Davidson's account, *'prima facie'* does not mark an attribute of the moral predicate of an action although grammatically this would appear to be the case if, following Ross, one were to say that a given action is *prima facie* obligatory. Neither does *'prima facie'* serve as an operator or modifier for a sentence as a whole, although grammatically it would appear to do so if one were to say of a given action x, *'Prima facie*, I ought to do x.' Like 'other things being equal' and 'all things considered', *'prima facie'* marks, rather, a relation between sentences or propositions, a relation of judgment and grounds. Specifically, what 'I have a *prima facie* duty to do x' expresses is that there is 'a relation between a judgment and a part or the whole of the system of principles that defines its grounds'.[11]

Now Rawls speaks of principles as grounds which 'allow the reasons they define to support contrary lines of conduct in particular cases, as indeed often they do, without involving us in a contradiction'.[12] And Davidson on whom he says he bases his account also speaks of the moral principles that are involved in the particular judgments we make about what it is that *prima facie* we ought to do. What sorts of principles are they?

For Davidson they are the quite familiar moral principles like 'lying is wrong' and 'promises ought to be kept'. Ross supposed that these are universally quantified propositions about all cases of lying and all cases of promising to the effect, respectively, that all cases of lying are *prima facie* wrong and all cases of promise-keeping are *prima facie* obligatory, where *'prima facie'* functions as a modifier of, respectively, the moral predicates 'wrong' and 'obligatory'. And in saying about a given act x on a particular occasion that *prima facie* one ought or ought not to perform it, he supposed that one could 'detach' the modifier *'prima facie'* from the ground specified by the relevant moral principle. Davidson's view is that the moral principle 'One ought to keep promises' to which, as principle, the concept of *prima facie* applies, asserts that there is a relation between something's being an act of promise-keeping and that thing's being obligatory such that the former serves as ground for the latter. And his view is that to assert that *prima facie* this particular act x, where x is the act of keeping a promise, is obligatory, is implicitly to invoke the moral principle which, as a *prima facie* moral principle, asserts that there is this relation of ground to moral judgment between something's being an act of promise-keeping and that thing's being obligatory. Davidson goes no further in attempting to set forth why it is that this relation of ground to judgment should hold. Indeed, he repudiates the view that it is possible to formulate principles that can function as universally quantified conditional propositions that might serve as premises in our moral reasoning; and he explicitly rejects the view that where there are cases of conflict between principles, there are ordering principles that tell us which take precedence over the others.[13]

Rawls, however, appears to take a different line. For while he regards the principle of fidelity, which states that bona fide promises are to be kept[14] as a *prima facie* principle — one that provides a reason sufficient or not as it may be for performing a given act, namely, that it is the keeping of a bona fide promise — he does attempt to explain why it is a reason. And to this end he cites what he takes to be fundamental principles which do appear to take the form of universally quantified propositions.

Consider an analogy employed by Davidson, that if there are red skies tonight, probably it will not rain tomorrow, where the proposition that probably it will not rain tomorrow cannot be detached from the proposition that red skies tonight probabilizes that it will not rain tomorrow, and where, too, 'probably' cannot be construed as an attribute of the event or state of affairs rendered probable. In this case (although this is not implied by Davidson's remarks) it is at least plausible that there are universally quantified propositions — the relevant causal laws of nature — which explain why it is that the occurrence of red skies tonight probabilizes the absence of rain tomorrow. In a similar vein Rawls argues that we can employ the principle of fairness which

holds that a person is required to do his part as defined by the rules of an institution when two conditions are met: first, the institution is just (or fair), that is, it satisfies the two principles of justice; and second, one has voluntarily accepted the benefits of the arrangement or taken advantage of the opportunities it offers to further one's interests.[15]

Now his principles of justice, although couched in the form of universally quantified propositions about what it is that each person is to have, and what arrangements are to be made, apply to institutions, not to acts. In order to maintain the parallel for the case of the presumed causal laws that explain why it is that red skies tonight probabilizes no rain tomorrow, we need universally quantified conditional propositions about acts that are morally necessary comparable to the events or states of weather that are causally necessary given the requisite causal facts and laws. And for this purpose we do appear to have, in Rawls's account, the universally quantified conditional proposition stated in the principle of fairness that anyone who has voluntarily accepted the arrangement of a just or reasonably just institution is required to do his part in maintaining it, this consisting in acting in conformity with the constitutive rule of the institution, namely, that if one has said 'I promise to do x', one is to do x.[16] Presumably the institution so-called of promising is just or reasonably just. If it is not, then the principle of fairness fails to apply and we are left completely in the dark as to why the fact that one has promised is any ground for the performance of the promise-keeping act. If on the other hand, as it indeed appears to be the case from Rawls's discussion of the matter, the so-called institution of promising is reasonably just, the argument proves too little or too much. Too little, for if the argument shows merely that the fact that an act of promise-keeping is a ground that may or may not be sufficient for establishing the rightness of that action, then Rawls's moral principles are inadequate to establish the moral rightness of acts, and require supplementation by means of other morally relevant considerations, perhaps his so-called natural duties. But Rawls nowhere offers us any priority rules on this matter, as he does in the case of his principles of justice, rules which would enable us to determine when the ground he offers for the rightness of promise-keeping acts is or is not sufficient.[17] It follows, therefore, that it is not only in the non-ideal world of unjust institutions but in the ideal world of a just institution that Rawls must abandon his anti-intuitional or anti-pluralistic position, one that calls for principles and priority rules that will enable us infallibly to resolve the conflicts that arise when we are confronted by competing moral considerations.[18] But if Rawls is to avoid this outcome, his argument proves far too much. Too much, because it seems to imply that every case of conformity with the so-called rule of promising — that if one has said 'I promise to do x', one is to go on to do x — is morally right, thus providing an explanation of the relation of ground to moral judgment, the relation of the fact that something is a case of keeping a promise to the fact that is morally right, which transforms that relation into one that makes the ground a sufficient ground that may never be overridden by any other consideration.

I shall postpone until later in Chapter IV an examination in greater detail of Rawls's treatment of the obligation of promising; but for the present it may be sufficient to remark that Rawls's discussion, in which he attempts to explain the reason why the fact that an act is a case of keeping a promise is a good reason for performing that act, omits mention of what is of central importance in the case of the so-called obligation of promises, namely, the fact that in the case of a promise, it is not a rule that we have — that if one has promised anything one is to do it, given that one is to be fair in enjoying the benefits of the 'institutional' arrangement of promising— but a right that has been conferred. I shall argue in the next chapter that this right is the consideration that provides a warrant for the promise-keeping act, not rules or principles that take the form of universally quantified propositions about what it is that one is (morally or not) required to do. And if this is correct, any attempt to provide any explanation of why it is that one may be morally required to keep a promise— analogous to that explanation which hopefully one could provide, in terms of the relevant causal laws and facts, of why it is that it is likely the case, given red skies tonight, that there will be no rain tomorrow—must be abandoned. It is the neglect of rights and the preoccupation with what persons are or are not *to do* that has led philosophers down this garden path.

Now it is precisely because of the preoccupation with what it is that persons ought *to do* that leads Ross to reject an interesting suggestion made by Prichard, namely, that we employ the word 'claim' rather than '*prima facie* duty'. Ross objects that this is in effect to restrict the cases that we want to consider to those in which the duty arises from a claim that one person makes on or has against another, these being cases in which, as he puts it, the duties involve just two persons or, as we might say, obligations involving the correlative rights of others.[19] Ross also remarks that 'claim' does not apply to 'that important part of duty which is the duty of cultivating a certain kind of character in oneself'; yet it seems hard to understand why one should want to qualify the duty morally to improve one-self. Could this duty to oneself yield in the face of a competing consideration? Would the supreme self-sacrifice be an example of a 'duty', one that takes precedence over the duty to improve oneself? In any case, the restriction to cases involving two persons is not quite accurate. For two can join in promising some cooperative action to a third which neither can make good by his own efforts. And, do I not have a claim on a number of persons to go about my affairs without interference from them? In any case, Ross does object to Prichard's term 'claim' on the ground that even those cases in which the duty in question is the correlative of a right, the word 'claim' is appropriate to the point of view, not of the agent who is concerned with the performance of his duty, but of the person having the claim on the agent, or, as we should say, the person having the right. And he remarks in this connection that for the case in which one person has a claim on or against another which the latter can honor by an act he performs, 'ordinary language provides us with . . . no correlative to "claim"' that is appropriate to the point of view of the agent.[20]

On this point, surely Ross is mistaken. It is quite natural to say, in those cases in which A has a claim on B (or, a right *vis à vis* B), that B is under an obligation to A, or that B has a duty to A. It is important that we notice the prepositional phrases that follow the words 'obligation' and 'duty'; for unlike the cases on which Ross fastens his attention, where the talk is about what it is that a person ought *to do*, the notion of an obligation or duty expressed by these quite natural sorts of locutions, is the notion of an obligation or a duty *to a person*, an obligation or duty that one can discharge or meet only by doing what this obligation or duty to the person requires one to do.

Now why should Ross, and others who have followed him, neglect the fact that 'obligation' and 'duty' can carry prepositional phrases that mark the moral relations between persons, on the basis of which there are requirements imposed upon agents to do certain sorts of things? It would be a mistake, in my opinion, to say that the neglect is simply an oversight. It is true that Ross like others was concerned to catch, in the same coarse net, the obligations we have not only to persons but the obligations we have to do the various sorts of things required of us in order that we might meet our obligations to others, and even the things we ought to do, which do not appear to involve any rights at all, such as the help and kindness we ought to extend to others, even strangers. The troublesome word here is 'obligation', philosopher's coin for any item of conduct, whatever its ground may be. This may appear to be nothing less and nothing worse than a typical philosophical craving for generality. But I believe that the neglect of the prepositional phrase that marks the moral relation of one person to another, that constitutes the right of one person *vis à vis* another, really stems from an unperspicuous view of the subject matter of morality itself. For given the pre-occupying concern of Ross, and of many if not most recent writers, with the problems that center on the notion of rights acts, i.e. the notion of what it is that one ought to do, the view of morality itself becomes constricted. It is not the neglect of linguistic forms or the craving for generality that leads to such a narrowed conception of the subject matter of morality, but the reverse. Given the preoccupation what it is that you and I, here and now, ought to do, with what generally or universally persons are duty-bound to do, inattention to these characteristic linguistic idioms follows. But there is much more to moral philosophy than what it is that we are required to do, and unless this much more is kept in mind, there can be no light thrown even on those matters on which the moral philosopher focuses his attention: the question of what makes right acts right.

There are very many things we ought to do, and for ever so many different reasons, many or most of which have nothing to do with morality. But among the moral reasons we have for acting in this or that way is the fact that we would be meeting some obligation we have to another person, i.e. according a person something to which he has a right. But to say 'I ought to do x because of the obligation I have to A' is not to stutter 'I ought to do x because I ought to do it'. Nor is this like a child's 'Because', which offers us only the verbal preface but without the content that might serve as a justification. On the contrary, 'I ought to do x because of my obligation to A' does refer to a ground for the act in question by citing a consideration that justifies the action. The justification here is the obligation to a person, or, correlatively and equivalently, the right that a person has that bears upon the given act. Without this ground the act may well be arbitrary, eccentric or unfair, an act that lacks any sort of justification.

III

My concern is not to argue that we must not employ *'prima facie'* in locutions about what it is that one ought to do. Clearly, sentences about what it is that ought to be done can be employed not only to state what it is that one is duty-bound to do, given due consideration to all of the relevant facts in a given situation, but also to state a relevant moral consideration to which attention needs to be paid in arriving at such a moral decision. And if one wishes, following Davidson's suggestion, to employ '*prima facie*' to mark the latter employments of sentences about what ought to be done, there need be no objection. My concern, rather, is with the question of why it is that the fact, for example, that an act is a case of promise-keeping is a good reason, insufficient as it may prove to be in a given situation, for performing that act. For here, and in other cases too, the notion of a right is of central importance.

Now it would be unfair to claim that the concept of rights has been completely ignored even by those who take the question of what one is duty-bound to do to be of central importance for moral philosophy. Ross, for example, does touch on the subject of rights, in a brief appendix to a chapter entitled 'What Makes Right Acts Right?' (*The Right and the Good*, pp. 55–64). Here, as in his earlier discussions of duty, he introduces the qualifying expression '*prima facie*', this time speaking of cases in which *prima facie* a person may be said to have a right, thereby suggesting (but not explicitly stating) that as in the case of duties one might wish to employ the expression '*prima facie* rights' in order to speak about the rights a person may be said to have even in the cases in which it may not be right to exercise them or for others to accord them. It is this suggested use of '*prima facie*' with which I am primarily concerned, for here the mischief can be and has proved to be much more serious.

We are often told, to consider a familiar instance, that the right of property is not absolute, but only *prima facie*. Now certainly no one is entitled to do what he wills, and as any passing fancy, whim, or emotion moves him, with anything he owns. That point was made long ago by Plato in Book I of the *Republic*. Conspicuously, there are many sorts of reasons why a person ought not to be permitted to exercise his property rights. But as a term of contrast with 'absolute' in this sense of the term, '*prima facie*' serves no useful purpose. Locke, for example, spoke about absolute rights but not in this absurd sense of the term. He recognized full well that, to consider only one type of case, a person is subject to fines and other penalties that deprive him of his property because of his misdeeds. Speaking of the absolute power— clearly, the right— of military commanders in the field to issue orders to their inferior officers and troops in the field, Locke explicitly declares that their power 'is not arbitrary by being absolute, but is still limited by that reason, and confined to those ends which required it in some cases to be absolute'.[21] But readers of

Bentham, who seem to have felt it unnecessary to read Locke and to discern what Locke intended, have felt it necessary to declare, apropos of Locke's declaration that men have an absolute right to property, that this right is not absolute but only *prima facie*. Yet this is to misconstrue the sense in which Locke employs the term 'absolute'. For an absolute right is a right that human beings have qua human beings and not, as in the case of special rights, rights that they have only if certain conditions, which pertain to their social relations and the transactions in which they engage with one another, are satisfied. A military commander, Locke thought, had the *de jure* power, i.e. the right, to issue commands to his troops, qua commander, and not as in the case of the right that he might have to withhold part of a subordinate's pay, only if the latter has authorized him to do so by means of a suitable legal instrument. There is no warrant for the popular misconception that in thinking as he did that the right of property is absolute, Locke ever intended that anyone could do whatever he wished and whenever he was moved to do so, for whatever reason that might be, with anything in which he has a property right.

Other writers not given to such talk about Locke, but mindful of the fact that a right may or may not be overridden in its justificatory function with respect to conduct, have followed Ross's suggestion that, as in the case of duties, rights may be *'prima facie'* or 'actual', the thought being that they are 'actual' only when they succeed in justifying relevant items of conduct. On this view while the right of property may not be absolute in the foregoing sense of the term, it will be 'actual' when in a given situation it prevails even in the face of competing rights or other moral considerations. In this way of speaking *'prima facie'* and 'actual' appear to serve as modifiers of 'rights', corresponding to the way in which they were supposed by Ross to serve as modifiers of moral qualities of acts such as 'right' and 'obligatory'. Accordingly, we are told that there are different senses of the term 'right', indeed, that this term may be ambiguous.[22] Indeed, one writer even speaks of a *'prima facie'* and an 'absolute' sense of 'right', once more citing the fact that in a given situation the right in question may justify the act of according the person his right, in which case it is an absolute right, whereas in other situations it may not, in which case it is only a *'prima facie'* right.[23] This merely compounds the confusion surrounding the use of 'absolute right' in the philosophical literature. For on this way of speaking, if a person's right to the ten dollars, which I promised I would give him, is decisive in establishing that I ought to give him the ten dollars, then his right is absolute. Whatever else may be said about this use of the word, it surely obscures the point of the popular clamor against any suggestion that there is an absolute right to private property according to which one is always justified, *no matter what*, in demanding or exercising it. In any case, it is surely strange, to say that a right in one sense of the term— a *prima facie* sense of 'right'— becomes a right in another sense of the term— an 'actual' (or absolute) sense of 'right', on the ground that in a given situation the right in question succeeds in its justificatory function. This would be like saying that a good reason or item of evidence that is not sufficient and hence decisive in a given case in establishing the truth of a given proposition becomes a reason or item of evidence in a different sense of 'reason' or 'evidence' when, in altered circumstances, it is indeed sufficient or decisive. And since one does on occasion encounter the philosophical talk about *prima facie* evidence and *prima facie* reasons—talk clearly inspired by Ross's earlier talk about *prima facie* duties— one should be prepared even for the suggestion that 'reason' and 'evidence' are employed for the reason given, in different senses. Talk about rights may or may not serve to justify claims that given acts are right; but this no more validates the conclusion that 'right' admits of different senses, than the fact that talk about cats may or may not serve to justify the conclusion that the speaker is a cat-fancier validates the claim that 'cat' admits of different senses — a cat-fancier's and a non-cat-fancier's sense of that word.

It is one thing for a person to have a right. It is another for him to be justified by virtue of that right in doing the various things involved in exercising it. Correlatively, it is one thing to be under an obligation to someone, and it is another thing to be justified by that consideration, in specific circumstances, in meeting that obligation. It does not follow from the fact that one may or may not be justified in exercising one's right, that there are different senses of 'right'; and it does not follow from the fact that in specific situations one may or may not be justified in meeting one's obligation to others, that 'being under an obligation to someone' has different senses.

Nor will it do, following a suggestion considered earlier for the case of the concept of duty, to contend that *'prima facie'* marks a relation between sentences ascribing rights to persons and moral principles, the force of this being that there is good (although perhaps not sufficient) reason for ascribing such rights to the persons concerned. The objection to this is not that such a move provides us with no ordering relation that would enable us to ascertain under what circumstances any given ascription of a right to a person would or would not give way in the face of any competing consideration. It is rather that it succeeds only in bringing into question every claim to the possession of a right for which the expression *'prima facie'* is appropriate. For on the present suggestion it will no more follow from the fact that one's moral principles provide reason for ascribing a right to a person that he *has* the right, than it follows from one's causal principles together with the fact that the sky is red tonight, that it will not in fact rain tomorrow. But if I have promised someone such-and-such then he does have a right to what it is that I have promised, and even when that right must give way in the face of an unexpected but more compelling consideration, the right that I gave him by the promise I made remains the troublesome factor it is. Unlike the case of the red skies of the previous evening which are followed by rain, we do not explain away the right and proceed happily to ignore it.

The use of *'prima facie'* in connection with rights, paralleling that introduced by Ross for the case of duty, suggests, in fact, that rights are putative or apparent unless they succeed in their justificatory function. If, however, one does have a right, its status as a right is not compromised by the fact that in special circumstances it must give way or yield in the face of other competing considerations. To have a right is to stand in a moral relation with respect to some one or more persons, and that relation does not simply disappear when, in recognition of it along with other relevant considerations, it is deemed appropriate to infringe or to refuse to accord a person his right. We need to look more carefully, not merely at the role of rights in justifying a given action as one that ought to be performed — the act of according or exercising a right — but also at some of the other complicated features of the conceptual terrain in which the concept of a right has its place. The mischief created by Ross's suggestion is that it simply obscures these matters from our view.

IV

Consider the case in which I have conferred a right on some person by means of a promise. Suppose that, unexpectedly, circumstances justify me in breaking my word. Surely this is not the end of the matter. Unlike an unrealized tendency, unlike the *prima facie* guilt of an innocent man that fails to stand up under examination, unlike the evidence for a conclusion that turns out to be insufficient, unlike a good reason for doing something which as it happens is counterbalanced by weightier reasons against the given action, and unlike a legal case that one person has on another which justifies holding a hearing but which is resolved in the latter's favor, the right one has conferred upon the person to whom the promise was made does not simply wither away or cease to concern us. Yet this is what is suggested by each of these models that have been proposed, in order to explain the fact that rights may yield to other considerations. It is noteworthy, however, that even Ross himself does acknowledge the fact that when we are obliged to break our promises we do so with some compunction, although why this should be so and why remedy, restitution or any other suitable form of conduct appears to be required of the promise-breaker, Ross does not venture to explore, and, understandably so, given his preoccupation with the bearing of the so-called obligation of promises simply upon the rightness of the promise-keeping act. But in giving a person my solemn word, I put myself under an obligation to him, that is to say, I confer a right upon him which he has *vis à vis* me, one which calls for a performance or abstention of the kind specified in the promise locution. It is this relation that is established by the transaction of promising, the features of which we need to articulate in some detail, a relation that characteristically is ignored by those who speak of *prima facie* rights, and which explains the compunction I must feel when, even justifiably, I break my solemn word. And it is this same relation that explains why in cases of this sort new requirements are imposed upon me, the promise-breaker. Indeed, attention to the complex moral character of this relation will enable us to see why it is that the person to whom I made my promise, invested as he was with a moral right, must be prepared for his part, possibly to waive his right, or even to relinquish it, and, should neither of these measures be open to him, to be ready to forgive and forget the transgression against him.

But, first, is there some order of relative stringency in which the right of promisees stands to other relevant considerations? To begin with, is it the case, as some might be inclined to think, that a right may yield only to another right, that, as Ross supposed Kant intended, the so-called perfect duty of promise-keeping takes precedence over any imperfect duty so-called, e.g. the duty we have to help those in need? Important as it may be for him, the fact that a stranger needs my help does not in itself establish that he has a right to it; and granted that I ought to give him help it is not always or even generally true that I ought to do so because I am under any obligation to him. The fact that my help will benefit him is reason enough; we do not need to inject any of the heavy moral overtones of the concept of a right in order to recognize that helping someone is a good moral reason for doing just that, and that an indifference towards those who are in need is reprehensible — because it is moral callousness, not because it violates the rights of a person. But it takes no great imagination to conceive of endlessly many cases in which the keeping of a promise, for indefinitely many different sorts of reasons (altered circumstances that affect the importance of what has been promised, to the promiser or to the promisee or to those who would be affected by the promise-keeping act, either because of their rights or because of other sorts of relevant considerations — one could go on to specify still other sorts of reasons without end) is far less important than the simple virtuous act of helping a needy stranger. Indeed, as Hume once put it, we are 'bound by the laws of humanity to give gentle usage' to inferior beings even though we are not 'under any restraint of justice with regard to them, nor could they possess any right or property'.[24] We ought to relieve animals of their distress; but it sounds queer to say, generally at least, that they have rights. Yet we can easily imagine cases in which the keeping of a promise, one that is of no more importance than the keeping of a casual engagement ('He promised to meet me here at one o'clock, but no matter— it isn't important'), is far less compelling than a humane act that relieves some beast of distress. And let the misery, indeed agony, of helpless creatures be great enough, then even a promise of very considerable importance may be weighed and found less pressing than the assistance we can give these creatures.

Is it more important to keep a promise than to help others — humans and even animals in need or in pain? Sometimes it is and sometimes it is not. Everything depends on circumstances. And so it is with any pair of considerations that in the widest possible sense of the term can be called moral. Any proposed ordering relation of priorities simply will not stand the test of instances.

It may be argued, however, that if there is any rationale to be found in the ways in which we do judge that any given consideration does or does not yield in such-and-such circumstances, there must be moral principles in the light of which such judgments are made. Otherwise, it will be contended, everything is left to intuition, than which notoriously nothing is more capricious.

But what sorts of principles are possible here? Not principles that set forth the ordering relations between rights, or between rights and other sorts of considerations; for there are no such rigid ordering relations. And it is not open to us to accept the utilitarian's method of attempting to deal with so-called conflicts of duties. A promise obliges, Period. Surely it is false that the recipients of promises have rights if and only if the acts of according them their rights is useful. Utility is one of the relevant considerations in the light of which we weigh the stringency of our obligations to those to whom we have given our word; but we do not establish that we are in fact under such obligations by determining whether it is useful to meet them. And even where we are led by the inutility of meeting such an obligation, to refrain from doing so, our moral debt is not thereby discharged. Nor will it do to opt for any other principles (the most recent conspicuous examples being those offered by Rawls) which omit any reference to rights. For without the involvement of rights there cannot be, as I shall argue, that attention to the relations between persons that is important to our moral concerns. In any case, the fact that there is some rationale in the ways in which we ponder competing considerations, and in the great majority of cases decide without hesitation which of them is to prevail, by no means establishes that there are principles that take the form of universally quantified propositions or imperatives. It may only show, as I shall argue in Chapter V, that the moral attitude is one in which we exhibit appropriate sensitivities in thought, feeling and action towards others out of a concern for them as we go about our affairs in ways that affect their and our own interests. It is this moral concern for others as persons, rather than principles and priority rules, which provides us with a rationale for resolving many or most of the moral conflicts that arise, easily and without any hesitation.

Second, suppose that there is some sort of conflict of duties. In some cases, rare as they may be, there may be no easy way out; indeed, we may be faced tragically with dilemmas in which we are morally damned if we do and damned if we don't, no matter how carefully we consider the situations in which we find ourselves enmeshed. Examples in literature readily come to mind from the *Antigone* on down to the writings of present-day existentialists; but there are on occasion terrible incidents that have in fact occurred which inspire only pity (not the reproof that is in order when moral blunders are made) for those hopelessly involved in such tragic situations. But let us turn to the vast majority of the cases in which a right competes with another and clearly a more compelling consideration. A solemn promise has been made and, with it, a right to a certain performance has been conferred. Much depends, let us assume, on keeping the promise, but clearly another and even more compelling consideration unexpectedly arises. The details for this outline of a scenario can easily be filled in: by all that is obvious and pertinent, the promise *must* be broken in order to meet an emergency. So one ought, in these circumstances and at that critical moment, unavoidably, to break the promise and in so doing infringe the right one has deliberately conferred upon another.

But this is not the end of the matter. It is not as if one had to choose between acting benevolently and acting prudently, where no consideration of rights is involved, and, where given the magnitude of the issues involved, it is clearly sufficient to point to them in self-justification, showing that a moderate display of beneficence would be purchased only at the cost of reducing one's own state to tatters. Here one can only regret that one's purse was not large enough to permit one to be both prudent and beneficent. Nor need there be any shame felt in the matter: there need be no sense of one's loss of moral stature, no painful sense of the loss of respect for one's self, and no sense of the loss of the respect that others might have for us, who might be or might have been witness to the proceedings. But reverse the situation, and let it be that in the specific circumstances of the case one had erred in an excessive concern with one's own interest, and suppose, therefore, that what one ought to have done was not to hoard one's goods for oneself, but benevolently to bestow some of them upon another. In such a case shame is surely in order. Yet this is not the sense of guilt one feels when, forced as one may have been by unlucky circumstances, one denies a person his right in breaking a solemn promise made to him. For the fact that reason requires that it is better to break the promise and act on the basis of a competing circumstance in no way shows that there is no infringement of a right. The lesser of two evils remains an evil however reasonable it is to choose it; and the denial of a right remains a transgression against another person, unavoidable as it may be. We do not blame someone who is required by circumstances to transgress against someone else in following as he does the right course of action. But we would morally fault someone who had no sense of guilt in the matter, who merely regretted the damage involved in his infringing the right of another. 'Regret' is too bland a term to employ for the state of mind of the person who realizes that he has infringed the right of another. It fails to convey what is important in the matter, not only that moral damage has been suffered by another human being — a matter of which any spectator may be sensible — but that it is *he*, the agent, who was responsible for it.

Third, whether the denial of a person's right derives from the superior force of some competing moral consideration, or from insensibility, indifference, negligence, forgetfulness, laziness, cupidity, stupidity, and so on, the person responsible must bear his appropriate moral burden. In some cases some form of reparation or restitution is possible. In other cases there is no way of making it up to the injured person. Depending upon circumstances, and with due regard to the degree of one's fault or guilt in addition to the feelings and sensitivities of the person who has not been accorded his right — apologies, an appropriate display of one's concern, remorse or sense of guilt, some excuse, explanation or even the act of begging for sympathy, forgiveness or pardon may be in order. This implies among other things, an understanding of and sensitivity to the feelings of others, an imagination that brings home the appreciation of the situation from the point of the person morally damaged, and a willingness to reconstruct for the better the moral relations with the other party. The abilities required are traits that are conspicuously absent in the boor, the self-centered and those of limited moral vision. The point here is not the platitude that these are, in general, virtuous traits, but rather the bearing they have on (a) the moral relations between the persons in preserving, promoting or restoring these relations in ways that foster the assurance that in the future the rights on both sides will be respected, and, if at all possible, accorded, and (b) the means they provide for the person who has violated the right of another, in one way or another, of purging himself of any guilt he may have incurred.

We need now to reverse the point of view involved in the two preceding comments and consider the situation from the point of view of the person who has suffered the moral damage. Accordingly, and in the fourth place, any person having a given right must be prepared for the possibility, however remote it may be, that his right may have to yield before more compelling circumstances, whatever these may be. He must be prepared for the possibility that it would be wrong for him to insist upon his right, and even when the other person is disposed to accord him his right, to proceed forthwith to exercise it. It may be right for him to refuse to exercise his right — there is no self-contradiction involved. In some of these cases, the person with the right ought to waive it, without relinquishing it, and still less without forfeiting it in the way in which parents forfeit their rights when, as we say, they are parents in name only. In other cases there is no further opportunity for according a person his right or for exercising it; nothing can be done later on to provide an equivalent. Parents who waive their rights in the interests of their children's happiness sometimes die long before their children are able to provide them with suitable recompense for their sacrifices. Yet it remains the case that a person with a right, but who recognizes that it should yield in the face of a more pressing or important consideration, may suffer moral injury in relinquishing his right. To say that he is wronged carries with it the notion that he is wrongfully denied his right; yet the injury he suffers, gladly as he accepts it when he waives or yields his right, is in its effect what happens to him when someone violates his right.

What precisely the nature of this *moral* damage is, as distinguished from the *natural* evils to which persons are prone through no doing of anyone, I shall have occasion to discuss in exploring how it is that a promise confers a right and why it is that the breaking of a promise constitutes the moral injury it is. For the present it is important to notice that we need not blame someone who willingly relinquishes his right or waives it. Similarly, *we* must recognize that in choosing reasonably, as other persons sometimes do, to infringe the rights of others when they are forced by competing moral considerations to do so, they bring moral damage to others without moral fault on their part, although it is not unreasonable for them— they would be morally insensitive if this were not so— to appreciate with a sense of guilt the moral damage they brought to pass.

And, fifth, however it is that one has been denied his rights, whether by the wrongful acts of others or by the forced but reasonable decisions they make when they infringe his right because of competing but more compelling moral considerations, there are moral burdens that he must bear in dealing with those who have caused him moral damage. Paramount is the requirement that he maintain unimpaired the good moral relations in which he stands to others. And if these relations are threatened or eroded by the apparent moral failures of others, he must endeavor, in response to the explanations and excuses they offer, the indications they give of their remorse and sense of guilt, the restitutions and amends they make for the violation of his rights, the pardon or forgiveness they seek, and so on, to help restore and make secure once more his good moral relations with them. To lust for revenge, to nurse one's grievances or to relish the sight of others' remorse or suffering from their sense of guilt, is not only to demonstrate one's own defects of moral character, it is also to cut off from us those who may well be worthy of our respect because of the measures they have taken to purge themselves of their guilt they have incurred and who are now prepared, if we give them the opportunity, to conduct themselves towards us as moral equals and in good faith.

V

One purpose of this work is to discredit the widely held assumption that what is of paramount importance is the question of what it is that one ought to do and, accordingly, that it is upon this matter that attention needs to be focussed. It has even been suggested that in reading Plato this question should be understood as the one with which he was really concerned in asking for the nature of justice.[25] But if we take Plato to be continually keeping his eye on the question, 'What ought we to do?' we shall surely miss what he takes to be of central importance in morals, namely, virtue and vice— the health and disease of the soul respectively — of which right and wrong conduct are only external manifestations. And if we adopt the modern lead of those who take moral philosophy's task to be that of delineating the good reasons for acts which establish them as right or obligatory, we shall lose sight of the important features of the moral relations between persons, and the moral requirements imposed upon them by virtue of these relations that constitute the rights and obligations they have with respect to one another.

A full treatment of the importance of rights in morals cannot be given in a few words, and I shall develop this topic as the argument unfolds.[26] But it may be useful at this point to comment on the singular insight revealed in a remark made by Frederick Douglass, the black leader in the Abolitionist Movement in mid-nineteenth-century America, when he broke with Garrison. Abolitionists in the north, presenting their case against the quality of the treatment of the blacks in the south, stressed the fact that blacks were endowed with those capacities exhibited by whites who were cultivated in the arts and acknowledged scholars and scientists. The appeal made was to the humanity, benevolence or sympathy of whites in witnessing the suffering of the blacks, and the failure in slave America to provide them with the opportunities to develop their talents and enjoy a measure of happiness through the cultivation of their intellectual and aesthetic capacities. So conceived, the role of the blacks in the Abolitionist Movement was passive, designed to demonstrate the claims made concerning their capacities, to offer whites the spectacle of suffering blacks and to elicit the sympathy of white audiences. It was this passive role that Frederick Douglass refused to play and, with an uncommon perception for the time, declared firmly that

the man who has *suffered the wrong* is the man to *demand redress* . . . the man STRUCK is the man to CRY OUT — and . . . he who has *endured the cruel pangs of slavery* is the man to *advocate Liberty*. It is evident that we must be our own representatives and advocates, not exclusively, but peculiarly — not distinct from, but in connection with our white friends.[27]

The point is that slaves do have rights and as slaves are wronged, and they are wronged because the rights that they have as human beings are violated. I shall not now argue the case for human rights— that belongs to a latter phase of this inquiry — although it should be mentioned now that such rights are presupposed by the possession of any moral rights that persons have by virtue of their transactions or relations with one another.[28] But the point made by Douglass, in respect of which he was far more perceptive than his abolitionist allies, is that the violation of any right calls for a complaint of a different order from those made against those who deal unkindly, ungenerously and even unfairly in failing to allot them the benefits accorded to others. In the latter cases, the complaint is not that a person has suffered moral damage or injury or that he has been wronged. Ungenerous, unkind, selfish, and, within limits, unfair treatment may induce shame when those who exhibit such forms of misconduct are reproved or reproached; but they do not invite that sense of guilt for which expiation and, if possible, reparation and redress are required in order to remedy the wrongs committed when the rights of persons have been violated. Nor may a spectator of such injustice be the sole complainant, in the way in which this is necessary when in the interests of children too young to be sensible of their rights only an adult can serve on behalf of someone else. For, this was the bone of Douglass's contention with Garrison and his fellow abolitionists: If there are rights that blacks have as human beings, then in this respect they are in a position of moral equality with any other human being, black or white. They are therefore in a position of moral authority. Only *they* can forgive those who transgress against them; no spectator can do that for them. And those who transgress against them are accountable to *them*, the victims of their injustice, not to the spectators of the scene. The transgressor may attempt to rationalize his misconduct to a disapproving spectator, but he cannot in principle make amends to the latter or offer him any redress by which he might expiate his guilt. A spectator can, in registering his disapproval, hold *his* head up high as one who in the best sense of that term is a member of the moral community; but unless the black who has been wronged demands redress in his own right, he fails to exercise his moral authority as the moral person he is and submits to the injustice perpetrated upon him. It is, therefore, the distinctive moral requirement imposed upon the victims of injustice that they assert their authority as persons with rights, failing which they acquiesce in the wrongs they suffer and continue as before to go about in fear and trembling as if they were beings devoid of any rights, and who as such are dependent for their limited fortunes solely upon the humanity and generosity of others.

Douglass perceived that if blacks were to achieve their normative status as persons they could not depend solely upon the assistance that others might give them, but must exert themselves in word and deed to demonstrate their status as the moral equals of their oppressors, by calling for their rights and for the redress of their grievances.

I shall make one more comment at this point upon the importance of rights. Consider the right of any person to go to the theatre, and the obligation of others not to interfere. Now others who meet this obligation do so not merely if it is false that they interfere. It is false that the man tending his garden in the interior of China is interfering with my going to the theatre. But what is required on the part of others is an abstention — not merely a non-performance — so that when I go about my affairs, I do so confident that others will abstain from placing impediments in my path. It is only in this way that they can meet their obligation to me, and only those with whom I have some form of contact as I go about my business — not the billions of people wholly unknown to me — can meet this obligation that they have to me. Contrast this case with that of the slave who went about his affairs — raising children, etc., etc. — only at the pleasure of his white master, with his permission or in his ignorance of what he was doing. It would have involved considerable personal risk on the part of a slave to resist the interferences of his master with his doing the many things any human being has a right to do; but the alternative to the complaint that his master had no right to interfere with him, an act that is already a declaration of his independence since it is a demonstration of his status as a person on terms of moral equality with others, is the acquiescence to his role as slave, and the acceptance of the wrong his master has done to him. By demanding one's right, when one has been wronged by the violation of one's right, we are, in asserting our rights, asserting ourselves as persons invested with moral rights. Such self-assertion, in circumstances of rank social injustice, can be dangerous. Yet it is incumbent upon us, in certain situations, to stand up, and, in asserting our rights, to demonstrate our status as persons who may not be trampled upon and dealt with as inferior beings.

To be able in these ways to demand our rights, to assert ourselves as the moral agents we are, is to be able to demand that we be dealt with as members of the community of human beings. This is what moral dignity involves, not some esoteric goodness that is intrinsic to human beings and that has its roots in some transcendent realm of which they are members. Nor is it the ability that we have, by deciding how to live our own lives, to achieve that good which, as the scholastics put it, is the fullness of our own being; for surely it would have been a shaky argument that the slaves, if freed, would be able to achieve happiness and in that way the fullness of their being. 'Dignity', as Locke once remarked about 'person', is a forensic term, one that applies to persons in the forum in which they conduct their affairs with each other. The moral dignity of persons is the dignity they have insofar as they show themselves capable of being full and unabridged participants in the life of a moral community, comporting themselves with others in the expectation that they will be dealt with on terms of moral equality, and prepared in a way that anyone can see to hold others to account for the infringement of their rights.

VI

In the above sketch of the philosophical terrain to be covered in this work, I have stressed the importance of the concept of rights together with those with which it is linked. I shall be arguing, in the next chapter, that the failure in the past to take due account of these notions is the major cause of the failure to explain the so-called obligation of promises. But the views elaborated concerning what I shall call paradigm cases of promising may well appear to be sharply at variance, not only with other philosophical doctrines, but with some features of everyday moral thinking. This is inevitable. It is no longer plausible to maintain with Kant, for one, that a sound moral philosophy can be extracted, as it were, from 'common human reason' without in any way departing from major segments of popular thought, as if 'ordinary reason in its practical concern' were simple, whole and complete.[29] There are too many conflicting strains to be found in what passes for commonsense moral thinking, too many traditions to which people are bound, and too much diversity of moral opinion on many issues even among those with the same general moral outlook. It would be a mistake to suppose, as some have supposed, that the task of the moral philosopher is to develop a kind of meta-ethical analysis, with complete neutrality, of moral concepts and judgments which are accepted without question as given and immune to challenge. There can be no such neutrality. For what passes for common sense turns out, upon closer inspection, to be a disorderly clutter of opposing judgments that reflect the idiosyncrasies of individuals and the variety of traditions of moral thought to which they subscribe. Moral reflection must inevitably come into conflict with some facets of everyday moral thinking. Who, then are *we* to say, i.e. by what authority can *we* declare, that a promise, for example, is anything more than a bargain, a tit-for-tat arrangement for the mutually advantageous exchange of benefits and burdens? Who are we to say, as indeed we shall in this work, what the moral background is within which a promise has its moral import? And if like Bentham, who recognized that philosophy cannot rest content with the variety of conflicting moral judgments of the time, we oppose our moral approach to those of others, how can we charge them, without begging important issues that need to be resolved, with being the unwitting and confused victims of tradition and social habit? How can we make good our claim that our own intuitions are sound and that the moral concepts we have selected for emphasis are viable and of central importance?

In the account of justice recently advanced by Rawls, which we shall examine in some detail in Chapter IV, the claim is made that no appeal need be made to the self-evidence of any general conceptions or particular convictions.[30] We are told that we need only seek to achieve a 'reflective equilibrium', i.e. a balance between our considered moral judgments or intuitions and the principles of justice to be chosen by anyone in the so-called contractual or initial situation. But the circumstances outlined in this hypothetical situation in which a rational choice of moral principles is to be made are themselves the product of moral reflection in which judgments and intuitions have been at work. It would seem therefore that the process of reflection is morally loaded from the outset; for the description of the circumstances in which a rational choice of principles is to be made will embody judgments of what alone are the morally relevant items that serve as the conditions under which this choice is to be made. Indeed the description given by Rawls of the process of reflection, the end product of which is to be this reflective equilibrium, as a process in which one goes 'back and forth, sometimes altering the conditions of the contractual circumstances, at others withdrawing our judgments and conforming them to principle'[31] offers us no assurance of any sort that the reflection in which one is to engage has not been unduly circumscribed from the outset by the choice of moral concepts with which one operates. And, as we shall see later in our more detailed discussion of Rawls's doctrine, there is no place in the account given of the data upon which a choice of principles is to be based, for any consideration of the rights and obligations of persons, these being matters that relate to the structure of the institutions within which persons conduct their affairs with one another. If this is so, the claim that the process of arriving at a reflective equilibrium is inherently rational and free from bias is suspect from the outset.

No moral reflection can operate *in vacuo*; we proceed from where we are and with the understanding we have and, in some measure at least, share with others. If this is circularity, it is unavoidable; but this kind of circularity is as unobjectionable in the philosophy of morals as it is in logic itself. It does not preclude those advances in moral understanding that occur in the life of an individual or in the history of a people. The moral development of a person may be arrested by his rigid adherence to the inflexible attitudes and 'first principles' of his parents, attitudes and principles that are taken to be definitive of the very limits of reason in conduct. And the moral progress of a people may be arrested by social habit and blind adherence to tradition beyond which, they imagine, lies only moral evil and unreason itself. But the cure for such hardening of the moral categories consists, not in refusing to reflect about prevailing moral attitudes and norms by continuing to focus attention upon what lies in the foreground of one's attention—the comfortable acceptance of received opinion and the easy conformity with the prevailing and socially accepted habits and practices of one's group — but by reflecting as we must in morals, even when it is difficult and disturbing, about what matters most in morals, namely, what it is to be a person and how it is that in our dealings with others, we can, with the sensitivity to them and to ourselves as the moral agents they and we are, achieve rationality in the lives we live with them. Just as in logic our concern is to set forth the rationale of the inferences we make by which truth may be preserved as we move from premises to conclusions, so in moral philosophy our concern is to set forth the rationale of, i.e. the reason that operates in, our transactions with one another, by which the moral relations between persons may be most effectively served in the lives they live with one another. Central to our task, therefore, is the understanding of the normative status of persons, not merely as the psychological subjects of good or bad experiences, but as beings who as agents owe each other the treatment that they are to give each other during the course of their lives with one another. It is for this reason that particular attention will be paid in this work to the development of a child's sense of others as persons. In the life of a person, as in the history of a people, moral development is ensured by the growing understanding and appreciation of this sense of others as the human beings, the moral agents, they are, with whom lives are lived. The idols of the moral market place cannot withstand the force of this sustained growth of understanding.

How then can we make good our claim that the moral intuitions that underlie this work are sound, that we ourselves do not suffer from bias, parochialism or any sort of moral tunnel vision? The way to check for error in one's reflection is further reflection about relevant matters, in this case about the manner in which we understand persons — ourselves and others during the course of our dealings with them — whoever we and they may be — parents, children, promisers and promisees, husbands, wives, friends and strangers. There can be no guarantee that error is impossible. Neither can we reasonably assume that the outcome of our own reflections will not embody substantial changes in our moral outlook — both in judgments and in the moral concepts to be employed in making those judgments of right and wrong. Whether or not this is so can be determined only by proceeding not only with the requisite technical skill in appraising the doctrines and arguments of our predecessors but, as we cross and criss-cross the conceptual terrain with which we are concerned, by maintaining a firm and perspicuous view of our subject matter — the moral relations of persons.

NOTES

[1] For further comments on Locke's use of the term 'absolute right' see pp. 12–13 below.

[2] Cf. *Man and the State*, University of Chicago Press, 1951, ch. IV.

[3] *The Individual, the State and World Government*, New York: The Macmillan Company, 1947, ch. II.

[4] See his discussion of the four cases in which Kant applies the principle of the categorical imperative in the Second Section of *The Foundations of the Metaphysics of Morals*.

[5] For a non-Kantian view which takes obligations to be more fundamental than rights, see Simone Weil, *The Need for Roots*, trans. by A. Wills, G. P. Putnam's Sons, New York, 1952. I owe this reminder to Professor D. Z. Phillips. It is not, however, clear to me that the obligation which has as its object 'the human being as such' (p. 4) can be made intelligible independently of the ascription of human rights to persons.

[6] *The Right and the Good*, ch. II.

[7] Op. cit., p. 28.

[8] Ibid.

[9] Ibid., p. 29.

[10] *A Theory of Justice*, by John Rawls, Cambridge: Harvard University Press, 1971, pp. 341–2. Davidson's account is to be found in

'How is Weakness of the Will Possible?' in *Moral Concepts*, ed. Joel Feinberg (London: Oxford University Press, 1969), pp. 105–110.

11 Rawls, op. cit., p. 342.

12 Loc. cit.

13 Cf. p. 105, loc. cit.

14 P. 346, loc. cit.

15 Pp. 111–12, loc. cit. I shall defer until later the examination of the view that promising as a practice can be viewed as an institution with offices or roles defined by certain so-called constitutive rules. See Chapter IV for a detailed examination of Rawls's view concerning the obligation of promises.

16 P. 346, loc. cit.

17 But see page 341 where he suggests that there must be such rules: 'Obviously, we are not yet in a position to state these rules for more than a few cases, but since we manage to make these judgments, useful rules exist (unless the intuitionist is correct . . .)'

18 Rawls's difficulty goes farther, if we accept this horn of the dilemma, than that indicated by Joel Feinberg in his discussion of Rawls's view in the essay 'Duty and Obligation in the Non-Ideal World', *Journal of Philosophy*, 10 May 1973, p. 268. For if Rawls is to avoid the other horn of the dilemma posed above, he must abandon his anti-pluralism even in at least the case of one so-called just institution. A more extended discussion of intuitionism as Rawls uses this term is to be found later in Chapter IV.

19 Loc. cit.

20 P. 20, loc. cit.

21 *Second Treatise of Civil Government*, ch. XI, para. 139.

22 Cf. Frankena, in 'The Concept of Universal Human Rights', in *Science, Language and Human Rights*, University of Pennsylvania Press, 1952, p. 196.

23 R. Brandt, *Ethical Theory*, Prentice-Hall, Inc., 1959, ch. 17.

24 *An Enquiry Concerning the Principles of Morals*, sec. III, part I.

25 Cf. P. Nowell Smith, *Ethics*, p. 23.

26 Cf. Chapter VI for an expansion of the points made in this section.

27 Quoted in Lerone Bennett, Jr. *Before the Mayflower, A History of the Negro in America*, 1619–1964, Revised Edition, Chicago: Johnson Publishing Co., Penguin Books, 1966, p. 149.

28 The manner in which the right of a person, qua person, is

involved in the right of a promisee is discussed in the next chapter and generalized in Chapter III for other special rights.

[29] Cf. the concluding paragraphs in the First Section of *The Foundations of the Metaphysics of Morals*.

[30] Op. cit., p. 21.

[31] Op. cit., p. 20.

II

The Obligation of Promises

I

Just as soon as we ask why and how it is that a promise obliges, we must face the fact that the word 'promise' is a veritable blanket-term covering a staggering variety of cases. Some promises are promises to do what is otherwise permissible or even desirable, others are promises to do the trivial, unseemly, offensive or even the immoral. Some are promises to do what is foreseeably manageable, practicable or in some strong sense possible, others are promises made recklessly, foolishly or stupidly to do what lies beyond anyone's ability, even of God himself, as in the case of a befuddled contractor who undertakes to build a house modeled precisely after an impossible design by Escher. Some are promises to confer a benefit; others are manifest threats. Some are made freely; others are made under pressures of one sort or another. Some are promises made to oneself; generally they are made to others. And so it goes— there seems to be no end to the possible sorts of variations and no single feature common to all cases, not even the use, as Hume put it, of a certain form of words. For one can indeed promise, in the appropriate circumstances, even by a simple nod of one's head.

Some of these and others too might be eliminated at the outset on the ground that they are cases of derivative, borrowed or in some pejorative sense deviant uses of the word 'promise'. No one is morally obligated to do the immoral or impossible. And in no unproblematic or straightforward sense of the word is a promise a threat or something one makes to oneself. But on what basis shall we pick out those that do involve what has been called the obligation of promises? — for these vary too broadly to support any simple generalization.

Shall we say that a promise is one we ought to keep if and only if we ought to have made it? But there are many things that I ought not to undertake; but once the die is cast I ought to carry on — I gave my word. Or, should I keep my word only if it confers some good or benefit upon the promisee? But what does the promise itself secure that is not secured by what independently of the promise most if not all of us would concede, namely, that one ought to further the good of others? In any case, a promise may be made to provide some good, not for the promisee but for a third person who is not party to the transaction. Further, one can imagine cases in which, independently of the fact that a promise was made, circumstances are such that there is no reason, both good and sufficient, for conferring that benefit. No doubt in these cases it is true that the promisee desires that the promised act be done, whether or not the good that it produces is conferred upon *him*, but this fact, that the act is desired, is too weak to support an obligation, for why should I do anything that anyone else wants me to do? Surely it is the fact that one has promised to do it that provides reason for doing the act that is desired, and *not* that what justifies doing that act is that it is desired. And this is quite compatible with the fact that if a promisee no longer wants the promised act done then the promiser does have *a* reason for not doing it; but this fact needs to be distinguished from what may well be false, namely, that in this eventuality the reason is sufficient and that the promiser by that fact alone is absolved from any further responsibility in the matter.

II

Let us try another tack. One can set aside, as of little importance, the fact that one can promise without using the verb 'to promise'. One could use any word or noise for that matter, as long as one understands the uttering of whatever word or noise we use to function in the appropriate way. One first learns how to employ the word 'promise' and then one understands other forms of speech, even an affirmative nod of one's head in reply to 'Do you promise to . . .?' What we have is a certain kind of language-game. One person says 'I promise . . .' and the other, who normally, even though not invariably, benefits from the act described, desires that the act be done and fully expects that the speaker will do what he says he will do.

This is the game of promising that children learn to play. To use the current philosophical jargon, it is a constitutive rule of this game that the person who says 'I promise . . .' (or gives an equivalent sign) is to perform the appropriate act.

But clearly it will not do to pattern promising after familiar sorts of games. Three times one has swung at the ball and missed; so one has struck out and must now leave the batter's box. One has said 'I promise . . .' and now one must do. . . . This is how, in each of these cases, one plays the game with others; and if one fails to do what the game requires one to do, one will not be permitted to play with others again. It makes no difference if one has swung at the ball inadvertently or involuntarily; one has swung if and only if the movement of the bat has been such-and-such. It makes no difference if the words 'I promise . . .' have been wrung from one under duress or under the pressure of temptation too strong for most persons to resist; one has uttered the operative words and now, except on pain of being ostracized by one's fellows, one must go on to do the thing one said one would do. That and how and why one should take account of the circumstances under which promises are made, paying due attention to compulsion and temptation in weighing whether and how much to fault those who later fail to keep their promises, are matters to which those who are bound in their moral practice by the simple game analogy are oblivious. And in the case of those, too, for whom any promise is sacrosanct, to be kept no matter what the cost may be, the price paid is moral collapse — like the collapse of all play in a game defined by inconsistent rules — in those occasional situations confronting moral agents when they are forced by circumstances to choose between the keeping of a promise and the meeting of another competing obligation, a choice reasonable moral agents are able to decide, in most cases without any hesitation or doubt.

On the face of it the game analogy presents us with much too external an account of promising. A child observes someone saying, 'I promise . . .' (or, giving some equivalent sign, verbal or non-verbal) and then later on doing the thing described or referred to. The effect of the initial verbal or non-verbal performance is dramatic and puzzling — the agent must go on to do what is called 'keeping the promise'; and if he does not, he is shunned by others. In order to dispel the appearance of magic the answer is that there is a (constitutive) rule. If one is to play the promise game one must first say 'I promise to do such-and-such' (or say or do something equivalent) and then do such-and-such. Why play this game? The answer is that it involves getting a useful return for something one wants to get now from the other person— and if one does not follow through one is shunned forever more. No one wants to suffer this penalty. Why then should one do the things called 'keeping the promise'? The answer is that one cuts one's losses by doing so.

III

If this seems childishly unperspicuous, it is nevertheless reminiscent of some recent moves allegedly inspired by Hume. It would be well, therefore, to turn to Hume's account, from whom we can profit, on this topic as on others, as much from his mistakes as from his insights.[1]

Hume declares that in order to promise 'a certain form of words' is necessary. This suggests that the form of words employed is cere-monial and fixed. However, Hume is correct in thinking that 'I promise . . .' is not a fact-stating sentence. He notes that a person using a promise locution 'in effect expresses a *resolution* of perform-ing' the action described or referred to by the promiser.[2] And he takes account of the fact that a promise is a socially useful device by means of which a person uttering the required form of words benefits by receiving some important present good, resolving in exchange for that benefit to confer upon the promisee, without undue hardship and presumably with a resulting net advantage to himself, some benefit provided by the action which, as we say, he promises later on to perform. From the recognition of the general utility of the practice of promising, Hume is led, incautiously, to declare that the promiser 'is immediately bound by his interest to execute his engagement and must never be trusted any more, if he refuses to perform what he promised'.[3] In effect, then, the promiser says 'Let me never be trusted again if I do not do . . .'

It is important to notice several things in this account. First, it does not apply to promises made, not out of a desire to profit from an exchange of benefits, but out of kindness or good will. Second, Hume supposes quite mistakenly, that the cost of not keeping one's promise is never being trusted again, but this is to ignore a fairly wide spectrum of mitigating or excusing circumstances, even the simple plea for forgiveness, which may suffice to restore or preserve the trust of others.[4] Third, by 'his interest' Hume means his advantage; and, similarly, no moral import is to be ascribed to the idea of trust. By 'trust', Hume means a psychological matter of fact devoid of any moral import, namely, the confidence with which those who receive promises expect that the described actions will be performed.

As Hume sees it, the presumed moral obligation of promises cannot follow from any advantage accruing to promisers. In this, Hume is surely right, since even where a promiser is moved to promise solely by kindness and good will and in no way stands to benefit from the affair, there remains nonetheless the obligation that was incurred. And this obligation need not be dependent upon the fact that a failure to keep a promise would induce a lack of confidence, disappointment or contempt for promise-breakers or the refusal on subsequent occasions to accept further promises from them when it would be useful for them to make them in exchange for benefits to be received. For no such loss of confidence need result from the failure to keep a promise — promisees may forget, forgive or exhibit a degree of moral maturity, apparently not appreciated by Hume himself, when they take due account of mitigating or excusing circumstances — but the obligations incurred remain even in those cases of unimpaired confidence. But even if every case of a promise were one which, directly or indirectly, it would be to the promiser's advantage to keep, it is quite clear from Hume's account that this would in no way explain the distinctively *moral* obligation of promises. It is for this reason that Hume appeals to a new sentiment which arises and concurs with self-interest. This sentiment, however, consists, curiously enough, in the feigning of 'a new act of mind which we call the *willing* an obligation',[5] a remarkable bit of self-deception reminiscent of those fictions of the imagination he introduces elsewhere to explain, not justify, the commonsense belief in personal identity and in the continued and independent existence of external objects.[6] For there is not, nor can there be anything that can possibly answer to the description given. Hume's argument is as follows: The obligation to be explained is the obligation created by a promise. The promise, it would appear, consists in the utterings of certain words after the fashion described earlier by him. This, however, cannot possibly establish a moral obligation however useful it may be to employ this device after the fashion in which we do employ it. We believe, however, that by promising we oblige ourselves. We imagine, therefore, that accompanying the uttering of these words is the very heart or substance of the promise, namely, a mental act of willing an obligation (which, remarkably, we suppose *must* accompany the uttering of the words in order to explain even the obligation of false promises). But there is nothing that can possibly answer to the question 'Whereby is one obligated?' except the promise itself, the very substance of which is the willing of the obligation and which occasions the very same question all over again. In Hume's words, 'the will has here no object to which it could tend, but must return upon itself *in infinitum*'.[7] In short, if, as commonly we do, we think we oblige ourselves by promising, the promise must be something we do in our hearts in addition to the uttering of the socially useful words 'I promise'; but the supposition that there is anything that will do the trick is 'naturally . . . altogether unintelligible'.[8]

The absurdity of an internal act of mind is, as we shall see, even more serious than Hume himself imagined. For the present it is important to notice that while there may be many reasons for keeping a promise— the advantage to the promiser, the preservation of a socially useful instrument for the mutually advantageous exchange of benefits, the avoidance of the contempt of one's fellows, etc.— the one reason of which one must not lose sight is the meeting of one's obligation which *as such* provides a reason for the action that is performed. And unless with Hume (and because, as I shall argue later on, of the quite unperspicuous view he takes of the transaction of promising itself) we suppose that it is quite impossible to incur or create an obligation by promising, it would be well to make a different start. Hume's skepticism here as elsewhere is the fruit of his own constricting preconceptions.

IV

More recent writers have been much more sanguine than Hume that the problem could be resolved. Frequently, it has been assumed that if saying 'I promise . . .' were understood as a moral performance by which formal notice is given that the speaker's moral credit or standing is now at issue in the performance of the described action, the obligation incurred could be explained. One learns, so the suggestion goes, that the uttering of these words is the representation to others that one is a person of moral integrity, that promising is staking one's moral reputation in such a way that one will lose one's moral credit if one fails to perform the action in question.[9] To promise is to put oneself out on a moral limb that will continue to sustain one if and only if one does what one says one will do. A number of comments are in order.

Surely this is an excessively hard-nosed view to take of what is at stake whenever one makes a promise. One fails, or refuses, to keep a promise; but *must* this be immoral or indecent? May it not be in fact precisely what one is required to do when confronted by circumstances in which one would keep a promise, say only at the expense of the life of one's child? Promises do vary in importance and there are, on occasion, other competing considerations with which morally responsible and reasonable persons must reckon. And even those that appear matters of urgency for the promisee at the time the promise is made, turn out to be, when circumstances are unexpectedly altered, of little or no importance to the promisee. Besides, there are all sorts of imaginable circumstances that might quite possibly reduce the degree of fault incurred by the failure to keep one's promise. And, finally, however reprehensible it might be for one's failure to keep one's word, there are occasions when it is to the moral credit of the injured party, not mere sentimentality, to forgive and forget.

But how does a person stake his moral credit, if indeed he does, when he utters the words 'I promise . . .'? One answer is that uttering these words is a performance the linguistic function of which is to serve formal notice that one has tied one's moral reputation to the promised action. But this needs to be distinguished from a quite different reply, with which it may be confused, namely, that it is a *consequence* of what one does in promising, that one's moral reputation is tied to the performance of the promised action. The first answer to which we must now turn is that it is a rule of language pertaining to the use of promise-locutions that this connection between one's moral credit or reputation and the action described or referred to is secured. It would seem to follow that if one's moral credit or reputation were not in fact at stake one could not, strictly speaking, have promised!

How is it possible for this connection to be secured? Surely when I say 'I promise . . .' I do not have to wait for what others later may do or think in order to be assured of the fact that when I say 'I promise . . .' I do indeed promise. If, then, the connection between my moral standing and the performance of the so-called promised action is made by me when in uttering these words I promise, then that connection is something I secure at that time. But how can my uttering of the words do this? Are we to suppose that there is some internal performance in which I engage, accompanying the uttering of these words, that consists in my connecting my reputation with the action promised? The latter, however, does not yet, and perhaps never will, exist; so even if it were intelligible to me that by some sort of internal doing I could connect my reputation with an action, this is hardly possible when the entity to which I tie to my reputation does not and perhaps never will exist. Nor will it do to allege that what I now connect with my moral reputation is the thought of the action promised. In any case my moral reputation is not something that can exist *in foro interno* there to be hitched to anything else. My reputation is something I enjoy or suffer in the eyes of others. If I cease to be in good moral standing with my fellows, the change occurs at their hands. *They* change their attitude towards me. *That* is their doing. But when I promise, the making of the promise is *my* doing. It would be a mistake, therefore, to attempt to import into that doing of mine that consists in my promising, the change that others make in their attitude towards me because of my subsequent failure to do the thing I said I would do. For supposing no such change occurred — others seeing that I failed to keep my promise feel certain that for reasons they might not themselves discern, I *must* have had a good and sufficient reason for breaking my promise — would it follow that I had not promised at all?

Still, one does put oneself out on a limb by promising in many cases at least, and one of the possible costs of not keeping one's promises is the loss of one's moral reputation. Shall we say, following a suggestion of Hume, that a promise is a formal invitation or solicitation to others, something like 'Think ill of me if I fail to do . . .'? But one puts one's reputation for honesty, truthfulness, or whatever, at stake in saying all sorts of things — about the quality of the stuff one offers to sell, about what happened when . . ., and so on — yet it seems absurd to say that what is understood but unspoken when each of these declarations is made is something like 'Think ill of me if what I say is not so.' Why then does one suffer the loss of moral credit (if indeed one does) when one fails to keep one's promise? Surely not because of such a tacitly conveyed request to which others, obliging chaps that they are, accede. It must be, rather, because one has failed to meet the obligation incurred in promising. But on the view that promising just *is* staking one's credit on the relevant performance, not keeping one's promise *is* losing one's moral reputation. And since the only relevant obligation appears to be the obligation not to lose one's moral reputation, one loses one's moral reputation because one has failed to meet one's obligation not to lose one's moral reputation. But if the explanation of why it is that one loses one's reputation is to avoid the triviality that one loses it because one does, the specific obligation incurred in promising — like the *specific* obligations to be truthful, deal honestly with our fellows, and so on — must be distinguished from the *general* obligation to maintain our moral credit, an obligation that each of us can meet only by meeting the specific obligations we assume in speaking, trading, promising or whatever else it is that we do when we go about our affairs with others. Unless the obligation of promises were distinct from the obligation to preserve one's moral credit, there could be no non-trivial and intelligible answer to the question 'Whereby does one preserve (or lose) one's moral reputation?'

But what is the specific obligation incurred by promising? Surely this is an obligation to the person to whom the promise was made. That obligation is the very same moral relation, viewed from the point of view of the promiser, as the right which the promisee has with respect to the promiser. In short, the promiser who ought to keep his promise is obliged to perform the act in question because of the right conferred by him upon the other person, a right to a certain performance on his part. And if the promiser who fails to engage in that performance is placed outside the moral pale or loses his moral credit because of his failure to keep his word, the reason for this loss can only be that he has violated the right that he himself has conferred upon the promisee.

V

The history of the attempts to explain the obligation of promises has been the story of the efforts to explain why one ought to keep one's promises simply in terms of what it is that promisers do and what it is that happens to them when they keep or fail to keep their word. Cudworth, Hume, Prichard and those who have followed them in more recent days demonstrate in their efforts to explain the so-called obligation of promises the futility of any attempted explanation that ignores the moral relation that holds between the promiser and promisee, and which focusses merely upon the promiser — imagining that by looking more closely at what it is that he does, or what happens to him, one could find the answer to the question of why it is that he ought to go on to keep his word. The consequence of this tunnel vision has been, inevitably, failure. And this is precisely what one would expect. Hume is clear at any rate in rejecting any internal performance called 'the willing of an obligation' as incoherent, but seeing nothing else that the promiser can possibly do that could explain the moral obligation of promises concludes that, incoherent as the notion of the willing of an obligation really is, we 'deceive' ourselves, on a commonsense level, by 'imagining' ourselves engaging in an impossible charade when we utter the magical words 'I promise . . .' This, of course, is in effect to reject as incoherent the commonsense belief that promises do in fact oblige. The lesson to be learned is not that promises, in strict philosophical truth, do not oblige, but that nothing whatsoever that happens to a promiser or that he does even *in foro interno* could possibly have this prodigious consequence: that a right has been conferred upon another person and, hence, that a moral relation has been established such that the failure to perform the promised act is or may be a violation of the right of another person. And whatever else may be said about more recent talk about the moral credit that promising places on the line, this offers us, as a reason for the keeping of a promise, an evil that may befall the promise-breaker; but it ignores once more, because of the preoccupation with the promiser — with what he does and with what befalls him — that which is of central importance, namely, the right conferred upon the promisee by the act of promising and in the absence of which the loss of moral credit would be quite inexplicable.

We need, therefore, to look more closely at some of the features of that moral relation created by the making of a promise. Unfortunately, however, it seems difficult to know where to begin, since rights including those derived from promises constitute a very broadly varied group of cases, without sharp boundaries, and without a single set of common features. We are back, therefore, to the problem raised at the beginning of this chapter.

The difficulty, however, is not insurmountable. A child's limited conception of a promise, important as it may be in marking one phase of its moral development, gives way as it acquires moral maturity and with that maturity the ability to deal reasonably and effectively with a broad variety of cases: those in which, for one reason or another, and in varying degrees, the fault of failing to keep one's promise is diminished or even completely removed; and those cases, too, in which there are competing considerations, of morality or common decency, and in which the agent must decide in view of these broadly varying sorts of complicating circumstances what line of conduct he should follow. How is this moral competence achieved? Surely not by learning some formula or recipe, nor by having been drilled that and how — but not why — an ill-defined and ill-sorted collection of randomly varying cases of kinds x, y, z are to be dealt with, respectively, in ways a, b, c, so that, seeing a new case of a given kind, one applies to it the prescribed technique without any further thought.

The cases to which the child's attention is directed are neither randomly distributed nor does the instruction for dealing with them take the form of recipes or directives. Rather, the child comes to understand, first, that there are certain central or nuclear sorts of cases to which a rich array of concepts may be applied. Second, it comes to appreciate the fact that certain other cases deviate from these nuclear cases in one or another of a variety of respects. And, third, it learns how the various sorts of differences that exist between such deviant cases and those central or nuclear cases — to which the fully enriched array of concepts apply unproblematically, without truncation or diminished degree— are importantly relevant, and how it is that this array of concepts must receive, in varied ways, limited or qualified application when in various respects the cases under consideration diverge from central or nuclear cases.

Let us, therefore, consider the central sorts of cases by reference to which, in the course of our own development as moral agents, we come to understand what a promise is and how to apply the fully enriched array of concepts in which the notion of a promise is embedded. In such full-blooded paradigm cases, the promise-locution (or whatever it is that functions in the same way) is employed (a) in good faith by a responsible agent, (b) freely and without constraint or duress of any form, (c) to assure the addressee that the speaker will do something clearly manageable by him without undue effort or sacrifice, something that in some strong sense is possible or manageable, (d) something that is morally acceptable and without hurt or moral damage to himself or anyone else, (e) something desired and indeed required by the person to whom the promise is given in order for him, or for someone else in whom the latter has an interest, to carry on with some program or line of action. Further, (f) the assurance thus given is accepted in good faith on the terms represented by the user of the promise-locution by an equally responsible agent, who (g) respects, and in turn is respected by the promiser, as a person who may be counted on to show a proper concern not only for the other party to the promise-transaction but indeed for anyone else whose interests may be affected by what transpires in consequence of that promise.

In this sort of central case a promise is no idle prediction, no mere expression of a wish, hope or even resolution, but a transaction between persons who are united by the bonds of mutual respect in some sort of moral community. This point is not rhetorical but substantive. It is that the good reasons that impel a responsible promiser, who is informed about the special circumstances in which a promise-keeping act may be performed, to keep his promise (or to refrain from doing so), will be recognized and accepted by the promisee (and all others affected by his decision) as legitimate. Unless this is true there can be no agreement between the parties to the transaction that the right created by the promise should be accorded, waived or relinquished as the case may be. Nor can there be any sense in our talk of forgiving a promiser who violated the right of a promisee, thus wiping the moral slate clean, since there could be no reasonable expectation of the promisee (or of any spectator of the proceedings) that in future cases that may arise the promiser would conduct himself in ways that he (or anyone else) would regard as morally acceptable, and no reason therefore for him (or anyone else) to rely upon the promiser as a person of moral integrity. The bonds of a shared moral understanding — this is what is essential to any sort of moral community — are conditions in the absence of which, and in varying degrees, the array of moral concepts in which the concept of a promise is embedded would cease to have any unproblematic application.[10]

It is not enough, then, to say about these central sorts of cases that the promisee expects that the promiser will perform the action in question, or that he believes truly that this will be the case; for these can be idle, in no way impinging upon or connecting with a segment of the promisee's life during the course of which the promised action

is an integral factor in the design of the line of conduct the promisee
follows. Nor is it enough to say that the promisee depends upon the
occurrence of the action in question in order that he may be able
successfully to carry on with his affairs; for this can happen in the
absence of any promise and simply on the basis of one's shrewd
estimate of another's habits or desires. Indeed, it is not even enough,
in order that there be that distinctive moral relation established by
the promise, that the action in question be one that a person ought to
perform. I ought to give a stray and hungry dog the food I have in
my outstretched hand, and which the dog fully expects me to give
him; but it would be queer to say that the dog had a right to the food
in my possession, that when I torment it by denying it the food it
tries to get, and later on when I come to my senses and feel the shame
I ought indeed to feel, that I have that sense of guilt that comes with
the realization that I have violated a right. Indeed, a man might need
money in order to buy food, but notwithstanding the fact that I
ought, out of common decency, to give or loan it to him, this is not
enough to establish that he has a right to that money, and I an
obligation to him that I can meet by giving him that assistance.

It follows that there are additional features of our central cases of
obligations incurred by promises that we need to underline. (h) The
obligation incurred is an obligation to the promisee such that the
recipient of the promise has a right, or is entitled by that promise, to
the performance of the action in question. (i) Failure to meet the
obligation, in the event that failure is willful, is a case not merely of
hurting, disappointing or frustrating the promisee, but of wronging
him as a person, i.e. doing moral damage to him because of the
violation of his right; and (j) the moral damage inflicted entitles a
promisee thus wronged to demand redress from the person guilty of
this transgression; and (k) the person to whom the promiser is
obliged has the responsibility, if circumstances warrant it, to waive
or relinquish his right, and to forgive the person who has transgressed against him given appropriate indications of the remorse
felt for the guilt that has been incurred.

A nuclear case of a promise, then, is no trivial matter lightly to be
tossed off and quickly to be buried as an event in the dead past. It
marks the establishment of a moral relation between the promiser
and the promisee which carries with it important moral burdens that
each assumes with respect to the other, both in the making and the
acceptance of a promise. Not all cases of promises, of course, are so

fraught with a moral import that continues to color the relations of those party to it, from the time they are made until that time when the obligations incurred have been fully met and discharged. Circumstances do change significantly, and what may have appeared to be of importance in the foreseeable life of the promisee may turn out to be of little or no consequence; but when this does occur it is the responsibility of the promiser to seek, and it is a requirement imposed upon the promisee to grant, a release from an obligation that has ceased to be of any interest or importance to the promisee. To be morally mature is to be able unhesitatingly and surely to deal with cases of this sort. And there are other — many other — off-standard cases, some of which are discussed in Section VII below.

VI

It is, however, with central sorts of cases that we are here concerned along with all that is implied in the ways I have enumerated. We need now to ask ourselves how it is possible for the act of promising to give rise to these features.

It should be clear now in view of the complexity of these features, which involves both parties to the promise transaction, that any attempt to explain the right conferred upon the promisee — correlatively, the obligation of the promiser to the promisee — simply in terms of what the promiser does in promising is futile: To adapt a remark made by Wittgenstein in a discussion of another topic, nothing of this kind could possibly have the required consequences. The reason for this lack of perspicuity is only one of the crippling effects of that obsession with right acts that characteristically has afflicted modern moral philosophers.[11]

I promise — this is what I do — and what I achieve in a central or nuclear case of promising is my doing too. What do I achieve, besides giving voice to the words 'I promise . . .'? Something quite important, clearly, in some segment of the life of the person to whom these words are addressed. The communication to him of a resolution on my part to perform the promised action? Suppose, however, I do not really resolve — the promise is a false one — then does that doing of mine collapse? Surely not. Is it, then, a confident expectation in the promisee that I achieve when I utter the words 'I promise . . .'? But if this is all, the promisee has no right to complain that his own purposes were frustrated through my failure to confirm his expectation. 'I expected you to do such-and-such'— this would be a lament and an explanation of what otherwise might seem foolish conduct on his part; but this can hardly serve as a complaint directed at me, a charge that I had wronged him because I had violated his right, and thus a reason for demanding redress from me. How then can what I achieve — this being the doing that is the making or giving of a promise— have these logical consequences which mere declarations of intention, expressions of resolution, etc. do not and cannot possibly have? The only thing that can possibly have these features is something that must connect crucially with his status as a moral agent, a *moral* status I damage when, subsequently, I let him down by breaking my promise. That status, in the paradigmatic and central cases with which we are here concerned, is that of a moral agent to choose, decide and act for himself as he pursues his interests— in food, clothing, shelter, in work and in play, or in any of the indefinitely many other activities in which he engages— interests that give point and purpose to his very many different sorts of endeavors. By letting a person down when I fail to keep my word I do more than frustrate or disappoint him; I do violence to the right he has as a moral agent to pursue his interests. Nothing remains, therefore, that counts as my achievement in promising, whether that promise be made in good or bad faith on my part, but which *he* accepts as one made in good faith, except this: The uttering of the words 'I promise . . .' (or whatever it is that I say or do which serves as its equivalent in signifying that a promise is being made) is a formal way of conveying to the person to whom it is addressed that, henceforth, he, as such a moral agent, may regard the future performance of the action described or referred to as a matter on which he is as fully assured as he is of those actions of his own that lie wholly within the scope of his competence as an agent in any line of conduct he may elect to carry forward.

A promise is not, therefore, merely an assurance one gives to help another, just as it is not merely an expression of a resolution to perform an action. It is, in addition, to *underwrite* any endeavor the other party to the transaction may choose to launch, by giving notice to him that he may henceforth regard the performance of the promised action as one which he may be as assured as he is of any action that he, as a moral agent, is capable of performing and as he himself chooses. The failure to keep the promise, therefore, is no mere defeating of an expectation, no mere failure to carry out a professed intention or to make good an expression of one's resolution. It is, as we commonly put it, letting the other person down; it is tantamount to interfering with or subverting endeavors he has a right to pursue. It is thus to subvert the person's status as moral agent, one who relies not only on his own resources as an agent but also, by virtue of the promise he has received and accepted in good faith, on the promised action as a virtual *fait accompli*. It is for this reason that the promisee is entitled to the promised action: he is as entitled to it as he is, as a responsible agent, to conduct his own affairs. He is wronged by a promiser's breaking of a promise as much as he is wronged by any unwarranted interference with his conduct which violates the right that he has freely to go about his affairs. He is peculiarly privileged, therefore, when he has suffered this moral damage to complain, to demand redress and to invite that sense of guilt, not merely shame, that anyone who violates the right of another should feel. And unless in the promise transaction, specific assurance has been given that relevantly qualifies the obligation assumed by the promiser, it is the responsibility of the promiser, when altered circumstances warrant it, himself to seek, and the promisee to grant, the waiving of, or even the release from, the obligation that has been incurred. Finally, given the function of the promise locution to provide the sort of formal notice described above, it is now intelligible that an obligation is incurred whether or not the promise was made in good faith; for the interest in performing the promised action, whatever else it may be, by virtue of the fact that it is the subject of a promise, is an interest in the promisee's status as a moral agent. Let it be that a promise was in fact made in bad faith, the fault of the promiser would be compounded by the failure to keep the promise since it would now become, in addition to the fault involved in deceiving another person, a failure to respect the other person as a moral agent.

Why, then, are promise-breakers subject, when in fact they are, to moral ostracism? Why should any penalty be suffered by the willful breaker of promises? Not because a promise just *is* a solicitation or invitation to others to impose such penalties in the event the promiser fails to do what he says he will do — this being a brute fact about the game of promising. The answer, rather, is to be found in the character of the moral relation that is established when a promise is made and accepted. The promisee proceeds with his affairs, to which the promised action is crucially important, secure in his conviction that the promiser will respect his right as a moral agent. The promiser, for his part, however it is that he goes about his own affairs, must now see the promised action as one that he performs if and only if he is to respect the other as an agent and hence doing him moral damage, i.e. damaging him as a moral agent, by his failure to make good. And whatever the cost suffered in the form of penalties imposed by others upon those who violate the rights of promisees there remains in addition to the moral damage visited upon promisees the moral cost such promise-breakers bring upon themselves: the guilt they must suffer in violating the rights of those to whom they have given their solemn word, the remorse they must feel and the redress they must offer to those whom they have wronged.

VII

It may be objected that either the view just presented implies that there are ghosts or it does violence to the commonsense conviction that a deathbed promise—and in general, any promise that can be kept only after the promisee has died—does not bind the promiser and serves only to comfort or relieve the anxiety or distress of the promisee during his last moments. Surely, once dead there is no one that is the bearer of the right. Or, are we to suppose that the promisee continues to exist after death in some ethereal form, haunting our earthly scenes, and able to engage in these performances albeit in some ghostly form? Alternatively, are we to say that the past, and with it both the promise and the promisee are dead and gone, no longer to enter into our present moral calculations except upon pain of our embracing the belief in the existence, in some shadowy realm, of the person to whom the promise was made?

I do not believe that the past can be drummed out of the ranks of the things that morally concern us in the quick and easy way suggested. The past events that concern us now are unlike the events in some fictitious account of the past. A person now dead is unlike a figment of our imagination or a figure in a vivid dream. These cease to concern us, when their unreality is disclosed, in ways in which those now dead and with whom we have had our moral dealings often continue to enter into our feelings, thoughts and actions long after they are gone. So much so is this true that understandably it nourishes the temptation, to which all of us are exposed, to imagine vividly and keenly that those dead to whom one was particularly attached are now present where previously they lived and worked and played. Hume would have said that the imagination, in his broadened sense of that term, is assisted here by present impressions, or, as we should say, by those feelings, emotions and convictions we now have which involve a reference to the past as one of their essential features. For it is not merely understandable, because of the *de facto* workings of the human mind, but, within limits, reasonable and eminently proper, that one should now feel grief for some who are dead, regret for some of the things that have happened, guilt for some of our misdeeds, remorse for the ways in which we have wronged others, and, towards some persons now dead who have had a special and important place in our hearts, the sense of what they were and are in the lives we now live. And we could go on to show, by still other examples, cases in which the past enters conceptually into the ways in which, in some morally important fashion, we characterize the incidents that now take place in our lives.

None of these items, however, is sufficient to warrant the belief that there remains, after death, a person, i.e. a moral agent, who retains a right that was conferred by a deathbed promise, correlatively, that the promiser remains under an obligation to the promisee after the latter's death. Even if one were ready to endorse the doctrine of personal immortality, that doctrine, supposing it to be coherent, would be inadequate to sustain that belief unless the self thought to endure after death were also thought to preserve enough of the features of a moral agent to enable it to preserve that moral relation in which it, as the possessor of a right, stands to the person, who, having promised is now under an obligation to it. Could such an entity, persisting after death, waive, claim, or relinquish its right? Could it demand redress for the wrong done to it by the promise-breaker? What line of conduct could it follow to which the promised act would be essential? Ghosts visit us, supposedly, but what do they do when they are not so occupied? The conclusion seems clear. There is no agent that remains as the bearer of a right conferred by a deathbed promise. There is, therefore, no right that persists as a right of the deceased, the violation of which damages him as an agent.

There are, however, other considerations that support our conviction that a deathbed promise does bind. And here it will be instructive to consider different sorts of cases.

Suppose that the promise has been made to someone close to one, to whom one owed much for the way in which he shaped one's own life, someone like a member of one's own family or a close friend, whose life had been so much a part of one's own life that one orders one's own life in ways that would have been impossible without him. It is not merely that one now remembers that person and that the failure to keep one's word would not be in keeping with what one would have done, had he been alive. For he survives, not merely in one's recollections, but in the character of one's life. One now lives as one does, supposing that one's own life has not disintegrated with the grief suffered at his loss, by continuing, after his death as before, to make his will one's own. Not to keep faith with him now is not merely to ignore the dissonance between recollections of the past and present conduct; it is not to keep faith with what one now cherishes and prizes in one's own life. 'Sacred to the memory of . . .' is no mere declaration of our present resolve to remember the past. It is rather to resolve to remember in order to continue in our own lives to remain steadfast to those commitments we shared, and continue to do so, with those who are now dead. And we tarnish their memories only by tarnishing ourselves.

But there are other cases in which deathbed promises are made, those in which the person now dead played a much less important role in one's life. Shall we say that, here, no commitment had been made and that nothing now remains after his death to support the conviction that one ought to keep the deathbed promise? There are commitments where there may be no promises. A man may commit himself to a social cause, a career or a way of life, where there is no vow of any sort, not even a promise uttered *sotto voce*. And we should fault a person in respect of his character, if not his performances, in these cases in which no vow is taken or promise is made, should he lightly dismiss his commitments when it was personally advantageous for him to do so. But suppose that a deathbed promise has been made, is there no commitment here at all, even if it was made in order to lay to rest the anxieties of the dying man? It would have been an offense against him as a person if it had been made without any intention to make good one's word, untruthfully, and only soothingly as one does in applying a damp cloth to his feverish brow. But even here one does commit oneself—it is a human thing, dying though he is, like ourselves a being with interests and concerns of his own—one who has rights even though shortly thereafter he will not exist to exercise them in carrying out any plans or projects he may have had. And that commitment—to care for his son or whatever it may have been—remains a moral burden one cannot slough off without loss of self-respect, even though the dying man ceases to exist and there is no longer the bearer of any right.

But there are other cases we can imagine in which still other moral constraints may operate independently of the rights of promisees. For let us now modify the example of a deathbed promise to care for the son of the dying man. Once more, the promisee dies, and there is no one who has precisely that right and only that right created by the promise. Only the possessor of a right can waive the right *he* has, forgive someone for violating *his* right, or relinquish *his* right. But the fact that the son of the deceased is made aware of the deathbed promise does present a new factor, the son's knowledge of the promise, and the reasonable assurance based upon the presumed integrity of the deathbed promiser that he can rely upon the help that had been promised. The situation here is similar to the one that arises in the case of a promise that A makes to B, who is about to go off on business to a distant place, to care for his son C in his absence (and where the right conferred by the promise is the right that B, not C, has) but where C is informed of the promise that A has made to his father. Here the knowledge of the promise surely makes a difference to the moral relation between A and C. C now counts on the help that A has promised to give him and while he cannot release A from the obligation he has to B—that can be done only by B if he learns, for example, that unexpectedly altered circumstances have rendered it unnecessary for A to look after C—surely C's attitude towards A in the event that A lets *him* down by neglecting to meet his obligation to B is justifiably different from that of a spectator. The latter cannot complain about A's misconduct, for he has not suffered the moral injury; he can only disapprove. Here the knowledge of the assurance given C entitles the latter to count on A's assistance in his endeavors and as such he does have a right, one that is consequential to the right that B has. This becomes evident if we consider what happens in the relations between A and C where A knows that the promise that he has made to B will be communicated to C. How, we may ask ourselves, does this new factor affect the matter other than to assure C that A will be more attentive perhaps to the moral interest of C, a moral interest that C already has because of his knowledge of the promise? And if as it may happen it turns out that C does not require A's help—unexpectedly a grandparent arrives on the scene and functions *in loco parentis*—C now can release A from his obligation to *him*, although A will owe B an explanation if he learns that A, during his absence, has himself gone away and ceased to care for C.

The deathbed promise is, of course, an extreme case in which a promised act does not play an integral role in a line of conduct the promisee undertakes because of the formal assurance usually provided by means of a promise. A promises to do x for B, the promise is made in good faith by A and it is solicited equally in good faith by B, not in order, for example, to harass A and burden him with a task for the malicious pleasure it gives him, but in order to carry on with his affairs. B now changes his mind about his endeavors; he no longer needs A's promised performance. Shall we say, therefore, that A, whether or not he is informed of this fact—and surely if it is possible for B to do so, he ought to inform A that he no longer requires him to go through with his promise—is no longer bound to B? But suppose that B once more revises his own plans and projects and now, for differing purposes, however, requires A's promised act for the success of his newly projected line of conduct. Are we to say that he no longer has a right to the promised act because at the earlier stage the act not being essential to any endeavor was no longer owed to him by A? Unless B had at that point released A from his obligation, A continued to be under an obligation to him even though the promised act did not, at that time, serve its usual function in respect of B's endeavors. Why should B have informed A of his first change of plans unless it was to release him from an obligation that A had to him? One can therefore imagine cases in which a given line of conduct is *not* served by a promised act but in which there is an obligation to the promisee, a right that he has.

But these cases, like the cases of deathbed promises, are not counter-examples to the thesis advanced for the central or nuclear cases of promising, that what is at stake in such cases is the right of persons, as agents, to go about their affairs in the pursuit of their interests. For these are peripheral cases in which one or more of the various features of the nuclear cases are absent. It does not follow therefore that there are no good moral reasons for performing the promised action. In some of these peripheral cases there are excellent moral reasons, but nothing that can be construed as the right of a promisee. In other cases there are rights involved, consequential or derivative rights that the beneficiaries of deathbed promises have.

And in still other less dramatic instances in which the plans and projects of promisees are unexpectedly altered, the obligation and the right remain unimpaired, the change of circumstances merely affecting the question of whether the right should be exercised and whether the person obliged should be released from his moral burden. But all of these cases are peripheral to the central or nuclear cases as I have described them earlier; and this is only to say that the account previously given is not intended as a generalized account of all promises but as an account of those promises that we need first to understand in order that we can intelligently and reasonably deal with those other peripheral cases.

VIII

Let us attend, however, to central cases of promising, and now summarize our results. In these sorts of cases and in important ways, limited as these may be, some segment of the lives of promiser and promisee are joined. The fact that in the past this has escaped attention is due to the unfortunate preoccupation of philosophers with the problems that cluster immediately around the notion of right action. The problem as it has been presented traditionally, was how it is that barely by uttering the words 'I promise . . .' one could be duty-bound to do. . . . So stated, the problem was of course impossible of solution. The remedy, I have argued, is to focus attention not only upon the promiser but upon the moral relation, in all of its rich conceptual complexity, that is established between promiser and promisee in the making and the acceptance of the promise. Given such a perspicuous view of what is involved, it is now understandable that and how a right has been conferred, correlatively, that an obligation was assumed. For the possessor of the right orders and conducts some portion of his life in such a way that a failure on the part of the person obliged to him is not merely to disappoint him or visit some misfortune upon him, but to wrong him, i.e. to commit an offense against him as a moral agent. For his part, the moral cost of such a failure is the moral blemish he suffers. The remedy for the person he wrongs lies in the redress he owes him. For himself redemption is to be secured through the guilt he feels, the remorse he suffers and the moral assistance he receives from others through their forgiveness and their indication to him that they are prepared to resume their moral relations with him, and once more to join their lives with his.

NOTES

[1] Hume's discussion is to be found in the *Treatise*, bk. III, part II, sec. 5, 'Of the obligation of promises'. All page references that appear below are to the Selby-Bigge edition.

[2] Ibid., p. 522.

[3] Ibid.

[4] Like Kant in his most moralistic moments, Hume seems altogether oblivious of the possibility that circumstances might force a choice between competing obligations.

[5] Loc. cit., p. 523.

[6] Professor Yoshinobu Kiso of the University of Kyoto has commented to me that unlike the case of the feigning involved in our commonsense beliefs in personal identity and the existence of external objects, it is possible for us wholly to free ourselves from the commonsense fiction of the willing of an obligation. In the former cases Hume clearly intends that the mechanism of human nature is sufficiently seductive in misleading us by virtue of those tendencies he cites, so that philosophic truth cannot long withstand the forces of our common human nature and must through sheer mental weariness give way to the commonsense beliefs; whereas in the case of promises it is possible for us to sustain the philosophic conviction that there is not and cannot be any consideration other than utility to warrant the keeping of promises. Certainly Hume does not appeal in the *Treatise* to the workings of our human nature to explain the feigning of the willing of an obligation, and in the *Enquiry* he appeals only to utility considerations as *moral* grounds for the obligation of promises.

[7] Ibid., p. 518.

[8] Ibid., p. 517.

[9] Cf. J. L. Austin's 'Other Minds', *Proc. Arist. Soc.*, Supp. vol. xx, and my essay 'On Promising', *Mind*, Jan. 1956.

[10] This is not to say that central cases of promiser can occur only in ideal moral circumstances, i.e. that it is only by reference to persons who deal with each other in morally impeccable ways that a promise is intelligible. If that were so, it would be quite unnecessary to

mention, as we have, the guilt incurred by violations of the rights of promisees. Nor does this account entail that we cannot speak of promises made to a stranger or even to some barbarian in the wilderness—we can and we do promise them or receive promises from them. But the more alien they are from us in their moral views, the more our guards are up and the more deviant or peripheral the use of 'promise' becomes in our 'promise' transactions with them. In such extreme cases 'promises' degenerate into empty verbal forms.

[11] It is small wonder that W. D. Ross, in *The Right and the Good*, confines his discussion of rights to a brief appendix to a chapter entitled 'What Makes Right Acts Right?'

III

Rights, Personal Relations and the Family

I

I have argued that in central cases of the right conferred by means of a promise the promised act plays an essential role in some line of conduct chosen by the promisee. There are, of course, ever so many different sorts of things that may be promised and which may function in this way. What is required for some plan of conduct and occurs therefore as the subject of a promise may be some performance, abstention or forbearance, verbal or otherwise. It may be some material object, item of exchange, some commodity, good or service. In general, it must be something that the promiser, not the promisee, can supply that is essential to some line of conduct elected by the promisee. Further, we must not impose too narrow a restriction on the sorts of things that come under the title of 'conduct' on the part of the promisee. It may be the overt behavior of someone who having planned to purchase an automobile now takes the necessary steps, relying on the promise of a loan that will make the purchase possible. But it may also include the manner in which thoughts and feelings, intentions, hopes and aspirations, as in the case of a child who has been promised a horse on his next birthday, are built around the item promised. For these too, like matters of overt conduct, are involved in the lives that we live.

Some qualifications, however, are implied by the account I have given. The promised item must not be involved in some improper or even mad urge or propensity that one might have. If it were, the failure to keep the promise which frustrates the efforts involved in the satisfaction of such tendencies would not constitute moral damage; the line of conduct served by the keeping of a promise must, in the central or nuclear cases to which we need to attend, be of the sort an agent is entitled to engage in, in the pursuit of his objectives. Nor need the failure to keep one's promise in the case of one who exacts a promise in order to indulge his madness or folly, occasion any sense of guilt or remorse, or call for the forgiveness of the promisee after he has returned to his senses. Another qualification implied is that the item promised must not be the object of some passing fancy or momentary whim of the promisee; for, if it were, it would play no role as an integral factor in some line of conduct undertaken by the promisee, and the failure to keep the promise, at best, would defeat only an idle wish or expectation. It would not, as an isolated item in the promisee's life, subvert his status as a moral agent by letting him down in an enterprise in which he is engaged. Why count on anyone else's agency, as much as one counts on one's own resources as an agent, if the promisee's interest, even supposing that it recurs in this same idle way at some later time when the promiser can make good his word, in no way engages the concerns that give point and purpose to his activities and thereby a measure of unity during some segment of his life?

There are, no doubt, other considerations that need to be mentioned; but I shall not now pursue this matter, although I shall return to certain of these later in this and in subsequent chapters as the argument in this work develops. It is enough for our present purpose to note that these considerations are by no means confined to the rights established by promises.

Consider the familiar requirement of veracity. On the surface it would appear that there is an enormous difference between this requirement and that of promise-keeping, so much so that the recent suggestion that the latter can be brought under the former as a special case has not found ready acceptance.[1] One objection is that on this view it would not seem possible that the recipient of a promise could have any claim on the promiser, i.e. a right that he enjoys *vis à vis* the person who made the promise. What is implied here is that while we ought to tell the truth, no one has a right to veracity on the part of others, the thought being that truthfulness, like kindness and generosity, are morally justifiable by considerations other than those of the rights or entitlements of agents. But everything depends upon the stage setting, i.e. the circumstances in which utterances are made; and those who are inclined to rank truthfulness with generosity and other forms of conduct which do not seem to involve the rights of agents nourish their conviction only by ignoring the details of the circumstances in which persons address their remarks to others. For here, as in the case of promise-utterances, there are cases and cases, radically different in kind.

Suppose, within earshot of others, I tell someone standing near-by—a stranger who has no interest in my affairs—that I plan to purchase a thousand shares of a high-priced stock. Why? I want him, and others nearby, to think that I am well-to-do; I enjoy this sort of thing. Now I ought not to do this; but does my fault consist in my violating a right that the addressee and others nearby have? Certainly I misrepresent the facts about myself, as much so as I would by my appearance and my conduct if I were to dress well and drive an expensive automobile, neither of which I am able to afford, in order to foster the impression that I am well-to-do. But is it the case that those who receive the wrong impression have a right to a more seemly form of conduct on my part, one that is commensurate with my financial condition? That strikes us as too strong a view to take of the fault involved in this sort of self-puffery and deception, one that once uncovered as the deception it is, elicits only a mixture of amusement and contempt, not moral indignation.

It is tempting to generalize from these sorts of cases in which deception occurs, verbally or not, and to deny that any issue of a right is involved in any sort of misrepresentation. But we need to attend to the details of particular cases, lest we conclude that persons have no right to truthfulness from others. Here we need to remind ourselves how utterances are employed in normal situations in communication. Persons ask questions, normally at least, not out of idle curiosity, but in circumstances in which their interests are engaged, in order that the answers they receive will enable them to pursue their interests more effectively during the course of their endeavors or to carry out with some hope of success the plans and projects they have. They ask questions perhaps in order to test the knowledge and competence of students or of those applying for jobs, etc. They ask questions, sometimes, only in order to draw the attention of those to whom they speak to matters which they might otherwise overlook. And there are many, many other interests and concerns that prompt the questions they ask and the inquiries they address to others. And in responding as they do by uttering indica-tive sentences, persons intend—unless of course some game is being played the purpose of which is concealment of fact—that those to

whom they speak will accept what is being said as having been said
with the intention of stating what they take to be true. But to accept
what is being said in this way is not merely to recognize this intention of the speaker, it is also to regard this intention as one that is
bona fide, so that what is being said may be taken as a correct
indication of the speaker's view of the matter at hand. Yet even this is
not enough. It is not enough as we saw in the case of the use of
promise locutions that we attend simply and solely to what transpires in the minds of those who employ such locutions, recognizing
their intentions and resolutions for what they are; we must also
attend to the service such recognition may play in the lives of those to
whom such locutions are addressed. Promise-locutions need to be
understood by reference to those cases in which they go through, as
it were, from promisers to promisees, and are not only offered in
good faith but accepted on this same basis by someone to whom they
are a matter of concern. And so it is with indicative utterances
generally, for unless these are received (a) with the recognition of the
intentions of those who employ them as (b) correct indications of
their views of the matter at hand, and (c) as matters that engage the
interests of those to whom they are addressed, what is said by means
of them may be heard idly and ignored as we do the words of a
chronic liar who recognizes the futility of his own remarks and
whom we regard with amusement and pity, or the verbal ditherings
of a compulsive talker whose words ramble on in a free-wheeling
manner, or the self-puffery addressed to someone who could not
care less.

It is, I venture to suggest, the consideration that communication is
not idle talk that comes and goes without engaging the interests of
those who receive it, that lies behind Kant's notion that telling the
truth is to be ranked with keeping one's promises as a perfect duty,
when, in the *Foundations*, he discusses the second of the four cases in
which he seeks to illustrate the manner in which the Principle of the
Categorical Imperative may be employed. For communication
involves a relation between persons in which the interests of
language-hearers rest in the balance with the veracity of language-
speakers, a fact that imposes the peculiar obligation that is involved
in truthtelling. It is in line with this thought that Prichard remarks
that 'the obligation to speak the truth . . . involves a relation consisting of the fact that others are trusting us to speak the truth, a relation
the apprehension of which gives rise to the sense that communica-

tion of the truth is something owing by us to them'.[2] There is no such trust where there is indifference to what is said; trust here involves the idea of dependence upon the truthfulness of the speaker because of some interest one has in the subject matter of his remarks.

We need, however, to distinguish between the right to truthfulness that anyone has against those who speak to us, from the right to the truth and also from the right of a promisee, both of which arise from special circumstances that go beyond those generally involved in communication.

No one has a right to the truth, generally and without qualification. A parent, for example, who has a right to the truth about his son, has a right only to certain matters of fact that pertain to his son, e.g. his performance at school, the medical diagnosis of his illness, etc.; and he has this right by virtue of his special relation to his son by virtue of which he is responsible for his son's upbringing and care. This right is one he has against specific persons— school administrators, physicians and, in those matters in which the son is accountable to his parent, from the son himself— whose obligation by virtue of the parent's right is to supply him with the information he needs in order to discharge properly his parental responsibilities. But an inquisitive stranger has no right to demand or to ask for the information to which a parent is peculiarly entitled because of the latter's moral relation to his son; the truth, for example, about the son's progress at school is none of his business. Nor is the right to truthfulness, to veracity in the verbal statements others address to us, the right anyone has to have his questions answered by those to whom they are addressed. It may be unpleasant or rude for one to ignore a request for information or to refuse to supply it, but depending upon circumstances it may also be the more reasonable course to follow rather than, say, to create embarrassment or mischief of any other sort by replying. And when the information requested is essential to saving someone's life (e.g. someone driving his car with a badly injured person he is taking for urgently needed medical attention, something of which I am fully aware, asks me for directions to the nearest hospital) the failure to speak up, and reply truthfully with the information requested is a failure to respond properly to the right to life itself. But if in normal circumstances one does speak, whether or not in response to a request for information, and in a matter in which one does have an interest, the person to whom one's remarks are addressed does have a right to an honest statement.

As for the right conferred by a promise, this right needs to be distinguished from the right that promisees have to truthful promises, i.e. promises made in good faith. For a promise binds; it confers a right whether or not it is made in good faith, i.e. with an intention on the part of the promiser to carry out the terms of his promise. A promiser represents himself as having such an intention and when the promise is accepted, even though it may have been made without any intention on the part of the promiser to keep his word, the failure to keep the promise is nonetheless a violation of the right conferred upon the promisee. But it is, in addition, a violation of the right of the promisee to a truthful expression of the promiser's intention, and it would therefore compound the fault of the promiser, if after having promised untruthfully, he failed to keep his word. This is why promisers, having promised falsely, will often have a change of heart and minimize their moral fault by keeping their word. The right of promisees is the right they have to performances and abstentions described or referred to by means of promise-locutions; but as persons to whom promise-locutions are addressed they have the right they have in common with anyone to whom any locution is addressed, of whatever sort this may be, to be dealt with truthfully in any matter of interest to them.

Utterances are addressed to persons, with interest and concerns of indefinitely many kinds, during the course of their encounters and transactions with one another. As Wittgenstein put it, 'the *speaking* of a language is part of an activity',[3] one in which, casually or not, the lives of agents engaged in the pursuit of their interests— when they report, describe, inform, promise, speculate, and so on— are joined. For during the course of those segments of the lives of those to whom such utterances are addressed, however brief these segments may be, what is communicated is employed by those to whom discourse is addressed in their thought and action, in ever so many different sorts of ways that mark the indefinitely many facets of the lives of agents engaged in the pursuit of their interests. In speaking as we do to others, we represent ourselves as truthful, and those to whom we speak must, generally at least if there is to be any communication at all, rely upon our word during the conduct of their own affairs, of whatever sorts these may be: intellectual, aesthetic or practical in the broadest sense of this term. To speak falsely, to mislead and misrepresent, whether in making a report, giving information, issuing an order, or making a promise, is, therefore, to put in jeopardy the interests of those to whom our utterances are addressed. And if so, then language-hearers are to be accorded truthfulness, or honesty in word (as much so as they are to be accorded honesty in deed) by language-speakers, if the right they have to pursue their interests is to be respected. It follows accordingly, that the sorts of qualifications mentioned earlier apply equally to the present case: the right to truthful performances presupposes that the interests with which such performances mesh are morally unobjectionable, and those to whom we speak must be rational in employing as they do the utterances we address to them. For we are concerned here, as in the case of promises, with persons, not disembodied pure intelligences, who are engaged in the pursuit of their interests in ways that are intelligible and acceptable to us as moral agents.

II

I have discussed, so far, only two sorts of cases in which moral rights occur. There are, of course, still others to be considered; and later on I shall say something about these. But in all of these cases of rights—certainly in those paradigm cases in which the full conceptual ramifications of the concept of a right are involved—the lives of persons are joined, not in isolated incidents quickly to be forgotten because of their irrelevance to the pattern of their lives, but in some event or events essential to some relatively unified segment in the life of the possessor of the right. Given a sense of this fact, there is a recognition of the importance of honoring a right if one is to accord a person the respect that is his due as a moral agent, and, in the event that one is derelict, the appropriateness of a sense of guilt.

It is clear, therefore, that the notion of a person as a moral agent plays a central role in this account. I shall not address myself here to the details of the metaphysical question of the nature of personhood and to the further question much debated in the recent literature concerning the question of how far, if at all, personal identity can be attributed to individuals over a period of time. These are matters that appear to lie on the periphery of the present discussion of the nature and the conditions of the possession of rights. But it is worth remarking, at this point, that if the argument so far developed is correct, then certain views of the nature of personhood will have to be rejected. And later, in Chapters V and VI, in dealing with special problems involved in ascribing rights, there will be further relevant considerations to which we shall need to attend if we are to do justice to the important features of our concept of persons.

One view, familiar enough, is that identity of person can be secured only (a) by supposing that that which is essential to being a person is the subject of the experiences that come and go in his life, and (b) by attributing to that subject a complete and perfect immunity to all change. For should it—the ego—change in any way then it is no longer what it was, but something else. If, then, persons preserve an identity over a period of time, then that which is essential to their personhood is an ego that is unchanging and unchangeable. In short, like faithful followers of Parmenides we can no more tolerate any change in the essential reality of the person—his ego—than we can tolerate a change in the number 2 during the course of our calculations. If the person with whom we are concerned at any given moment is the same, now and later, then he is no more changing and is just as timeless as the number 2 or any other eternal object to which at different times our thoughts may be directed. Perfect identity, one wants to say, is the identity of a thing with itself at a given instant, in which there can be no change because there is no before or after possible with respect to it. And if there is to be real identity (for how can it fall short of that identity provided in the formula x = x?) in an entity which, like a person, appears to be in time and is subject to change, then the reality of that entity is to be found in an eternal present with respect to which there can be no before and no after and hence no alteration to which it is subject. But perfect identity, so conceived, is purchased at too high a cost, namely, the perfect irrelevance of this idea to any of our moral concerns. For is it intelligible that an unchanging and unchangeable ego can be a subject, i.e. *have* experiences without in any way participating in or being affected by the changes that take place as those experiences come and go? And how shall we understand the fact of agency itself, if the person *au fond* is utterly immune to the passage of time, yet brings things to pass now and then? Nor need we dwell at any length upon the complete irrelevance of the idea of a timeless ego to anything that counts for or against the identity of persons over time, or the identity of Smith as contrasted with that of Jones, indeed, to anything in the person whom I might love, admire or respect or whose life I have joined with mine by virtue of the right I have conferred upon him, the obligation to him that I have assumed. I can no more love, admire, respect or concern myself with an ego from whom all salient temporal features have been removed than I can love, admire, respect or involve myself with an unchanging and unchangeable billiard ball suspended in splendid isolation in infinite empty space.

More recently, interest has been revived in a view suggested by Hume, who having rejected any appeal to an immaterial substance or ego in the account of the self, likens the soul or the self to a republic or commonwealth.[4] Just as the latter is to be understood as a collection of individuals related in diverse sorts of ways, so the self is to be understood as a changing set of experiences connected more or less with each other through memory. For Hume, the soul or self consists of nothing more than experience contents—impressions and ideas—related by association and memory. Modern writers, who share Hume's antipathy towards the doctrine of the ego, are prepared, in their account of personhood, to introduce a reference to the body and even to lean upon the possibility that the diverse sorts of entities connected through memory, such as feelings, thoughts, emotions, desires, intentions, etc. are identical with bodily events or states. In any case, personhood, on this view, is a complex matter. Setting aside the reference to the body, it is constituted not by a single and thus simple item, an ego, but, rather, by the persistence of memory together, perhaps, with psychological propensities, interests, etc., which confer the unity that is constitutive of personhood itself.

But personhood, so understood, is a matter of degree. Am I the same person I was as a child? Surely the differences, bodily and psychological, are enormous between the child and the man into whom he was transformed. So it is with the difference between the ardent young bridegroom and flabby, pot-bellied middle-aged man about whom his restless wife complains: 'You are not the man I married two decades ago!' Change is an ever-present fact of life. Shall we say, then, that any change of personality—let it be substantial and not those minor changes in mood and temper that occur from day to day as new and different experiences crowd in upon us—is a change of the person such as, for example, the change from a Dr. Jekyll to a Mr. Hyde, so that one can say in truth and with good moral purpose, 'He—Dr. Jekyll—did not commit those foul murders and is to be pitied, not punished, for the deeds of a Mr. Hyde into which he had been transformed!' Shall we deny too that it was I who forty-odd years ago committed such and such an indiscretion, or that it was I who decades ago took *this* person to be my wife? And if this is the conclusion to which one is impelled, what sense can there be in the claim that I should feel remorse for misdeeds I committed long ago, beg for forgiveness and attempt to make amends? Punishment itself, or any of the familiar grounds upon which philosophers have based their justifications of its retention, would seem to be without point or purpose if the person punished is not the person guilty of the misdeed. And *whose* wedding anniversary am I now celebrating, what right does she have and what obligation do I have, if the she here-and-now is not the she long-ago and the I here-and-now am not the person who put that ring on the finger of the she long-ago in the wedding chapel? No praise, no blame, no guilt, no remorse, no punishment, no obligation, no right—none of these can bridge the chasm that separates one person from another. And so too with human agency itself in any line of conduct that would seek in vain, for good or ill, to bridge the gap of change in personality.

Indeed, the alleged analogy between persons and nations is patent nonsense. Let it be that a nation is nothing over and above its citizens in their complex relations, institutional and otherwise, with one another. Let it be that a nation has no duties, no obligations, no rights, and that all such talk is metaphysical nonsense. Let it be granted that only citizens have rights, have duties, and are under obligations to each other. What is there in the case of a person, now viewed on the analogy with a nation or republic, that has rights and obligations? An experience? That makes no sense. And neither does it make sense to suppose that it is the whole complex series of interrelated experiences that has rights or is under any obligation. Or, shall we say that it is the events constituting the body that is the bearer of rights? There would appear to be nothing in the events allegedly constitutive of the person, corresponding to the citizens of a nation, to serve as the bearer of rights and obligations. Or, are we to suppose that just as our talk about the subjects of experiences, e.g. that it is Smith or Jones that has this or that experience, is no more than a grammatical fiction which philosophical enlightenment dictates that we replace by complicated talk about experiences and their interconnections, so our talk about the rights and obligations of persons is misleading talk that must be replaced, in the interest of clarity and truth, by talk about the relations between experiences (and, in truth, with the events or states constitutive of the body)? It is no good saying, 'Give us time— perhaps endless time because of the endless complexity of the task, and all of this and much more involving the rich fabric of our moral talk about persons— their guilt, remorse, punishment, forgiveness, etc., etc.— can be spelled out by specifying the requisite relations between the events that constitute the person!' That response is not only reminiscent of the forlorn hope expressed a few decades ago by phenomenalists in their programmatic accounts of material objects, it is far worse off, since in the present instance we have no idea of how even to begin the hoped-for analytic reconstruction. Or, shall we say, 'So much the worse for all of this morality talk!' Philosophical analysis may require making some changes in our attachments to some of our everyday convictions, retaining, perhaps modifying some and abandoning others as we proceed with our reflections, but if the cost of the alleged demands of ontology or metaphysics is the wholesale repudiation of morality itself, then the claim to philosophical truth exceeds the limits of credulity.

We need, in our conception of what it is to be a person, to bring that concept back to where it has its place in our practical discourse about persons. Our concept of a person applies to a being who is born helpless; completely dependent upon those who have prepared for its birth and who nurse and care for it; reciprocating the love and affection it receives from them as it is brought increasingly into the life of the family; learning first in this context and, later on, as its moral education progresses, in the wider community of which the family is only one small part, how within the limits imposed by concern with and respect for others, to conduct itself in various sorts of enterprises in many of which it counts on others for the success with which, as it grows in stature as a responsible agent, it pursues its affairs, first within the family circle and later with friends, acquaintances, and strangers.

III

It is clear that the growth of an individual, from its helpless condition of early infancy into that of a full-fledged partner in its activities with others, both within and without the life of a family, is one in which his life is connected in various ways with the lives of others. It is one in which there is increasing understanding developing out of the obscure and confused beginnings in infancy that his status as agent, extremely limited as this agency may be at a very early stage, is dependent upon the contributing support of others. And as he grows in his understanding of the contributions that his own activities make to the plans and projects of others, there is also a growing understanding on his part of the ways in which he is counted upon to support the hopes and the aspirations his parents have for him, and also the life of the family itself in which, increasingly, he plays a part.

In such developing circumstances, rights and obligations are distributed among the members of a family as their lives are joined and the agency of each, in different and changing ways, supports the agencies of others. The fact that, normally, there is love and affection that unites the members of the family in many of their activities in no way undercuts the fact that there is a characteristic distribution of rights and obligations within the family circle; it shows merely that, to use Kant's term, inclination plays a reinforcing role and would operate, even in the absence of any explicit recognition of the moral relations that bind the members of the family, to insure the support that each provides the others. For what is essential to the existence of rights and obligations is the mutual understanding, which need not even be expressly formulated, that exists between them, of the crucial ways in which they are linked, as supporting agents, in their various lines of conduct.

Nor should we be misled into supposing that the obligations, say, of child to father, of brother to sister or of husband to wife, is based on nothing more than the requirement that one reciprocate favors and benefits. For such reciprocity may be called for in the absence of the mutual understanding that exists between those bound by that moral relation constituted by the existence of a right that one person has *vis à vis* another. If unexpectedly someone favors me with his assistance—he sees me in need and extends his helping hand to me without my having solicited him to do so, and without any expectation on my part that he might do so since he is at best only the most casual acquaintance—I ought to demonstrate my gratitude not only by my thanks but by means of some benefit I can give him in return. And even if this sort of unexpected assistance were received from a sibling, this need in no way occur on the basis of any understanding that might exist between them that help of that kind would be provided. What is essential, not only in the case of a promise, but also in the case in which the lives of siblings are joined in such a way that rights and obligations may have application, is the mutual understanding that exists between the parties and that certain performances or sorts of performances— the performance described in the promise locution or those brotherly or sisterly actions in which siblings give each other special consideration (e.g. the sharing of their resources with each other)— which support each other in their endeavors, and in normal cases at least are assured as anything that the recipient of the special consideration can do on his own. But for benefits reciprocated there need not be any right at issue at all, not even the issue of whether it is fair to enjoy the benefits generously accorded one without in some way recompensing one's benefactor. For in some cases of reciprocity, one ought to make some suitable return for a benefit one has received at no cost to the donor simply in order to demonstrate one's own good will towards someone from whom one had least expected any help at all— someone towards whom one had been cool and distant. What is sometimes called *the* obligation of reciprocity can be any one of a number of different things, all of them distinct from an obligation that is the correlative of a right. Here as elsewhere we need to think of cases and cases in order to guard against mistaken generalizations.

But are there, really, any *moral* as distinct from *legal* rights and obligations that bind the members of a family? There is, of course, a substantial body of common law and statutes that define the legal rights and obligations of certain members of a family with respect to legal persons, within and without the family circle, and to which appeal is made when there is recourse to litigation in order to resolve the disputes that sometimes arise. But to argue that because there are covering legal rights and obligations established by common law, statutes, and prior legal decisions, that these rights and obligations have no moral force or import would be as fallacious as arguing that because the marriage ceremony by which a man and woman are joined as husband and wife is a legal contract to which a well-defined body of law applies, it is not therefore any kind of promise that each makes to the other and by which they are morally bound to each other. A contract *is* a promise, although not every promise has the legal status of a contract, and it would be absurd to argue, because a contract has a legal status, that it is not any promise at all, as much so as it would be to argue, because of the ceremonial character of the proceedings at a marriage, that there is no exchange of promises and no moral rights and obligations created by what is said and done during the ceremony. It is hardly necessary for our purposes to explore the complex and difficult topic of the relation between morality and the law; for it should be clear that rights and obligation talk invested with legal import as it may be by virtue of legal precedent, common law and positive statute, and to which recourse is made in order to secure legal remedy in the event that certain rights are infringed or violated, does have moral import, and moral force even where there is no such recourse taken, contemplated or even possible because there happen to be no statutes, precedents or common law that apply in the given case. Nor is it necessary to invoke the idea of a natural law, paralleling the positive law of a state, in order to provide the proper footing for the moral rights and obligations that are distributed among the members of a family, still less to regard the marriage ceremony as an empty ritual, a mere custom, unless it is taken to be conducted in the eyes of the Lord. We do not need a heavenly Overseer in order to insure that the two main participants in the ceremonial rites, religious or civil, are mindful of the moral burdens that each assumes with respect to the other, and of the entitlements with which these burdens are linked. It is enough that they are agents who join their lives and undertake to conduct themselves with respect to each other in order to support each other in the lives they are to live together. We need neither a shadowy parallel of the positive laws of man nor some heavenly equivalent of a human court to fill in the gaps in our juridical system, as a necessary foundation for the range of moral rights and obligations that are distributed among the members of a family.

We should be on our guard, too, against a confusion that stems from the consideration that the family is a social institution. This fact is sometimes supposed to be sufficient to establish that whatever rights and obligations members of a family have are 'institutional', in the same way in which the rights and obligations of, say, the members of a legislative assembly are institutional, since these are specified by a set of 'constitutive' rules that define the offices or positions within the institution. What is meant by 'chairman', for example? Here we have nothing more than those rules or regulations that state what the chairman is required to do, or the entitlements he has in preparing for, or in conducting the business of, the body over which he presides. If, therefore, there are any moral considerations distinct from the rights and obligations that define his office, these might appear to be those involved in his assuming his office when he undertakes, faithfully and fairly, to discharge his duties. Accordingly, if as some have supposed, we can employ this model, not only in dealing with political institutions but with social institutions like the family and even with the practice of the making and receiving of promises, we should look upon the rights and duties of the members of a family as institutional rights and duties that go with their several offices, positions or roles.

Some of the philosophically pernicious effects of the current talk about institutions and practices will be dealt with in the next chapter in connection with the recent attempt by Rawls to employ this model in the explanation of the obligation of promises. For the present I wish briefly to examine this approach to the social institution of the family. And the first thing that we must do is to look at cases, to recognize that there are institutions and institutions. For an institution may be a practice with written or unwritten rules, but there are practices and practices, some of which are hardly institutions in any literal and unproblematic sense, e.g. the practice of many Americans religiously to turn on the television to watch 'The Game of the Week' on the screen. And if, as we do, we speak of the social institution of the family, are there rules—written or unwritten—that state what husbands and wives, parents and children, brother and sister, are required or entitled, each of these by his particular status within the family, to do or to abstain from doing? We do have precepts like 'Honor thy parents' and precepts and admonitions that call upon us to give special consideration of one sort or another to our siblings, parents or children: to obey our parents, care for our children or our aged and needy parents, and to love, honor and obey (or cherish) one's husband or one's wife. Some would call these 'rules' in some quite extended sense of this much abused term. But setting aside their inherent vagueness or generality (in which respect they are *not* comparable to the constitutive rules that specify the rights and duties of office holders in an assembly or the positions of players in a game of baseball or football) these precepts and admonitions are not in any way constitutive rules for the following reasons. First, a constitutive rule defines a term; it informs us that a given term is to be applied to those who are entitled or required to do such-and-such. But such a rule cannot inform us of a matter that goes beyond the definitional function served by the rule; specifically, it cannot inform us of what anyone, who does in fact satisfy the requirements for the application of the defined term, is morally required to do. Definitional considerations, such as the entitlements and duties that define a given office or role, need to be distinguished from moral considerations such as the fairness or justice with which anyone holding the given office performs his (institutional) duties and exercises his (institutional) rights. But, that one ought to honor one's parents, cherish and protect one's wife, care for one's children, and so on, are moral requirements imposed upon the relevant members of a family, and they are moral requirements imposed upon them because of their moral rights and obligations. Second, if such moral 'rules' or precepts were constitutive rules, there could be no meaning given to such terms as 'father' or 'son', 'husband' or 'wife', 'parent' or 'child' independently of the rule so-called that applied to these terms. We could not understand what was meant by 'husband' independently of the 'rule' that husbands are to honor their wives, if the 'rule' were a constitutive rule, any more than we can understand what is meant by 'chairman' independently of the constitutive or defining rule that chairmen are required to prepare agenda, preside at meetings, etc. But whether or not a given husband loves, honors and cherishes his wife is a moral matter that is independent of the question whether or not he is in fact a husband; unless this were the case there could be no question of moral fact to be resolved, since there could be no meaning given to the query whether someone who is a husband does love, honor and cherish his wife.

But are there any constitutive rules at all, since the familiar moral precepts will not do as candidates for this title? Well, how in fact does one establish that A is father, B is son, and so on? Is A father because he lives in the same household with B? Not necessarily, even when A is step- or foster-father of B and provides the latter with financial support, although normally A and B are members of the same household. Is A father because he provides financial support for his son as the breadwinner for the family, this being what by definition he is (institutionally) required to do? But sons sometimes remain within the family circle even when it is *they* who are the breadwinners. Is the helplessly cripped father (or mother, for that matter) qua father (or mother) institutionally because definitionally required to provide financial support for the family, and therefore because helplessly crippled and penniless no more father (or mother) than a stranger wandering into a legislative assembly is institutionally or definitionally entitled to introduce a motion or vote on one before the house? To say that A is not *really* a father because he does not provide the needed financial support for his son is to say that he is not fatherly, i.e. that he does not act in the way fathers should, or, given that because of his incapacity he is not to be blamed, that he is unable, because he is crippled or whatever, to meet the obligations that fathers, who are neither incapacitated nor unable by circumstances that lie outside their control, have towards their son and to the others in the family. Yet A remains father, incapacitated or thwarted as he may be, to do what fathers in normal conditions and circumstances are required to do whether or not they are blood fathers, step-fathers or foster-fathers of their children. Even for those living within the family circle there are familiar ways in which persons may be identified as fathers or son, husbands or wives. But these ways do not depend upon the fact that we have at hand constitutive or defining rules that set forth criteria that must be satisfied if familial terms are to be applied. Rather, we have multiple and alternative criteria each of which is often but not necessarily satisfied: the father is often, but not necessarily, the blood parent, for he can also be step- or foster-father. The husband, like the father, is male; but must he have exchanged marriage vows with his wife? There are alternative possibilities with respect to the criteria to be employed in determining whether a given individual is the father of this child or the husband of this woman. And so it is with other terms that we apply to the various members of a family.

Besides, if the rights and obligations of the members of a family were institutional because of certain constitutive rules that define, say, 'father' and 'son', they would not change as manifestly they do even though the relation of father to son continues.

The infant son surely has no obligation to his father, but he does have a right to the care and protection the father is able to give him; and this right exists as no mere augury of the future but as a right that he has then and there even as infant. Granted that certain conceptual linkages of this right are missing—for it makes no sense to speak of infants claiming or asserting their rights or forgiving those who violate them—the talk of the rights of infants is no mere *façon de parler* which could be put in a more straightforward and literal manner by speaking of what they need or ought to have in order that they may develop into beings who in a literal sense of the term have rights. The infant enters significantly, although passively, into the lives of his parents. They involve its life in their own lives, supplying for it the hopes and interests it itself is far too immature to have in organizing what it is unable to do for itself, namely, the program of and the means for its development into a responsible person who can carry on its own affairs. And they function as surrogates in claiming and even waiving its rights, and less and less so as he develops his agency and his understanding of his moral relation to his parents. There is, therefore, enough similarity between this and other standard cases to support our talk about it as a being with rights.[5] If the infant son does have rights *vis à vis* his father, these are moral rights grounded in the way in which their lives are joined then and there, and not merely in some future status into which hopefully the infant will develop. He has a right to the care and protection he can receive from his father, and to whatever the latter must now do in order to insure that he will develop properly as a moral agent, although some things, e.g. the right to an education in a school or university, are future rights only, i.e. rights that he will have if he develops properly. But the rights and obligations of father and son with respect to each other do change. It makes no sense to speak of the infant's obligations to his father; that is a matter that lies wholly in the future. And even when the son does acquire a sense of the moral constraints imposed upon him, his obligations to his father and the latter's rights against him are subject to modification as he grows in maturity, develops self-reliance and gains his independence. Yet he remains the son. His moral relations to his father are one thing, and his familial relation is something else.

But surely the social relations of father and son change as the latter matures. Have we shown, therefore, that the rights and obligations that bind them are moral rather than social or institutional?

What is at issue here is whether these social relations are those which hold between the occupants of offices defined by the rights and duties specified by constitutive rules. Suppose such rules could be found which delineate the social structure of the family in terms of the rights and duties that define the several roles or offices within the family. Since the social relations between father and son change, there will be different offices designated by the terms 'son' and 'father'. Accordingly, these terms will be inherently and typically ambiguous since they will be applied to individuals who in the natural course of events occupy different offices within the structure of the family. So it is not the son John who at birth is and remains in the same sense the son of Henry as he develops from infancy through childhood and adolescence into adulthood, but rather that he is son in sense 1, then son in sense 2, still later son in sense 3, and finally son in sense 4 of an individual, Henry, who correspondingly is father in different senses as his roles and with them his rights and duties with respect to John change. This does seem fishy.

We can, of course, imagine family arrangements in a primitive society, with rigid institutional structures, in which each individual is supposed to undergo a series of fixed and predetermined changes in the roles he plays, each role being defined by a well-defined set of rights and duties. And we can imagine a morality consisting simply of the requirement, stemming from some imagined divinity or divinities, that each individual conduct himself within the family in accordance with such institutionally prearranged rights and duties. But in such a society there would be not a single word 'son' or 'father' to mark the social role of an individual as he grows in maturity, but a set of quite different terms to mark the successive social relations in which he stood to his parent. Now we do have the words 'infant', 'child', 'adolescent' and 'adult' which we apply successively to the same individual who, nonetheless, remains the son of his father. But we use these terms, not because we believe that there are abrupt and well-defined changes which occur at specified points in the life of the son. Neither do we use these terms because we think that the son changes his offices or roles in the way in which a person does during the course of his participation in the life of a political organization, when he is, first, a member of an assembly, later a member of its executive committee, and still later the chairman of the organization with executive powers and duties. We use these terms, rather, in order to convey, very roughly and imprecisely because of their inherent open texture, something about the character of the different phases of the life of a human being, so as to provide reasonable expectations of the ways in which those to whom we apply these terms will conduct themselves, given the conventional form of family life, with others within this social unit. 'He is an infant' (and so too with 'child' or 'adolescent') serves to inform or remind one, not of the specific rights and/or duties that define the role of an infant (child or adolescent) within the structure of the family, but of the manner in which one may or may not reasonably expect the individual to conduct himself with others within the life of the family.

Consider the terms 'husband' and 'father'. These are employed in legal contexts, and by statute or common law there are certain legal rights, duties and immunities granted to individuals to whom these terms are correctly applied. And a common-law husband (or wife) is defined by statute as one who without benefit of formal marriage vows, religious or civil, has cohabited with a woman (or man) for a specified length of time. But while a person may acquire the legal status of common-law husband (and the woman that of common-law wife) and with it the rights, duties and immunities that go with this legal title, it would be absurd to claim that there are no moral rights and obligations incurred during any period of time before this legal title is acquired, that there are no such moral constraints upon the persons who subsequently became common-law husband and wife. Nor need there have been any promise of any sort made by the cohabitants—to love, honor, cherish, or whatever—any more than in Hume's example, of men seating themselves in a rowboat and proceeding to ply the oars, we need to suppose that there has been any *sotto voce* declaration that each has made to the other, to play his part if the other also does his, in order that by acting in concert they would be able to move the boat to the other side of the stream. Persons may establish a common household and join their lives with one another in the familiar ways in which legally married husbands and wives do without striking a preliminary bargain, and only by deciding in ways evident to both, not by word, but by demeanor and deed, to live together.

The story is the same in the case of the moral relations between parents and their children. Blood parents are peculiarly obliged to their offspring in the ways in which step-parents are not. The latter bind themselves by oath to serve as surrogates for the blood parents of the child they adopt and in providing a place for it in their household take one more step to join their lives with it. But blood parents complete their own lives by bringing a child of their own into the world and making it part of the life they share with each other from the time they first become aware of its existence in the womb, preparing for its birth, and planning for the life that lies ahead for it as the person in whom their own lives are to be continued.[6] But however it may have taken place, the rights and obligations of parents and children, husband and wife, depend on the ways in which their lives are joined within the social institution of the family, not upon the structure of this institution as defined by a set of constitutive rules.

Nor should we imagine, given the very considerable variations in the ways in which father and son, husband and wife, play their roles within the life of the family, that their moral rights and obligations are limited and restricted to the roles they happen to assume with respect to one another. The family is a social institution, part of our social inheritance, which needs to be adapted to and modified in the specific form it takes by the changing and complex circumstances of the larger society of which it is a part. The family, in the relatively primitive circumstances of frontier life in early America, maintained, of necessity, at least a considerable degree of autonomy no longer possible in present-day industrial urban America. The education of children is no longer a matter that falls wholly within the province of parental decision and administration. The automobile alone has effectively and drastically altered the extent to which the lives of teenagers are subject to parental direction and control. And a father who conceives of his role in the lives of his children on the model of a biblical patriarch and joins his life with theirs in accordance with the mutual expectations and dependencies appropriate to that model of family life, will have, we think, a distorted conception of his and their moral rights and obligations. The family, in short, as a social institution is subject to moral scrutiny and appraisal for the propriety of the ways in which its members join their lives with one another and depend upon each other's support for the success of their endeavors. And a wife who meekly accepts the regimentation of her life by her husband and whose own interests as a human being have been largely washed out and circumscribed by her responsibilities within the kitchen and in the bed she shares with him, supports, and is supported by, the agency of a person in ways we do not approve.[7]

The point applies not only to the moral rights and obligations distributed among the members of a family, but to other rights as well, including the right to truthfulness discussed earlier in this chapter. This right, I argued, as in the case of the right created by a promise rests on the right that persons have to pursue their interests. But the interests of human beings are enormously varied and they may include, unfortunately, the interests of terrorists plotting mass extermination. Clearly, morally self-defeating interests such as this one need to be excluded from the set of interests to the pursuit of which human beings as such have any moral right. But there are other, less radically defective sorts of cases. For we may or may not share the accepted standards of a given social group and the requirement of truthfulness must not therefore be tied too closely to those purposes and interests that are featured in the prevalent lines of conduct in which, typically, its members engage. And the requirement of truthfulness without which the activities of the various members of a family must founder must not be tied to the specific interests they happen to have in maintaining, for example, the authoritarian rule of a parent who dictates how he and others are to live under his tight control, lest the appeal to the right to truthfulness in imposing restraints upon the conduct of others become a shibboleth that serves only to preserve morally askew arrangements. Truistically, the pursuit of the interests to which agents are entitled must not be morally self-defeating as in the cases of terrorists bent on mad and immoral conduct. And it is unhelpful, because circular, to specify the interests as those which agents are entitled to have. In any case, *which* interests are agents entitled to pursue and on what ground that avoids circularity? The trouble is not only that the interests of persons are enormously varied, differing from one individual to another even within the same social unit, but that everything depends upon the circumstances in which these interests are carried forward as to whether or not their pursuit contributes to morally acceptable arrangements. The interest of a wife in devoting herself to the maintenance of a household may be desirable and necessary, given her husband's role as a breadwinning factory employee; but it may also be that in playing this role as housekeeper she is, willingly as this may be done, bolstering an unduly sensitive male ego and blighting her own life by abandoning aspirations she may have had to a career of her own for which she is eminently qualified.

It is an old story that truth-telling, promise-keeping, etc. may be pernicious in special circumstances, as much so as the loyalty that binds the members of a group of political scoundrels; and so it may well be with the pursuit of interests that persons may happen to have to which, in normal circumstances, they have, as we often express it, 'every right'. In the instance of a family arrangement in which the husband and father assumes the role of ruler and imposes, even with their consent, the roles of subjects upon his wife and children—theirs being not to reason why but how to do and obey—there is no room for pride or self-congratulation on the part of a wife who blights her own life by confining her role to her servile chores. She *ought* to acquire interests of her own. And her husband, in channeling her interests as he does even with her acquiescence, is treating her as one would a race-horse by putting blinders on it in order to render it more efficient in the performance of the function for which it has been groomed.

Why then *should* she broaden her horizons and develop her own interests? Is it that this would enable her to enjoy a comfortable existence? That may be one reason, but it is not the sole or even the most important consideration. For even if this outcome did not result, we should still feel that it would be a more desirable state of affairs. Our sense of the impropriety involved in relegating our housewife to her servile role is that it is an offense against her as a human being, that her husband owes her, as a matter of her *right*, the kind of treatment that will enable her to develop interests of her own, as the particular human being she is with her native endowments and the capacities she may acquire, and that in imposing his will on her he has seriously undermined and even forfeited the rights which, in normal and acceptable arrangements, husbands have with respect to their wives. For as a human being with rights of her own, she is on terms of moral equality with her husband, and entitled to the assistance and encouragement she needs from her husband in order to broaden her interests and to live a life with him in which she is able to carry on her affairs within and without the circle of family life with dignity, as the particular individual she is, with her temperament, endowments and the opportunities that are made available for her to pursue interests of her own, interests that do not merely cater to the wishes, whims and demands of her husband. It is in the ways in which she joins *this* kind of life with the lives of others within the common life of the family that there are, paradigmatically, the moral rights of husband and wife, father and sons, to truthfulness and promise-keeping.

I have argued that the right to truthfulness from others, to their making good the pledges they have given us and to the support that the members of a family give one another rests on the right of persons to pursue their interests. But these interests are not to be specified unhelpfully, and circularly, as the interests persons have a right to pursue. Neither are they to be identified with the interests they happen to have, impoverished as they are in radically defective social arrangements. Human interests are of course a function of the periods in which human beings live, the particular historical and social circumstances of their time and place, of the specific circumstances in which human beings conduct their lives and within which they develop, given their endowments and the opportunities that are available to them. But the conception of the right of a human being is the conception of a normative status that he has with respect to others, and it is to be understood, if at all, only in terms of its place in the scheme of related concepts in which it has its place. Specifically, it is to be understood by reference to the role it plays when the appropriate setting for its enjoyment is present, when those who possess such rights are given the opportunities to develop their capacities, acquire the interests suitable to their endowments and training and the opportunities to pursue these interests in ways that establish them on terms of moral equality with others and with the dignity that is theirs when all concerned recognize and deal with them as beings to whom others are accountable, as they are to them.

In short, an appropriate conceptual setting is required in order to make sense of our talk of the rights of persons to pursue their interests—the kind outlined in Chapter I—and of our talk of the right a person has to interests he does not in fact possess. Rights cannot be construed as mystic badges that exist *in vacuo*. And our talk about them needs to be made intelligible in terms of what is implied by their exercise and enjoyment, including the circumstances in which individuals develop interests and conduct themselves in ways in which it is apparent to all concerned that the conditions of accountability apply not only to them but as persons with rights to anyone else in his relevant dealings with them. Unless this normative condition is at least moderately satisfied, the 'right' to pursue one's interests may be no better than the 'right' of a member of any morally askew social arrangement to conform to the oppressive constraints imposed upon him by the social role to which he or she is confined. Unless this normative condition is at least moderately satisfied, the rights of the members of the group with respect to one another may be forfeited or seriously eroded.

The argument presented here is that it is not by virtue of a set of rules that define offices within the family structure or by virtue of the *de facto* roles that persons play in any form of family life that its members have their characteristic rights and obligations as parent or child, husband or wife, but rather by the ways in which they join their lives as the individuals they are, given the normatively appro-

IV

Justice, Institutions and Persons

In the account so far given of moral rights, the concept of a person, as an agent who is sensitive to a variety of circumstances in those situations in which his life is joined with that of others, is of central importance. Persons are individuals, with their specific hopes and aspirations, projects and programs, sensibilities and personalities—matters to which those who have rights and obligations with respect to them must attend, if properly they are to bear their moral burdens. But the view thus advanced stands in such marked contrast with the doctrine presented by John Rawls in *A Theory of Justice*,[1] that it may be well before proceeding further to examine that doctrine lest it appear that the present account is altogether misguided.

I

I shall begin with an exposition of the relevant and salient features of the theory of justice advanced by Rawls. I shall then turn to a quite detailed examination of the account given by Rawls of the obligation of promises, where, as he puts it, the obligations are owed to particular individuals, in order to test, in this important instance, the adequacy of this new form of Kantianism and, as I shall argue, moral institutionalism. Finally, I shall conclude with some observations, on the basis of the discussion of Rawls's treatment of the obligation of promises, concerning the conception that is implicit in the doctrine advanced of the morally relevant attributes of personhood, i.e. the attributes to which we need to attend in judging that conduct is just.

Rawls's view is admittedly Kantian but with considerable differences, notably in the manner in which it admits empirical considerations of various sorts on a number of issues. It professes to be contractarian, but this is hardly accurate since the sort of agreement upon which it attempts to provide a basis for the determination of the justice of institutions and individual action does not take the form of a contract or covenant between persons by virtue of which certain rights and obligations of the parties concerned are brought into being.[2] Neither does the agreement in question involve, in the way in which the traditional Lockean contract theory does, any reference to fundamental rights that need to be honored if the continued exercise of political power is to be justified. The agreement is not a bargain or contract entered into by those party to it; it is not agreement *to do* anything, but, rather, *to accept* certain moral principles. It is not even an agreement among persons, but something, rather, that a single person could accept or choose. But if so chosen or accepted it is supposedly something that would be chosen or accepted by any rational person. In short, what is fundamental in Rawls's account are certain moral principles of justice on which all rational persons would upon reflection agree and which can be applied, so Rawls argues, in an ordered manner in appraising, first, political and other forms of social arrangements and, only then, the particular actions of persons that fall under them.

This Kantian requirement that the fundamental principles of justice be acceptable to any rational person can be satisfied, clearly, only if a wide range of facts that differentiate persons are ruled out as morally irrelevant. For Kant the exclusions are extreme; all empirical facts about human beings are set aside, the only relevant consideration in respect of the so-called fundamental principle of morality being their nature as rational beings endowed with will. For Rawls, on the other hand, the condition that in choosing each chooses for all, is that of persons in the so-called original position—the circumstances in which the choice of principles is to be made—from which some but not all empirical considerations are to be excluded from consideration. What is left as a basis upon which the choice of principles is to be made are matters that are available and applicable to all.

Consider the information that is available to persons in the original position. They are supposed to know certain general facts about society.

They understand political affairs and the principles of economic theory; they know the basis of social organization and the laws of human psychology. Indeed, the parties are presumed to know whatever general facts affect the choice of the principles of justice. There are no limitations on general information, that is, on general laws and theories, since conceptions of justice must be adjusted to the characteristics of the systems of social cooperations which they are to regulate, and there is no reason to rule out these facts. It is, for example, a consideration against a conception of justice that in view of the laws of moral psychology, men would not acquire a desire to act upon it even when the institutions of their society satisfied it. (pp. 137–8)

Further, the parties concerned recognize certain primary goods, i.e. things that any rational person wants: health and vigor, intelligence and imagination and, in addition to these sorts of natural goods, certain *social* primary goods indispensable to any person who has any sort of rational plan of life: rights and liberties that social organizations distribute among their members, powers and opportunities of action in the realization of desire and ambition, income and wealth, and, centrally important, the primary good of self-respect (p. 62). But those specific conceptions of the good which particular individuals have and which are likely to bring them into conflict with each other (e.g. the desire for political leadership or supremacy) are to be ruled out from the list of items to be taken into account. What they know, in short, are facts about themselves that apply to every person; only in this way will it be possible to achieve unanimity, so that in choosing principles of justice each will be choosing for all. It is assumed, of course, that the persons involved are rational, mutually disinterested, i.e. neither altruistic nor envious, and endowed with a sense of justice that will enable them to adhere to whatever social arrangements are made in accordance with the principles of justice that are chosen and thus insure the stability of just arrangements. But beyond these matters which are common to all parties in the original position, and in which, therefore, complete equality obtains, everything else is hidden behind the veil of ignorance: the specific place in society of each particular person, his social and economic class or status, his fortune, good or bad, in respect of a wide variety of natural endowments, of birth, abilities, intelligence, etc. In short, in choosing those principles that just social arrangements must satisfy, each chooses as a representative man, on terms of equality with everyone else. Finally, the choice to be made is a rational one in the sense that it is the choice that is most prudent for a person to make given the situation of equality with respect to others in the ways described.

Whether these conditions of choice compel the acceptance of the principles of justice as Rawls defines them is a matter I do not wish here to discuss. Nor is it a small matter to be granted without serious reflection and discussion that no particular conception of the good by which men are often brought into conflict with each other may operate as a constraint upon the principles of justice to be selected. For it could be argued that the veil of ignorance obscures too much and leaves us with too impossibly abstract a conception of human beings to provide an adequate basis for rational choice. Thus, one might argue, we need more information about the character of human beings, about the manner in which the interests and concerns of persons operate and develop in the diverse and changing relations between human beings in order for us to make reasonable choices of moral principles. No doubt the requirement of unanimity with respect to fundamental principles of justice requires the abstraction provided by such a heavy veil of ignorance; but perhaps this requirement itself needs to be brought into question. The issues here are complex and important and should not be allowed to slip by undetected and unexamined. Indeed I shall return to some of these later in the discussion. Nor should it be argued that the conception of justice is essentially egoistic because it is posed in terms of what an individual in the original situation would be led on grounds of prudence or considerations of possible gains and losses to accept. For to decide what principles to accept given the veil of ignorance is already to adopt a moral point of view and to exclude as morally irrelevant just those empirical considerations of private interest that prudent and even egoistic men employ in their calculations. The veil of ignorance is simply a heuristic device employed in order to establish the disinterestedness involved in the moral attitude; and Rawls's talk of the prudential weighing of gains and losses by persons in the original position is an unnecessary and obscuring shuffle in an argument designed to show that the satisfaction of the principles of justice by any social arrangement is most advantageous even to those who are most disadvantaged by virtue of the deprivations to which they are subject by the accidents of birth or by their shortcomings in respect of intelligence, abilities and other endowments.

What is necessary and essential in Rawls's view is its egalitarianism. Justice is the fairness with which benefits and burdens are distributed among persons; and the principles that such distributions must satisfy are those chosen by any and all persons on the basis of considerations that apply, and are known to apply, equally to all, and are correctly weighed and pondered. These principles are, first, that each person is entitled to 'the most extensive basic liberty compatible with a similar liberty for others', and, second, that 'social and economic inequalities are to be arranged so that they are both (a) reasonably expected to be advantageous to everyone, and (b) attached to positions and offices open to all'. (p. 60. But see also the later formulation on p. 250.)

All of this relates to the justice of institutions; and, clearly, further matters need to be adduced in order to deal with the justice of the actions of individuals. We need to distinguish at this point between two sorts of cases, those in which the social arrangements in which the actions performed are ideal since they satisfy the two principles of justice, and those in which they are to varying degrees imperfect. The latter sorts of cases often involve competing considerations for which there is no simple solution that can be reached in any straightforward manner. Rawls thinks that they are less fundamental cases than those in which the actions are performed in institutional arrangements that are ideal. Accordingly, I shall ignore them in this exposition and discussion of his views.

Given that institutions do satisfy the principles of justice, what sorts of requirements would anyone accept as constraints upon his conduct? Consider what sorts of constraints anyone in the original position would accept. To begin with, any person in that position would accept certain natural duties, the most important of which is the duty 'to support and to further just institutions' (p. 334). Another natural duty is the duty that each person has to respect every other person as a moral being, this being manifested in a willingness to see the situation of others from their points of view, and in each being prepared to give reasons for his actions whenever the interests of others are materially affected (p. 337). And there is, also, the natural duty of mutual aid. In these, as in any other natural duty, everyone benefits, and in accepting them any person in the original position accepts them on behalf of all.

But there are other requirements distinguished from the preceding by virtue of the fact that they derive from voluntary acts.

These acts may be the giving of express or tacit undertakings, such as promises and agreements but they need not be, as in the case of accepting benefits. Further, the content of obligations is always defined by an institution or practice the rules of which specify what it is that one is required to do. And, finally, obligations are normally owed to definite individuals, namely, those who are cooperating together to maintain the arrangement in question. (p. 113)

The fact that their content, i.e. what it is that one is morally obliged to do, is defined by an institution or practice, should not lead us to identify the moral obligations in question with the duties that define the particular position or office in a given institution or practice. The office of president, whether of a corporation or of a nation, is defined by certain duties as well as prerogatives, liberties and so on, but the moral obligation to perform these duties is distinct from the duties that are constitutive or definitive of the office. The identification of this moral obligation with the duties of the office is one form of ethical conventionalism, the consequence of which can only be to render pleonastic the phrase 'the moral obligation to perform the duties of the office' and, incoherent, the question whether one is morally obligated to perform those duties.

How then can the (moral) obligation to perform the duties of any office arise? The principle appealed to by Rawls is the principle of fairness which holds that

> a person is required to do his part as defined by the rules of an institution when two conditions are met: first, the institution is just (or fair), that is, it satisfies the two principles of justice; and second, one has voluntarily accepted the benefit of the arrangement or taken advantage of the opportunities it offers to further one's interests. (pp. 111–12)

I shall not here discuss the question of the rationale of decisions made when the first condition is not satisfied— the issues this question raises are too complex to be dealt with here— but turn rather to the question of why it is that one should accept this principle as stated. The reason, we are told, is this: the two principles of justice define what is a fair share for anyone, whatever his office or institutional role may be in the structure of any social arrangement. If, therefore, this structure is just, each person receives a fair share when all, including himself, do their part. But in addition to this statement of the matter, Rawls also tells us that

> when a number of persons engage in a mutually advantageous cooperative venture according to rules, and thus restrict their liberty in ways necessary to yield advantages for all, those who have submitted to these restrictions have a right to a similar acquiescence on the part of those who have benefited from their submission. (p. 112)

It might appear that this latter justification of the principle of fairness is different from the former in that it appeals to the rights of individuals, and that this along with the remark by Rawls that 'obligations are normally owed to definite individuals' (p. 113) introduces a consideration of rights that goes beyond the egalitarianism in Rawls's account of justice as fairness. This, however, would be a mistake. For here as elsewhere, and first appearances to the contrary notwithstanding, there is, as I shall argue, a failure to recognize the relevance of rights to obligations and indeed to considerations of justice in general; and, because of this fact, the conception of a person as a moral agent, which is implied in Rawls's account of these matters, is far too abstract to mesh with our ordinary moral intuitions. And we can do no better, in my opinion, than to begin with the account Rawls gives us of the so-called obligation of promises.

II

Philosophers have applied the terms 'moral rule', 'precept' and 'maxim' to the moral requirement that one ought to keep one's promises. Rawls uses the expression 'principle of fidelity' and this, he tells us, is 'that bona fide promises are to be kept' (p. 346). The restriction of the principle to bona fide promises would appear to be too stringent, for, as we should all concede as soon as we reflect upon the matter, we are bound even by promises that are not made in good faith. In any case, this principle, restricted or not to bona fide promises, is distinguished by Rawls from the rule of promising. The former is a moral principle, whereas the latter is simply a constitutive convention.

Promising, (we are told), is an action defined by a public system of rules. These rules are, as in the case of institutions generally, a set of constitutive conventions. Just as the rules of games do, they specify certain activities and define certain actions. In the case of promising, the basic rule is that governing the use of the words 'I promise to do x.' It reads roughly as follows: if one says the words, 'I promise to do x' in the appropriate circumstances, one is to do x, unless certain excusing conditions obtain. This rule we may think of as the rule of promising; it may be taken as representing the practice as a whole. It is not itself a moral principle but a constitutive convention. In this respect it is on a par with legal rules and statutes, and rules of games; as these do, it exists in a society when it is more or less regularly acted upon. (pp. 344–5)

The comparison of the so-called rule of promising with a rule of a game such as e.g., the rule in baseball that a man is struck out at the plate when he receives three strikes, is one that needs special emphasis. Just as striking out is defined as, or is constituted by, receiving a third strike, so promising is defined as or is constituted by the uttering of the words, 'I promise to do x', (or, as we might add, by its equivalent). *That* is what being out at the plate is; and so *this* is what promising consists in. There is a certain form of activity governed by certain formulated (or formulable) rules (for one can play a game even when the rules have not as yet been codified, but are understood). And there is a certain kind of practice called promising governed—the implication is clear from the account given by Rawls—by a set of rules (conveyed somehow to us when we are taught what it is to promise). It is understood what the appropriate circumstances are in which the verbal performance of uttering the words, 'I promise to do x' (or its equivalent) constitutes promising, or what the possible excusing conditions referred to by the clause 'unless certain excusing conditions obtain'; but given that the circumstances are appropriate and the excusing conditions are absent, the rule of promising tells us that 'one is to do x'. This is the game, practice or institution (all of these terms have been applied to describe the activity) of promising. And if there is any sort of parallel between constitutive rules of games and the constitutive rule of promising, the appropriate circumstances along with the excusing conditions can be defined, i.e. spelled out in detail.

I shall leave this last point for the moment, in order to complete Rawls's account of the matter. The rule of promising is publicly understood by all who engage in the practice, and it is a just one, for the offices of promiser and promisee are open to all, and all benefit from the arrangements. Accordingly,

in making a promise, that is, in saying the words, 'I promise to do x' in the appropriate circumstances, one knowingly invokes the rule and accepts the benefits of a just arrangement. There is no obligation to make a promise, let us assume; one is at liberty to do so or not. But since by hypothesis the practice is just, the principle of fairness applies and one is to do as the rule specifies, that is, to do x. The obligation to keep a promise is a consequence of the principle of fairness. (p. 346)

For remember what the principle of fairness tells us: that a person is morally required to do his part in a just institutional arrangement when one has voluntarily accepted the benefits it provides. One ought morally to leave the batter's box when one has received three strikes and thus struck out—it would be unjust because unfair to remain there and demand that the pitcher throw the ball again so that one could continue to swing at the ball, a privilege no one else had enjoyed. And in the same way one is morally obliged to do x, given that one has uttered the words, 'I promise to do x', (in the appropriate circumstances and in the absence of excusing conditions); the practice of promising is just, and how unfair it is not to do x if, after having been the recipient of the benefits of promises in the past, one now refuses to accord someone such benefits.

A. One ought to keep one's promise— why?— because the failure to do so is unfair; and it is unfair because one is thereby prepared to accept the enjoyment of benefits for oneself while refusing to accord them to others, thus doing violence to the terms of equality in which one stands morally with respect to anyone else. But this sort of consideration is clearly irrelevant to the matter at issue. No doubt, if I am to give myself or anyone else preferential or unusual treatment, then some special consideration is required in justification of this fact. But the issue in the present case is not whether I am to rest content with benefits enjoyed by me in the past while depriving others who are similarly situated of receiving corresponding benefits, as a matter of fairness or reciprocity. It is, rather, the question whether in the case of one who has made a promise there is some special feature of the circumstances *then present* that justifies one's giving another person special treatment by performing the given action. And the answer is that the special feature of the situation that justifies that special treatment is that in so acting one is according the person the right established by the solemn promise one has given him, or, equivalently put, that one is meeting the quite special obligation one has assumed.

Rawls's discussion completely misses what is central in the case of promises, namely, the rights that these confer, and, consequently, the fact that the keeping of promises is the honoring or according of these rights, equivalently, the meeting of the obligations to the recipients of those promises. It is, in fact, astonishing that he could think that this issue can be identified with a quite different one, namely, the question of whether or not it would be fair to make use of social or institutional arrangements in one's own case in ways that depart from the norms that we are prepared to insist upon for others on the basis of equality. One may be unfair to others in not assuming on equal terms with them the burden of supporting a social arrangement that is beneficial to all those who participate in it and hence worthy of support from all concerned. But it is one thing to be charged with being a slacker in being unwilling to bear one's fair share of a burden that falls equally upon all and quite a different matter with violating the right that one has freely conferred upon another, and, in so doing, morally damaging him. Those who parasitically enjoy the benefits of a given institutional arrangement without being willing to contribute their fair share of the effort required to insure that it remains viable are at fault; but there is another, quite different sort of fault, more obviously involved in the breaking of a promise that one ought in fact to keep, namely, the willful disregard for the right of the promisee, thereby doing him moral damage and, I should add, in this way committing an injustice against him.

Rawls's remark that obligations that arise in cases of promises, unlike natural duties, 'are normally owed to definite individuals' is, therefore, quite misleading. Suppose that it is unfair to others— those who keep their promises and help to preserve promising as an eminently useful social arrangement—if, after having promised I now 'cop out' when it is to my advantage to do so. And let it be granted, for the moment, that in doing this I am unfair to all those who engage in promise-making and promise-keeping. Still the obligation of promises is an obligation to those to whom they are given. The obligation I assume in making a promise is *not* the obligation I assume to all those, past and present, here and everywhere else, who make and keep promises, but an obligation I assume to the particular person to whom I make that promise. At best, others, whoever they may be and who are not party to this specific promise transaction in which I engage with this particular person, are entitled, with respect to this obligation, to disapprove if they are spectators of what does happen, and in the event that I break the promise I have given that particular person, of my having failed to meet my obligation to *him*, of my having been unjust to *him*, of my having violated *his* right, of my having willfully let *him* down. But these are disapprovals that involve *him*, not those uninvolved in that moral relation between promiser and promisee.

Surely it is this consideration, not the alleged unfairness upon which Rawls focuses his attention, that is crucially important. Rawls speaks of a right which those have— who are and have been involved in promises as promisers and promisees, here and now, and past and present, and who have performed conscientiously and properly in such transactions—'to a similar acquiescence' on the part of all others who have benefited from past transactions of promises (p.

112), the thought being that since I have benefited from the promise-keeping acts of others, that if I did not provide a similar benefit to a person to whom I have made a promise, I would not be according those, who have made and kept *their* promises, a right that they have to a similar performance on my part. But suppose, for a moment, that I would be unfair to others—the many conscientious persons who have made and kept their promises—would I, if unlike them, I were now to break my solemn promise, violate *their* right? What right do they have in the present matter? Is it a right that I would now violate, if in breaking my promise, I would be unfair to them? Or, is it a right that they have to complain that I am unfair to them? Would I do violence to their status as moral agents by subverting those endeavors in which they are engaged, acting in a way that is tantamount to interfering with those endeavors? I neither know *who* these people are—all those conscientious promisers and promisees, past and present, here, there and everywhere. Nor are these numberless persons, in most cases, even alive to serve as the bearers of a right that they have; they have no right, for they no longer exist. The idea that *they* have a right in the present case is, on its very face, preposterous. At best, what could be argued is that if there are any such persons around who were aware of my moral malfeasance, they would be entitled, in the sense that they would be justified in doing so, to complain that I was being unfair, not that I had violated their right, or that I was guilty of wronging them, or that I ought to redress the moral damage to them that I was perpetrating.

If I have a dozen candies and proceed to distribute them among the dozen street urchins clamoring for them, but give one of them two candies leaving none for the last member of the group, he has a right to complain that I am unfair, but not a right to complain that I had violated his right to one of the candies. He has no such right. My action may be arbitrary, inconsiderate, wrong, or unfair, but hardly a case of violating his right. And to say that he has a right to complain is only to say that he is justified in or has sufficient warrant for, complaining. But there are all sorts of grounds one might have for complaints against others in which there is no consideration of a right that has been abridged or violated: the inconsiderateness they show, their boorishness, unkindness, rudeness, etc. And, further, none of these need involve any injustice as we understand this term. It may be true that if one is treated unjustly, one is treated unfairly —just conduct is the general rule and injustice a departure from the generality of cases and in this way discriminatory or unfair—but it is not obvious at least that the converse is true and, hence, that the notion of the fairness with which one shoulders along with others, and on equal terms with them, both the burdens and the benefits of any sort of venture in which one engages with them, captures our sense of what is involved in the concept of justice, namely, the recognition in our thoughts and our deeds of the rights of others, the violation of which would constitute the injustices we commit against them.

B. But is it in fact unfairness against all those who are or have been conscientious promise-keepers—persons who have availed themselves of the benefits of promising but who have redeemed the pledges that they have given—if now, after having promised, I fail to keep my word? We can assimilate this sort of case with those cases in which there does seem to be ground for the charge of unfairness, cases to which the principle of fairness does seem to apply, namely, those in which one enters into some institutional relation with others in such a manner that all participate in a 'mutually advantageous cooperative venture according to certain rules and thus restrict their liberty' so that 'those who have submitted to these restrictions have a right to a similar acquiescence on the part of those who have benefited from their submission' (p. 343). Here, it would seem all who are involved cooperate in various ways in accordance with rules that define the several offices or roles of the cooperating persons. Several points are noteworthy here. The institutional arrangement is one in which its viability depends upon the cooperative activity of its members. Each of the members occupies a role or office defined by rules that set forth the duties, prerogatives and privileges involved. The submission to the restrictions imposed by these rules is advantageous to all who participate in that institutional arrangement. And, finally, the failure to submit to these restrictions, while enjoying the benefits of the particular office that depend upon the submission to restrictions on the part of others, is unfair to them.

(1) To begin with, who are the cooperating participants in the practice or so-called institution of promising? These, it would appear from the account given by Rawls, are the persons who engage in promising including not only I who have promised and the person to whom I have given my word, but all others who have availed themselves of the device of promising, in order advantageously to exchange benefits by giving and receiving promises. But this *is* fishy.

For nothing I now do, in refusing to keep *my* promise, interferes with the benefits that others may obtain by entering into promise transactions with each other. If I now shirk my duty in willfully breaking my promise, in what way am I failing to cooperate with others who in no way are party to the present transaction in which I am now engaged with that one and only one person to whom I made the promise? In what way am I failing to cooperate with the countless and indeed unknown persons who make, have made, or will make promises to others, or who receive, have received, or will receive them from others? Surely I do not interfere with *their* enjoyment of the benefits that *their* promising or their accepting of promises have provided or will provide *them*. The case is altogether different from an institutional arrangement that depends, for the benefits that each obtains, upon cooperative activities in accordance with the appropriate rules, statutes or regulations that define their various offices or roles. In the case of a promise transaction there are only two persons, normally, who are involved. If there is any cooperative activity from which both benefit, it is the cooperative activity in which these engage with each other.

(2) But it is not even obvious that the two persons involved in the promise transaction are engaged in the sort of cooperative activity involved in institutional arrangements. For this would imply that there is some joint venture in which they are involved which depends for its success upon both parties doing their different parts in some sort of cooperative activity; and, unfortunately, there does not seem to be any independently specifiable venture in which they are supposed to be engaged, in the way in which this would appear to be the case in institutional arrangements or games. In the case, e.g., of a legislative institution, the joint venture is the enactment of laws, statutes, etc. that requires that each of the persons involved perform his activities in accordance with the rules or regulations that define his office. In the case of a game, there is victory (or defeat) towards which all of the participants may contribute in one way or another. But what is that joint venture in which promiser and promisee are supposedly engaged and to which each contributes by performing the duties that define his role in the transaction? One can imagine cases in which there is a joint venture, e.g. a modified form of Hume's example of a tacit covenant in which, however, the two persons who seat themselves in a rowboat proceed on the basis of an explicit promise that each makes to the other to do his part in

rowing the boat across the stream. But this is a *very* special case since the joint venture in which both parties are engaged is the subject of a promise that each party makes to the other: each promises to do his part if the other will do his. But if A promises to do x to B, where there is no reciprocal promise on the part of B to anything at all, there is no such joint venture in which both A and B are engaged. Is the joint venture a mutually advantageous exchange of benefits and burdens? Promises often provide a *quid pro quo*, the promiser assuring the promisee that in return for a benefit now received he will provide the promisee with a benefit at some later time, where the benefit that each receives from the other outweighs the burden he assumes. But no such mutually advantageous exchange of benefits need be involved even in central cases of promises, for that would represent every case of a promise made out of consideration or kindness or compassion for another as a calculating estimate of the profits and losses involved in the transaction. There need be no bargain involved in a promise transaction. Or, is it that there is a cooperative joint venture in this respect, that the promiser in keeping his promise supports the line of conduct the promisee is supposed to be considering and hence the latter's agency in that intended venture? But how then does the promisee cooperate, i.e. what is that joint venture towards which *he* contributes that is specifiable independently of the performances in which he is to be engaged? There does not appear to be anything that would qualify as a cooperative activity in which promiser and promisee are engaged, in some joint venture towards which in their diverse ways they contribute. What we have, rather, is that distinctive way in which in thought and action, each responds to the other, during some segment of his life, in ways that are dictated by his respect for the other as a person, a moral agent.

(3) Perhaps it will be alleged that both promiser and promisee, and in their different ways, contribute to a larger enterprise in which they are engaged, namely, the continued practice of promising in which countless others have been and will be engaged. The practice of promising serves in some way, if not in the form of a barter system that allows for the mutually advantageous exchange of benefits, then in some other way, the needs of human beings. No man is an island, complete and self-sufficient; all require at some point or another the assurances that promises provide that they will be given the support they need in the activities in which they are engaged. To fail to keep

one's promise willfully is to weaken the general confidence upon which the continued existence of promising depends, that promisers and promisees will act responsibly in their relations with each other. Is *this* the joint venture in which you and I are engaged, namely, maintaining the practice of promising, the success of which depends upon the fact that you and I responsibly do our different jobs as promiser and promisee?

Of course, the continued general confidence that promises will be kept (one is reminded here of Hume's argument that all promises must be kept because of the indirect effect of promise-breaking acts upon the utility of the general rule that promises are to be kept) can be maintained, as Mabbott suggested long ago, by keeping dark the failures of promisers.[3] This, however, is not to the point. In general, legislators attempt to conceal their failures to discharge their duties, and the response to the case of promising can be made as indeed Rawls does to cases of malfeasance in legislative offices, namely, that even if the general confidence in promising is maintained, promise-breakers are as unfair as legislators who secretly fail in their duties. In both cases, the benefits that go with the offices are enjoyed without a fair assumption of the burdens imposed by these offices.

Nevertheless, the suggestion will not work. A legislator is unfair to those who cooperate with him in his joint venture—those who serve with him in their diverse offices; but a promise-breaker who merely appears to be maintaining the practice of promising is said to be unfair to those who have nothing to do with him, those who are completely unknown to him or as yet unborn. The only person with whom the promise-breaker is engaged in any sort of venture is the promisee; and, as we have seen, not only is there no joint venture with him in which the promise-breaker is engaged, but it would be as misleading to say that he was being unfair to the person to whom he had made his promise as it would be to say that a murderer was unfair to his victim.

Further, what contribution do I make towards the maintenance of the practice of promising when, whether in fact or merely in appearance, I represent to others that I am faithful to my word? One thing I show, or appear to show, is that I am a person to be trusted, and that others can, with some ground, accept a promise from me as one I shall keep. But do I thereby encourage third parties to accept promises made to them by fourth (and fifth, sixth, etc.) parties? Suppose, in fact, I break my promise, do I thereby in any way weaken or undercut the practice of promises? Hume and his followers to the contrary notwithstanding that surely is not at all clear. What I certainly do is to provide some reason, certainly not sufficient, for others to raise the question of whether *I* am trustworthy; but in the event that I am found to be untrustworthy, does it show anything at all to the effect that *others* are equally untrustworthy? Surely, it must do this if there is any substance to Hume's claims. Certainly promises are not made or accepted without regard to the situations, character and indeed the personalities of the individuals concerned. They are not, therefore, made to or accepted by persons who are strangers to or uninformed about each other; unlike contracts they are even made between persons who are bound by the ties of love and affection.[4] For it is by no means any Tom, Dick or Harry with whom we are prepared to enter into promise transactions. We enter into such transactions with persons for whom the moral sanctions are sufficient to ensure responsible performance, quite unlike the case of a legal contract for which there are reinforcing sanctions available in the form of legal penalties and compensation. Those who like Hume see any indefensible act of promise-breaking as corrosive in its influence upon the general practice of promising are oblivious to the fact that it is only in special circumstances, and with quite special sorts of persons, that we enter into promise relations; and, if we are at all sensible and responsible, we conduct ourselves with respect to each other on the basis of our understanding of each other's interests and traits. And should either of us misjudge the other in unwisely making or accepting a promise, the lesson to be learned by one of the persons from the moral dereliction of the other is not that promises are not much good, but only that it is not much good engaging in promise transactions with that particular individual. And should this sort of thing happen with any considerable frequency, the net effect is not that the practice of promising is threatened but, rather, that the domain of persons with whom one engages in the transaction of promising is narrowed. In the case of contracts, the sanctions are legal, determinable by judicial decision and imposed with the aid of enforcement agencies. Where there is no remedy for breaches of contract, we do not, as in the case of promises, reduce or change in any way the population of the class of persons with whom we enter into contracts, we simply give up the contract as an instrument for the exchange of goods.

(4) Is the practice of promising properly describable as an institu-

tion, with constitutive rules that define the offices or roles of its participants? The short and fast answer of many philosophers, including Rawls, is in the affirmative. For, do we not have as its participants the roles of promiser and promisee? And do we not have as a constitutive rule the following, as Rawls expresses it (on p. 345): 'If one says the words "I promise to do x" in the appropriate circumstances, one is to do x, unless certain excusing conditions obtain. This rule . . . may be taken as representing the practice as a whole. It is not itself a moral principle but a constitutive convention.' Certainly, we have the roles of promiser and promisee. Shall we then say that the practice of telling and listening to jokes, and the practice of issuing orders and obeying them are also institutions? And shouldn't one also say that, as in the case of promising, so in the case of joking, there is a constitutive rule that 'if one tells a joke, in the appropriate circumstances (not in one's sleep, or under hypnosis, etc.) and in the absence of excusing conditions, one is not to laugh at it oneself; and the person to whom the tale is told, in the appropriate circumstances, is to do such and such'? And so too in the case of ordering and obeying; one could also formulate its so-called constitutive rules that define the roles or offices of those who order and those who obey!

In his preface to *Philosophical Investigations* Wittgenstein remarked that he was publishing that work with some misgivings. Those misgivings were well-founded; and here is new confirmation. There are language-games of various sorts: promising, joking, ordering, etc., etc. But to construe these as institutions on the ground that they involve roles played by persons involved in these language-games, and to suppose, therefore, that there are constitutive rules defining these roles, is only to mangle the central idea involved in the notion of a language-game. Promising, like praying, joking, ordering, requesting, asking, etc., etc. are language-games—human activities in which language is employed in communication. They are not themselves institutional practices, however much the latter may presuppose them. The existence of our institutions of justice requires that there be the language-game of asking questions and eliciting answers in the cross-examination of witnesses; but asking a question and receiving an answer is not itself an institutional practice. It merely marks a characteristically human form of activity, one form that human life takes, without which other activities, including those performed in the course of one's institutional duties, could not occur.

(a) Institutions may be established by formal agreement. They are often the product of social habit and custom. Their continued existence depends upon a number of factors—the circumstances of human life, the success, real or imagined, in the achievement of their purposes, and the observance at least generally of the restraints imposed upon individuals which are associated with their roles or offices within the institutions. An institution is therefore a relatively fragile form of association between individuals; for one reason or another it may cease to be viable and come to an end. Is this equally true of the practice of promising?

Certainly we can imagine all sorts of cases in which the practice of promising, with the moral implications it has for us, would cease: The human race could conceivably, and if pessimists are correct should certainly, be extinguished. Conceivably, human beings could be transmuted into beings of a radically different order, so that the moral background or setting required by the creation of rights and obligations by promises would be missing, just as it is when these same locutions are employed by the members of a band of ruffians or fanatical terrorists committed to some insane enterprise. Promises are given and accepted by persons between whom there is a substantial basis of confidence that this moral background will in fact enable the persons concerned to join their lives in the manner in which this occurs in those central or paradigmatic cases to which the array of moral concepts, in which our concept of a promise has its distinctive place, has application without severe truncation or attentuation.

Now our concept of a person applies to beings who are engaged in a wide variety of everyday transactions—the language-games in which orders are given and obeyed, questions are asked and answered, reasons including moral reasons are advanced or weighed, predictions are made and later judged for their accuracy, and among many, many others, the formal assurances that are conveyed to persons, whether in the context of their institutional relations or informally during the course of their everyday activities, that they may proceed fully confident of the support that the actions and omissions of others provide their own agencies. To suppose that we can understand what it is to be a person simply in respect of certain psychological and physical attributes or properties—never mind the social and moral relations in which they go about their affairs with each other—is indeed to miss the point of Wittgenstein's insistence that any elucidation of a concept must proceed by bringing the relevant parts of our speech back to the language-games in which they have their function in our language. Locke's insistence that the concept of a person and of personal identity applies to beings who are concerned and accountable, that 'person' is a forensic term, in this way makes good sense, far more than the familiar philosophical talk about persons as beings who can be understood in psycho-physical terms and for whom any assurances of the support that persons provide each other in their daily affairs are institutional in character and like any of these that are capable of coming into being or passing away, external adornments or trappings that can be sloughed off but in no way are essential to them.

It may be of interest in this connection to consider the manner in which Kant, in Section 2 of *The Foundations of the Metaphysics of Morals*, argues against the validity of the maxim discussed in the last of four cases in which he illustrates the manner in which the Principle of the Categorical Imperative may be employed. Kant takes it to be a purely contingent fact that human beings 'need the love and sympathy of others' including, one might add, their need of the support that others may provide for their plans and projects. Kant argues, accordingly, that there is no conceptual incoherence—the form of which he takes to be self-contradiction—involved in the supposition of 'a universal law of nature' that accords with the maxim that one should be indifferent to the needs and hardships of others. He would, therefore, consider it conceptually coherent at least that one might will never to provide any support for the agency of others under any circumstances whatsoever. Kant's argument against the propriety of the maxim involved in this case appeals to the fact that, as he puts it, the willing of the maxim conflicts with itself since, as a matter of fact, 'instances often arise in which anyone needs the love and sympathy of others' and, presumably, the help that others can give us. The will to seek help from others would conflict with the willing involved in the universalizing of the maxim not to want just such help for oneself. (The text should serve to dispel the widespread but mistaken view that Kant nowhere makes any reference to inclination in the determination of our moral duties; and for those already disposed to subscribe to this misinterpretation, his express declaration in a foot-note in this same Section 2 of the sense in which he employs the terms 'perfect' and 'imperfect' duties, according to which the latter does involve consideration of inclination, is either ignored or taken to be a concession that is inconsistent with the general line of Kant's thought.)

But what would it be like for individuals never to offer help of any sort to one another, never to cooperate in any form of enterprise, never to exercise any mutual restraints in their affairs with one another, and, most important of all, wholly lack that moral background involved in the recognition of the right of someone else to pursue his interests, without which the use of promise-locutions ceases to have the moral import it has for us? Would this be intelligible or merely bizarre? Even if we admitted the intelligibility of this limiting case, even if we thought that our concept of a person could then apply in an altogether unproblematic fashion, it would imply a far more drastic change in human life than would be afforded by the disappearance of any of our social institutions. For if promising were to cease to be a viable form of moral transaction between human beings, the nature of human life itself would have to be radically altered in such a way that the moral background and the moral understanding that exists between promiser and promisee would be missing, and with it the mutual restraints, support, cooperation and help that makes possible training, education, discourse, culture or social relations of any sort. Or, are we asked to consider the possibility that promises would cease to perform any useful function if persons were far more generously disposed towards others, ideally altruistic in their readiness to offer each other the assistance they require in order to carry out their plans? But here again the supposition, that everyone need only ask in order to be given, presupposes that the interests of persons are completely congruent; this, even if imaginable, is practically impossible.

In short, to think of the practice of promising as an institution is to put it on all fours with any specific institution that can be established or dissolved, develop or fade away. And this is at the very least problematic.

(b) According to Rawls the content of the moral obligation involved in promising, i.e. what it is that a person who promises is morally obliged to do is specified by a rule that defines the action of promising (p. 113). To ask, therefore, what it is that those who engage in a promise transaction are morally required to do is to ask what the rules of the institution or practice of promising are.

Now

promising is an action defined by a public system of rules. These rules are, as in the case of institutions generally, a set of constitutive conventions. Just as the rules of games do, they specify certain activities and define certain actions. In the case of promising, the basic rule is that governing the use of the words 'I promise to do x.' It reads roughly as follows: if one says the words, 'I promise to do x' in the appropriate circumstances, one is to do x, unless certain excusing conditions obtain. This rule we may think of as the rule of promising: it may be taken as representing the practice as a whole. It is not itself a moral principle but a constitutive convention. In this respect it is on a par with legal rules and statutes, and rules of games; as these do, it exists in a society when it is more or less regularly acted upon. (pp. 344–5)

Several comments are in order. First, the words 'I promise to do x' must be uttered 'in the appropriate circumstances', e.g. when the speaker is fully conscious, when not suffering delusions or hallucinations, and so on, and he is required to do x 'unless certain excusing conditions obtain'. Since the rule is on a par with legal statutes or the rules of games, we need more than a few examples of the required circumstances and the excusing conditions if we are to be able to apply the rule of promising in the way in which we apply legal statutes and rules of games. On this score Rawls tells us that 'in general, the circumstances giving rise to a promise and the excusing conditions must be defined so . . . as to make the practice a rational means whereby men can enter into and stabilize cooperative agreements for mutual advantage. Unavoidably the many complications here cannot be considered' (p. 345). Why not, if the rule of promising is on a par with legal statutes and rules of games? One might argue that it is not possible so to state any rule or statute that every thinkable eventuality is anticipated and incorporated in the statement of the rule or statute in such a manner that it could then be applied without further reflection, as a kind of airtight directive, to any situation to which it applies. Any rule or statute has its characteristic open texture. Is there a rule in baseball, for example, to cover the following conceivable case: the batter hits a high fly and the ball is caught by a pelican in its beak as it is flying overhead above the field of play? Nevertheless, while rules of games or legal statutes unavoidably exhibit an open texture and cannot be construed as airtight directives that can be applied in a simple-minded fashion to any and all conceivable cases, they do involve much more than general policy guidance for determining when the circumstances are appropriate and what will count as excusing conditions. In the case of legal statutes, in addition to the general policies pertaining to social welfare and the basic rights of individuals spelled out in constitutional documents, there are other items that guide judges in their decisions:

precedents and an existing complex body of codified law of a considerable degree of specificity relevant to the duties, privileges and prerogatives of persons in institutional offices of various sorts. And in the case of rules of games even relatively rare occurrences are explicitly brought within the purview of rules, as experience in the playing of games mounts and as more and more contingencies are taken into account: consider, for example, the ruling that referees must make when the batter, in baseball, hits a ball that strikes his teammate running between bases. In short, the statement that 'unavoidably the many complications' cannot be considered in determining when the circumstances are to be appropriate and when the conditions are excusing, is fishy. Far from its being the case that they cannot be considered, they can and should be considered if the content of the moral obligation of promises is given by a rule as in the case of legal statutes, rules of games or rules that specify what it is that one is required to do in any institutional arrangement.

Second, the rule is represented as '*the* rule of promising', '*the* basic rule', 'as representing *the* practice as a whole' (italics mine throughout). It would appear, then, that there is one and only one sort of content to any moral obligation of those involved in the transaction of promising, indeed that there is one and only one obligation that the promiser has, either to do (or not to do) the action that is the subject of the promise— a matter determined by the considerations that the circumstances are (or are not) appropriate and that the conditions do (or do not) excuse. Someone might object that this could easily be remedied, by the addition of supplementary rules, rules about the remedy or redress that is in order if there are such-and-such excusing conditions, mitigating conditions that do not wholly excuse but do reduce the degree of fault, and so on. I shall not here argue against this claim or the contention that is even less plausible that additional rules could be formulated, in order clearly to show that the rule (or the rules of the practice of promising) is (or are) 'on a par with legal rules or statutes', and which have to do with the order of priority of promise-keeping in relation to truth-telling and other sorts of things one is morally required to do. Instead, I shall ask what provision can be made for the requirements that manifestly are imposed upon the promisee. Is he not required to act responsibly with respect to the promiser, in accepting or rejecting the promise he is given? Perhaps this can be handled by means of a supplementary rule. But there is, however, a great deal more in the way of moral requirements imposed upon promisees, and can *their* content be specified or defined by rules 'on a par with legal rules or statutes'? The difficulty here is that there is nothing in Rawls's account of the content of moral obligation in terms of rules of the sort in question, supplemented as it is by the principle of fairness, that can possibly seem to specify *what* it is that promisees are morally required to do. And the reason is that the requirements in question are imposed by the *rights* that are conferred upon promisees and correlatively, the obligations assumed by promisers, and there is nothing in the account given of the so-called practice of promising that renders these matters intelligible. For, as I have argued before, the concept of a right is embedded in a complex network of associated concepts, and there can be no rules of the sort to which Rawls's account is restricted, to render intelligible the requirement, under appropriate circumstances, that promisees waive or relinquish their rights, that they forgive and forget. Indeed, there is nothing in Rawls's account, since it provides no room for the notion of a right, for the idea that promisers who willfully break their promises violate the rights that they have created, are guilty of moral damage against those upon whom they have conferred such rights, and are required to take whatever steps are necessary in order to purge themselves of their guilt, a matter in which, depending once more upon the specific features of the case, the promisee himself is subject to moral requirements of one sort or another.

To all of this one can imagine the following defense: Why not enlarge the conception of the kind of rules involved in the practice of promising and, in addition to the so-called constitutive rule or rules suggested in the foregoing discussion, add rules that specify the rights no less than duties that goes with the office of promisee? For in the case of at least many institutional offices there are not only rules which, by specifying the duties involved, define the activities in question, but also those that stipulate the entitlements of those who perform these duties. Given this emendation— by way of addition to the alleged basic rule— will it not be possible to meet our objections?

But this will not do. The institutional rights of those occupying some position role or office in a given institution would appear to be rights designed to enable them to discharge the duties of the given office. The rights of promisees are, however, not institutional rights; they are, rather, moral rights. Further, the conception of a moral right is embedded in a whole framework of moral notions that extend far beyond the scope of the promise-transaction itself; the recipient of a promise may quite justifiably waive or relinquish his right on grounds of considerateness for the promiser, kindness to him, or any one of a number of competing and compelling moral considerations that lie wholly outside the relation established by the promise and have nothing to do with the socially beneficial results of the activity of promising.

In summary, the account offered by Rawls of what is morally required of those participating in promise transactions is radically defective. And the reason for this is the view adopted by him that the content of the moral obligations of those participating in such transactions is specified by constitutive rules for institutional activities, rules that define those activities by stating what it is that those performing the duties that define their offices must do. And the same conclusion applies to any moral obligation whose content is given, allegedly, by means of constitutive rules; however unfair it may be not to meet such an obligation, no violation of a moral right is involved. Here as in the case of the attempt to derive the moral rights and obligations of members of a family from the institutional arrangements in which they conduct their lives with one another, the blunder encountered in Rawls's account of the obligation of promises, given the confusion that promising is an institution with its constitutive rules which define the roles of those who engage in this practice, is that of supposing that, because there are institutional arrangements for those who play these roles, the rights and obligations that bind promiser and promisee derive from constitutive rules which allegedly prescribe the form of the transaction in which they engage with one another, rather than from the manner in which, as persons who give and receive promises, they conduct their lives with one another.

III

I want now to turn to Rawls's formulation of the fundamental principles of justice. We shall find that here, as in the case of obligations, there is an omission of any reference to moral rights.

A. But, first, consider the similarity between Rawls's conception of the moral obligations of persons in a society satisfying his principles of justice and that of the absolute idealists. On that older doctrine, supposedly no longer fashionable, moral persons are viewed simply as place-holders in the institutional framework of society. Each person has his particular likes and dislikes, hopes, temperament or other qualities of his personality. In respect of these qualities, his will is particular. But as a moral person his will is universal, since qua moral he accepts the universality of law that applies equally to him and to everyone else. Compare this with the account given by Rawls of the rationality of a person in the original position, making a choice of principles of justice, and doing so under a veil of ignorance that shuts off from his consideration all that differentiates him from others, and that is, therefore, morally irrelevant. Under these conditions the principles chosen would be chosen by everyone. For the idealist, if the universality of law is to assist us in determining what a person's moral requirements are, we need more than the universality of law itself. Specifically, what is needed is that the law be embodied in the society of which a person is a member and in which he has his specific station. Only in this way will he—that particular person with his particular will, in contrast with that universal will that he has in common with every other person, be subject to the specific constraints imposed upon him as the particular individual he is. For Rawls, only if the principles of justice that anyone would choose as a rational being for everyone else are embodied in the institutions of society, in which there are specific roles or offices for any particular person, will there be the specific constraints of moral obligation to which any individual is subject. Rawls himself recognizes this similarity. He writes that 'when Bradley says that the individual is a bare abstraction, he can be interpreted to say, without too much distortion, that a person's obligations and duties presuppose a moral conception of institutions and therefore that the content of just institutions must be defined before the requirements for individuals can be set out' (p. 110). Indeed, the similarities are even more striking in Bradley's apparent identification of justice with the fairness with which one abides by the rule, identified by Rawls in effect with what is required by one's station or office in a moral or ideal society.

'Injustice is, while you explicitly or implicitly profess to go on a rule, the not going merely on the rule, but making exceptions in favor of persons. Justice is the really going by nothing but one's ostensible rule in assigning advantage and disadvantage to persons.'[5]

Finally, there is the striking similarity in the treatment of the conception of the rights of individuals. For Rawls, the moral obligation of promisers derives its content from the alleged constitutive rule that specifies the duty of those in the role or office of promiser; and, as we have seen, this simply leaves out of account what is central in promising, namely, the conferring of a right upon the promisee and, correlatively, the assumption of an obligation to that particular individual. For Bradley it is only insofar as the will of the promiser is universal as this is embodied in his station as promiser, and thus brought into perfect congruence with the duties that anyone in that station has, that his will is right. But in that case there are no individual rights that he has against others, since his individual will no longer stands in opposition to that of others. His will, insofar as it is universal, is shared by all, not only by those in his specific station as promiser, but insofar as that universal will is embodied in all of the stations of the good society, by anyone whatever his specific station may happen to be. The analogue for the idealist of the fundamental principles of justice in Rawls's theory is the universal will which particular persons, insofar as they are rational beings, share with all others. It is therefore no surprise to find Bradley collapsing the concept of rights into the concept of duties. There are no moral rights distinct from those duties that the rule specifies for one's station in a good society. 'There is no right which is not a duty, no duty which is not a right.'[6] And later he remarks that my particular will 'has rights only because the sphere of its exercise, and therefore what it does therein, is duty. And it must be respected by others only so far as it thus expresses the universal will. If it has not right on its side, it has no rights whatever.'[7] What right does a person have? The answer is clear: to further the right. To fail in this, is not to violate the rights of individuals; it is, rather, to set one's individual will against the universal will and thereby demean oneself as a rational being.

Rawls sees his own view as a modified Kantian doctrine. I have so far emphasized the striking resemblance of his view with that of idealism, in particular with the views expressed by Bradley in his essay, 'My Station and Its Duties'. I have done this because of Rawls's institutionalized conception of the content of the moral obligations of individuals—a conception, as we have seen, that will not apply to the so-called obligation of promises for a number of reasons including the central consideration that it simply ignores the fact that in promising one assumes an obligation to the promisee and, correlatively, confers a right upon him. My purpose has been to bring home a point on which Bradley, unlike Rawls, is explicit, and with respect to which he does grasp the nettle firmly, in denying as he does that justice consists in honoring, and injustice in violating, the rights of others. But of course any attempt to place either the moral philosophy of Bradley or that of Rawls in proper historical perspective cannot stop short of Kant. I now turn therefore to the Kantian features of Rawls's view in order to prepare the way for the discussion of the question raised earlier concerning the nature of those features of personhood that are morally relevant to the rights and obligations of persons.

B. It will be recalled that, on Rawls's view, the veil of ignorance under which the fundamental principles of justice are to be chosen is designed to exclude from consideration any information that distinguishes one person from another. Only in this way can the choice be made by one on terms of perfect equality with everyone else, so that in choosing as he does he will be choosing for everyone else. Apart from general information he may have about the facts about human nature or social organizations, he must set aside as irrelevant from the moral point of view any facts about himself that might possibly bring him into conflict with anyone else. He must exclude from consideration, therefore, as irrelevant from the point of view of morality or justice, any matters concerning his particular personality, abilities, sensitivities, interests including those guiding concerns by which he organizes his activities, mode of life, ambitions and plans, in which those to whom he is attached by love and friendship may figure in important ways.

The point of view is admittedly Kantian.[8] In choosing rationally with these exclusions of information on the ground of their alleged moral irrelevance, a person in the original position is expressing his nature as a rational being freely and on terms of perfect equality with everyone else (p. 253). The principles selected are categorical, i.e. their validity is in no way conditional upon any particular aims or desires other than those primary goods that it is rational for anyone to want (p. 253). The principles selected 'are indeed those defining the moral law, or more exactly, the principles of justice for institutions and individuals' (p. 255). Accordingly, in acting on these principles we act as free and equal rational beings. 'Our nature as such beings is displayed when we act from the principles we would choose when this nature is reflected in the conditions determining the choice. Thus men exhibit their freedom, their independence from the contingencies of nature and society, by acting in ways they would acknowledge in the original position' (p. 256).

It follows from this Kantian account of Rawls's view, that in acting unjustly we act in ways that in demeaning others at the same time demeans our own nature as rational beings; that in failing to respect others we diminish our own self-respect.

Kant speaks of the failure to act on the moral law as giving rise to shame and not to feelings of guilt. And this is appropriate since for him acting unjustly is acting in a manner that fails to express our nature as a free and equal rational being. Such actions therefore strike at our self-respect, our sense of our own worth, and the experience of this loss is shame. (p. 256)

And this is to show that we have, certainly in Kant, and it would appear on Rawls's own view, not an ethics of law and guilt, of austere command, but 'an ethic of mutual respect and self-esteem' (p. 256).

C. This last point might not appear to apply to Rawls's own view, if one recalls the statement of the first of the two principles of justice, that 'each person is to have an equal right to the most extensive basic liberty compatible with a similar liberty for others'. For here there does appear to be the conception of a fundamental right that all persons have. It would seem, therefore, that any social organization that violates this principle will violate this right, and should occasion on the part of all who support the organization a sense of guilt, not shame.

This appearance is, however, illusory. The first principle does not refer us to a moral right that any person has, qua person, and on grounds independent of the character of any social organization of which he is a member, in the way in which this is done on the classical contract theory of Locke. If it did, the question of the justice or injustice of any social arrangement or institution could be settled by examining whether the institutions of society honor or violate the moral rights that human beings as such have. The rights referred to in Rawls's first principle are the rights established by basic law or legislation; they are political rights that men ought morally to have; and they are not as such moral rights they do in fact have, to an equality of liberties of a variety of sorts: 'political liberty (the right to vote and to be eligible for office) together with freedom of speech and freedom of thought; freedom of the person along with the right to hold (personal) property; and freedom from arbitrary arrest and seizure as defined by the concept of the rule of law' (p. 61). Unlike the Lockean contract theory according to which both the exercise of political authority and the specific forms of political organization are to be justified by reference to the moral rights of persons, the Rawlsian view is that on moral grounds, which involve considerations *other than rights*, political institutions are just if and only if they establish political rights to equal liberty for its members.

The fact that the justification of the institutions of rights to equal liberty involves no reference to moral rights of persons, becomes clear as soon as we look into the grounds given for the first principle of justice.

We are told that the principle is 'a special case of a more general conception of justice that can be expressed as follows. All social values—liberty and opportunity, income and wealth and the bases of self-respect—are to be distributed equally unless an unequal distribution of any, or all, of these values is to everyone's advantage' (p. 62). But unlike the cases of other goods such as income and wealth, where increases in the benefits of those worst off can be achieved by increasing the benefits of those best off, it is not possible, in general and permanently, to increase the basic liberties of those worst off (e.g. those disenfranchised) by increasing the basic liberties of those best off. Increases in the basic liberties of those worst off can be achieved only by closing the gap between those worst off and those best off. In short, the only way in which the basic liberties of all may be maximized is by securing equality.

Now assuming that the basic material needs of persons have been met, the equality of basic liberties is necessary given the fundamental interest that any rational person has to determine his own plans and projects on the basis of the knowledge that he has of his own situation and circumstances, whatever these may happen to be. Inequality, on the other hand, can only place this interest in jeopardy. For example, the cost of waiving the equal liberty of conscience that a just society would assure all of its members is the opportunity it would provide this group with the dominant religious or moral ideology to persecute or suppress others who deviate from its views. Accordingly, equality of conscience is the only principle that those in the original position, who are concerned to maximize the benefits of everyone, can reasonably acknowledge (cf. p. 207). In short, in choosing any principle that everyone would accept, whatever his particular plans, beliefs, etc. might be, a person would choose the principle that equal liberties are to be provided for all—this being most beneficial to everyone—and, therefore, choose to establish the legal and political rights to equality of basic liberties. Another reason is 'the central place of the primary good of self-respect and the desire of human beings to express their nature in a free social union with others. Thus the desire for liberty is the chief regulative interest that the parties must suppose they all will have in common in due course' (p. 543). Anything less would create a loss of self-respect (or self-esteem) and an occasion for shame, in short, a demeaning of one's nature as a rational being. The various goods in life, including the basic liberties that just social organizations establish for their members as their political and legal birthrights, are goods from everyone's point of view. To deprive anyone of these liberties is to deprive him of a good and in one's own self to suffer the loss of a good through the loss of the esteem in which one is held by others. This is, at once, to demean and to be demeaned; and the sense of this is shame, not guilt.

Rawls does distinguish, clearly enough, between guilt and shame. The former, he tells us, occurs when someone has acted contrary to his sense of right and justice. 'By wrongly advancing his interests he has transgressed the rights of others' (p. 445). Unfortunately, the right to equality of basic liberties is a political and legal right; and unless we suppose, in addition, that this right is instituted in order to reinforce the moral rights persons have to these liberties—by providing for the application of penalties and other sanctions against those who deprive others of their liberties—there is no violation of a moral right involved in the violation of the requirement that all persons are to have equality of basic liberties. We should in such cases feel shame, not guilt; we should 'sense the diminishment of self from our anxiety about the lesser respect that others may have for us and from our disappointment with ourself for failing to live up to our ideals' (p. 446).

Strictly speaking this is an ethics, not of guilt, but of shame. There is no basic moral right of persons to liberties of any sort, the denial of which would be a violation of these moral rights and a warrant for a sense of guilt on the part of the person responsible, whether he be sovereign or subject. The point is, rather, that a society that is just will provide equal liberty for all because that is beneficial to all and thus fair to everyone involved. And this is a radically different sort of view from the contract theory of Locke according to which the justification of political sovereignty, no less than of the forms of our political institutions, can be given by reference to fundamental moral rights, including our right to the liberty that is our common moral birthright.

IV

We recognize that human beings are endowed with their distinctive personalities, situations and personal relations, their hopes and ambitions and their dominant interests in terms of which persons, unlike animals and infants who are the creatures of their passing feelings and impulses, organize their desires and fashion the very pattern and direction of their lives—in short, all this and much more that fall under the heading of the idealist's terms 'particular will'. These, idealists and Kantians—and now Rawls—tell us, are morally irrelevant both in the rational choice of fundamental principles of morality or justice and in the determination of the justice of individual action. Does this claim make moral sense?

The differences between persons in respect of their aptitudes and intelligence obviously do play a role in determining what sorts of positions they are at least likely to hold in many of the institutions, professions or other sorts of organizations within our society. Whether this truism provides good ground for the kind of social regimentation proposed by Plato or the social engineers of our own day is, of course, another matter. Natural endowments that fit persons for those offices in which they can prosper are the accidents of fortune; and whether they are morally relevant to the assignments of individuals to any social office I shall not here discuss, although it is at least arguable that the public good requires that talents and natural endowments be adequate to the specific duties of a given office or role. Nor shall I here explore in detail the question that should be raised in connection with the demand for unanimity in the choice by persons in the original position of the fundamental principles of justice, a demand that requires that any person making a choice do so only as Everyman. It may be true that only in this way will it be possible for agreement by everyone on a single set of principles of justice to which any and every just society must conform regardless of the specific traits of its individual members. Perhaps a good deal less is required than the heavy veil of ignorance that shuts off as morally irrelevant so many personal characteristics and features of individuals. For it is not at all self-evident that there must be a single set of principles on which all may agree; it may be enough that persons agree upon the general sorts of considerations they are prepared to accept as moral reasons that count for or against any moral judgment, in the absence of which it would not be possible to agree or disagree about any moral issue. But agreement on the kinds of things that count as moral reasons does not entail agreement on a set of principles and the order of priority for their application; for it may be that, Rawls to the contrary notwithstanding, no straightforward deductive method is possible for the resolution of moral disputes. But these are questions that carry us beyond the questions of relatively limited scope I wish to raise here and which bear directly on the matters that precipitated the discussion of the moral philosophy of Rawls, namely, the determination of those attributes of personhood that are relevant to moral rights and obligations. It is enough for this purpose to raise the question whether the sorts of items that have to do with the distinctive personalities of individuals, their temperaments, character, dominant interests, personal style and the pattern of their lives in which their personal relations with others figure, are morally irrelevant to considered judgments of one's moral responsibilities. Put in another way, can we rest content with this essentially idealist conception of a moral person as a place-holder in an institutional or organizational schema, so that in this way the quite abstract person in the original position is made sufficiently concrete for moral purposes?

Since, as I have argued, there is no place for moral rights in the account Rawls offers of moral obligations, or, for that matter, in his account of the fundamental principles of justice, the answer must be in the negative. In the discussion of the obligation of promises I called attention to the moral requirements imposed upon both parties to the transaction. Specifically, there is the requirement imposed upon the person invested with a right by virtue of the promise he received and accepted in good faith, to waive or even relinquish this right in unexpectedly altered circumstances, and, when the promise given him has been broken, either willfully or not, to take into account possible excusing or mitigating circumstances of the promiser, and even to forgive and forget, given appropriate indications of regret or remorse. We have, therefore, a broad variety of circumstances and factors that need to be considered by those invested with a right. Some related to the unexpected changes in the fortunes of promisers, which promisees must take into account in determining how they are to be disposed towards promisers who do not keep their word. In such cases, the keeping of a promise might well, and unpredictably so, involve a sacrifice of an important good by jeopardizing the promiser's hopes, ambitions and the very structure and pattern of his life. Should a person ruin himself in order to keep a promise, a contingency he had no reason to foresee when he made that promise? And should the promisee ignore this as a matter of no moral concern to him? And surely when willfully a person breaks his promise, then feels that remorse he ought indeed to feel for the guilt he has incurred, and shows in this way that he is prepared to provide redress for the wrong he committed and to receive forgiveness for his fault, it would be absurd to suppose that the promisee is under no moral constraint in the manner in which he must dispose himself towards the other person, and that, throughout, he can ignore the latter's feelings, his temperament and his sensitivities in the manner in which he deals with him. In a similar way, a person bearing an unexpectedly heavy burden by virtue of a promise he has made, must take into account the promisee's conception of his good, given the style and structure of his life and the plans he has for himself and for those to whom his own life is closely bound; and he must take into account his personality in determining how best he is to conduct himself, whether to secure release from his obligation or if this is not possible, how best to make amends, or, if even this is out of the question, how if at all he is to secure the other's understanding and forgiveness. In all of these sorts of cases, responsible persons must attend to a variety of matters shut off from view by the heavy veil of ignorance that Rawls along with Kantians and idealists recommend that conscientious moral agents wear in their moral deliberations.

Nor can we accept the idea that a person's plans and projects play no moral role in any of his moral decisions. Persons do have the right as moral agents to plan their lives and to structure their activities in accordance with their chosen ends. But to do this is to form a conception of what, from the point of view of his dominant interests, is his own good, a good that is not common to all persons but only to those who share his own specific plans and projects. This, of course, is to bring him into possible conflicts with others in the competition for the things that are needed for the achievement of his purposes: goods, services, opportunities, offices, etc. And it involves much more than a knowledge of the primary goods which, according to Rawls, it is reasonable for all men alike to desire, and which alone are relevant to anyone's moral deliberations. But it is not irrelevant to anyone's rational judgment of what it is that he ought to do to consider the interests that govern and structure *his* activities as distinct from those of others, and that gives *his* life the purpose that it has in being lived. Nor is this simply a matter of a calculation of what is best for those with his plans and projects. For given that all is clear as far as his own moral relations with others are concerned, and given, too, the right that he has as a moral agent to go about his affairs in the pursuit of his objectives, it is, in addition, exercising a right that he has as an agent freely to go about his own affairs.

None of this is intended to bring into question the idea that all persons are equal under the law; neither is it to argue that race, creed, sex, etc. are to be ignored in dealing justly with the victims of discrimination. It is, rather, to argue that some of the features in respect of which persons differ and which are possible sources of conflict are morally relevant.

It is, however, with the relations between persons that I am mainly concerned in this discussion of the morally relevant facts about persons. I have already discussed the example of a promise transaction in which a wide variety of facts about persons, which include among others the temperaments, plans and character traits of the individuals concerned, are relevant factors that need to be taken into account in judgments of the moral requirements imposed upon those involved. This is only one case among many others that need to be considered in which some segment of the lives of persons are joined and during which it is incumbent upon them to respond to each other on the basis of their situations and their sense of each other's traits, aspirations, plans, and projects. There are, however, even more striking cases in which this is true and to which Kantians have been notoriously insensitive. Shall we set aside as irrelevant from a moral point of view the personal attachments of individuals that color their lives and in which they are bound to each other as friends, or as husband and wife?

Kant's idea that the regard and concern that friends have for each other can be lumped together as inclinations, on a par with the passing fancies, likes and dislikes that casual acquaintances and total strangers have for each other, and brushed aside as morally irrelevant in any issue that arises, surely will not do. It is not merely that it is impossibly insensitive to the facts in question, as if what constituted friendship could be made out in terms of the occurrence of certain internal impressions of pleasure or uneasiness, thus failing to recognize, in addition to the appreciation that each has for the individuality of the other, the manner in which in ever so many ways the lives of those united in friendship are bound to each other. It is also oblivious to the material difference that friendship with any person makes in justifying preferential treatment given him. Many philosophers, while conceding the value of friendship, think of it as something that lies outside the domain of morality. They distinguish the reasonable expectation friends have that they will receive special consideration from each other from the minimal demands that morality places upon all persons alike. But that is the nub of the matter, namely, the supposition that the demands of morality fall equally and indiscriminately upon all, that such minimal demands are also morally maximal. Is the expectation of favored treatment from friends merely a reasonable prediction? If, as it seems reasonable to suppose, we are morally obliged to those from whom we have accepted generous treatment,[9] (correlatively, that they have a right to reciprocity from the beneficiaries of their generosity), then *a fortiori* there is ground for supposing that friends are bound, morally speaking, by the ways in which they have dealt generously and appreciatively with each other. Certainly the disappointment we feel towards those whom we have had every reason to suppose were friends, when they deal coldly and inconsiderately with us, is not like the regret we feel when our predictions fail to come true; for in that case the failure is our own. It is, rather, the hurt that one, whom we have taken for a friend, has caused us, and for which we blame *him* because he has been false to us: after having joined our life to his and in that personal relation with him found purpose in our own life, we now discover that it was tarnished by deception. We are in that way let down, surely as disastrously as are promisees, who are let down by the fact that a portion of their lives, in a line of conduct they have followed, is brought to naught by the failure of promisers to keep their pledges.

Writing in the shadow of World War II, when everything dear seemed precarious as the Nazis were prepared with fanatical determination to trample on every decency in order to realize their ends, E. M. Forster was moved to write in praise of what the ideologues of his day, both on the right and the left, were only too ready to sacrifice: personal relations, theirs and anyone else's.

I hate the idea of causes, and if I had to choose between betraying my country and betraying my friend, I hope I should have the guts to betray my country. Such a choice may scandalize the modern reader, and he may stretch out his patriotic hand to the telephone at once and ring up the police. It would not have shocked Dante, though. Dante places Brutus and Cassius in the lowest circle of Hell . . . [10]

In these more settled times our reaction may not be as extreme as it was likely to be in 1939 when these words were written. It may strike some today as hyperbole; but it is not rubbish, and it is worth considering for the lesson it contains for the Kantian moral philosopher.

Nor should we regard as absurd the idea that those who like husband and wife have lived together in understanding and love, who have shared their sorrows and joys, and have made each other part of their very lives, have rights and obligations with respect to each other. The idea that a husband in any moral decision he must make, e.g. whether to save the life of his wife or that of a total stranger, may not give special consideration to his wife—whatever his station may be—but must deal, morally, with his wife on terms of equality with everyone else, is only one more example of the folly to which Kantism is committed. It may be undesirable for husbands and wives to raise the question of their rights and obligations during the course of their affairs with each other—for that shows that their relations are strained, as much so as it would be in the case of friends—but the fact that it would be better if neither claimed or demanded their rights does not in the least show that there are no rights there to be exercised or respected.

Whatever the sorts of relations between persons may be, in which rights and obligations are involved, some portion at least of the lives of those morally related in this way are joined in ways that call for special and preferential consideration that each must give the other. On the part of the person morally obliged, there is the requirement that by his own agency he support the endeavors of the person to whom he is under the obligation, during some segment at least of the latter's life; and, along with this, there is the requirement that in his conduct he take account of the other party's individuality no less than his own plans and projects in deciding how, when and indeed if at all, to meet the obligation that is his moral burden. On the part of the person who has the right, there is the reciprocal requirement that in carrying forward with his own endeavors, for which he depends crucially upon the other's support, he take account not only of his own plans and projects, but the circumstances, needs and even the personality of the other—waiving or even relinquishing his own right and thus abandoning his own endeavors in the light of his sense of the other's interests, circumstances and situation; and, if he is let down to any degree by the latter's failures or omissions, there is the requirement that he deal with him in ways that are sensitive to the characteristic and peculiar ways in which he bears the burden of his guilt. In these matters, we have far more involved in the moral requirements imposed upon persons than their stations and their duties, or those factors in their external circumstances and situations that afford them opportunities to meet their obligations or prevent them from doing so. In short, we have persons, responding to each other as individuals, with those characteristics and features of their personalities that distinguish them as the individuals they are from those faceless entities, each indistinguishable from every other, that the Kantian regards as the appropriate object of moral respect.

V

I turn now to that feature of personhood the neglect of which by Kant and by Rawls is fatal to their account of morality and obligation.

It will be recalled that for Kant the fundamental principles of morality are those which apply to any person, not on account of any particular desires or inclinations that he has, but simply and solely by virtue of his status as a rational being. Insofar as he is a rational being he is on terms of equality with every other rational being; and insofar as his will is rational, he acts autonomously on the basis of principles that his and every other being's rational nature requires. What are these principles? They make no reference to any empirical fact about human beings but only to the requirement of the lawfulness that follows from the rationality of his and any other rational being's will. Nor do they, insofar as they are principles that apply even to God himself, make any reference to duties or obligations; for these arise only in the tension that obtains between the constraints of man's rationality and his inclinations in particular circumstances, from whose influence God is wholly free. The paradox embraced by Kant is that it is only insofar as we are something less than rational that we have any duties at all. 'Duty is the necessity of an action done from respect for the law.' (*Foundations of the Metaphysics of Morals*, First Section.) We submit to the lawfulness that expresses our own nature as rational beings; but it is only insofar as we are something less than rational that there is submission and respect.

It follows that there is nothing in the fundamental principle of morality itself, as God himself understands it, that involves the concept of duty. Kant's statement of the principle, in each of the several forms in which he offers it, is put in the imperative mood, since it is only in this way that it is intelligible to beings who, like ourselves, are on occasion less than rational and hence corruptible by inclination. Here, surprisingly enough, and in morals where we are least prepared to expect it, there reappears the Kantian duality between the noumenal reality of the thing in itself and the phenomenal forms in which things are given to us; and one might well ask how one could state the fundamental principle in such a manner that it would convey nothing more or less than what God himself grasps when he, as a perfectly rational being, apprehends it. But even in the fundamental principle of morality when put in the imperative mood, it is not at all clear that what is conveyed by that imperative mood is the concept of duty, rather than of the submission of our will and the sense of this submission which Kant calls 'respect'. What the fundamental principle states is what it is that the rationality of will requires, namely, lawfulness, and hence the universality of its application to any being endowed with a rational will. To discover the concept of duty we need to turn to those maxims or principles of action which are performed in particular circumstances out of respect for law and which, accordingly, satisfy the criterion of universality of application that our own rational nature requires on terms of equality with that of everyone else. When, however, we look to those maxims that pass this test and which state what sorts of things human beings, as free and equal persons, are duty-bound to do, there is no reference to rights and their correlative obligations. Indeed, Kant's distinction between 'the stricter or narrower (imprescriptible)' duties and 'the broader (meritorious)' duties (in the Second Section of *The Foundations of the Metaphysics of Morals*) simply conflates under the blanket-term 'duty', cases in which one may be duty-bound to meet one's obligation to another by virtue of the latter's right (as in the example of a promise) with those in which one is duty-bound to help another person where he, however, has no right to the assistance given him.

In any case, in acting morally, one expresses one's own rational nature on terms of complete equality with everyone else. To fail to meet the requirements of morality is to fail by doing violence to our own nature as rational beings. And since rational nature exists as an end in itself and with an intrinsic worth of its own that has no price or market value, in failing morally we demean ourselves. With this comes the sense of the loss of our own worth. This is shame (not guilt), the sense of our own diminished worth and the diminished regard that any other rational being has for us.

Conspicuously, this account neglects rights, and with it the moral damage we inflict upon others when we fail to meet our obligations to them and with it too the sense of guilt that comes with the violation of their rights—a matter that pertains not merely to our sense of the loss of our own worth, but to the evil inflicted upon others which cannot be equated with a demeaning in ourselves of something we have in common with them. And this, finally, is to neglect what is essential to persons in their moral relations with each other, namely, the fact that personhood is a notion applicable to human beings, not in virtue of some common attribute like rationality which they have in common with other human beings, but in virtue of their dealings with each other as individuals, not only in the public forum but privately in their personal relations with each other.

Rawls does avoid the difficulties inherent in the idea of a noumenal rationality from which all empirical content has been stripped away. The veil of ignorance, it will be recalled, does not exclude as morally irrelevant considerable bodies of general information about individuals and social groups, nor does it exclude from view those primary goods all reasonable persons desire. But the concern, throughout, is to articulate principles any just institution must satisfy so that, whatever anyone's station or office may be within the structure of that institution there will be fairness with which benefits and burdens will be allocated to those participating in their institutional activities. Persons are agents and they have their distinctive personalities, ambitions, character traits, interests, etc.; but what is morally relevant and important about persons, in respect of which they are all alike, is their status as psychological subjects who bear burdens and enjoy benefits in accordance with their stations, and their duties. Corresponding to what in Kant's view is taken as central, namely, the rationality of persons that constitutes their worth, there is in Rawlsian doctrine a person's sense of his own worth when he bears his fair share of the burdens in sustaining just institutions, at the same time that he enjoys the benefits made possible by a like contribution from others.

This Kantian preoccupation with the person as the possessor of worth and self-respect in the manner in which he contributes to the fair distribution of benefits and burdens—rather than with that alleged intrinsic worth Kant professed to find in a wholly abstract rationality—simply ignores what is of central importance to the rights of individuals and to the obligations that are their correlatives, namely, their status as agents with the individualities they exhibit during the course of their dealings with one another, within and without the surrounding structure of institutional arrangements. For it is only as persons in respect to this status they have as the particular individuals they are—not those faceless subjects of benefits and burdens who function as place-holders in an institutional arrangement—that they are entitled to go about their affairs in the pursuit of their interests. And it is only as such persons in whose faces, speech and conduct are revealed their hopes and aspirations, their feelings and their dispositions, and the whole gamut of other factors that are embodied in characteristic ways in their personalities, that they join their lives with others and give each other the support which they require in accordance with their rights and obligations.

In short, we need to bring the concept of a person, if it is to apply to our moral life, back to the language-games in which persons with their individualities interact and communicate with each other in the quite concrete circumstances of human life. In these circumstances, in their thought and action, they carry on their multifarious affairs with one another, in the course of which, as the quite particular agents they are, they bring their lives together and support each other's agency.

VI

Let me review briefly and in outline the main points in this lengthy chapter. I have first outlined the salient features of Rawls's conception of justice. I then examined in considerable detail the kind of analysis to which he is impelled of the crucial case of the obligation of promises. That analysis I have endeavored to show is nothing short of an unqualified disaster. The result is not unexpected, for as I have gone on to argue, there is nothing in the account given of the 'content' of the obligation of promises—supposedly specified by an (institutional) constitutive rule—nor in the account given of the fundamental principles of justice that allows any room for the right conferred by promises and the obligation promisers assume to those to whom they give their word. I have then gone on to draw parallels not only between Rawlsian and Kantian theory, but between the former and the Bradleyian conception of morality in his essay, 'My Station and Its Duties'. And the conclusion I have drawn concerning the morally relevant features of personhood—in contrast with that offered on the Rawlsian account, according to which persons morally speaking are faceless place-holders in institutional arrangements and the subjects of the benefits and burdens distributed among them—is that nothing less than persons as individuals with their distinctive personalities are required if we are to give proper attention to their rights and their correlative obligations.

NOTES

[1] Published by Harvard University Press in 1971.

[2] Cf. Joel Feinberg in his review-discussion of Rawls's book in *The Journal of Philosophy*, Vol. LXX, No. 9, 10 May 1973.

[3] This reply to Hume's indirect argument is to be found in an article in *Mind*, April 1939, pp. 155–7.

[4] Consider the example of a husband, weary after a long tiring day of work, promising his wife to take her to see a movie on the next night if he can stay home and relax that evening.

[5] 'My Station and Its Duties', in the concluding note on rights and duties, on p. 146 of *Ethical Studies*, The Liberal Arts Press, New York.

[6] Loc. cit., p. 144.

[7] Ibid., p. 145.

[8] Cf. Section 40 entitled 'The Kantian Interpretation of Justice as Fairness'.

[9] This point is conceded by Rawls, who puts this on a par with promising (p. 113).

[10] In the essay 'What I Believe', in *Two Cheers For Democracy*, Edward Arnold & Co.: London, 1951, p. 78.

V

Rights and Goods

In deliberating about what it is that one is to do, is it possible
reasonably to weigh competing moral considerations, conspicuously but not exclusively, those involving a consideration of the
rights of persons and of the goods that may be achieved by action?
Or, are we faced, in instances of this sort, with incommensurables
concerning which no reasonable decisions can be made? Is there no
relation between the right of a person, one's own or that of others,
and the needs that persons have for the assistance that one is able to
give them, the love and affection one can extend to others for which
no ground of any sort seems to be required?

These are important practical issues, a detailed discussion of which
is hardly possible here; but perhaps some light may be thrown on the
rationale of the moral decisions we make when faced by competing
considerations by examining, to begin with, the relation between
rights and goods.

I

Traditionally, intuitionism has been understood to be the view that
in morals we are concerned with one or more unique and unanalyzable qualities or attributes. Whether or not the view is that proposed
by Plato in his account of The Form of the Good in Book VII of the
Republic as goodness in itself, in respect of which Richard Price in *A
Review of the Principal Questions of Morals* and G. E. Moore in *Principia
Ethica* can be seen as his philosophical descendants, the thesis
advanced by intuitionists addressed itself to the question of whether
or not there are certain basic moral predicates that are unique, simple
and therefore unanalyzable, the objects of a special non-sensory
mode of apprehension or intuition. But intuitionism has also been
understood in another way, e.g. by Henry Sidgwick, as the doctrine

that there are certain moral principles of a substantive or non-trivial nature the self-evident truth of which can be ascertained by an immediate act of intellection or intuition. For Sidgwick the basic moral principles of Prudence and Benevolence admittedly pose a problem for which, inevitably, he could not in principle provide a satisfactory solution: how to deal with those instances in which rational self-interest or prudence is brought into conflict with the requirement of benevolence. It is worth noting, perhaps, that one could adopt an intuitionist view in either of these senses without adopting an intuitionist position in respect of the other, although not infrequently intuitionism in both senses of this term are embodied in the same view. In any case, there is a third way in which, following Rawls, the term 'intuitionism' has come to be used in a quite untraditional manner to stand for views which exhibit these two features: 'First, they consist of a plurality of first principles which may conflict to give contrary directives in particular types of cases; and, second, they include no explicit method, no priority rules, for weighing these principles against one another; we are simply to strike a balance by intuition, by what seems to us most nearly right.'[1] Here Prichard and Ross come to mind. Unlike Sidgwick for whom his fundamental principles are morally binding upon agents in specifying what they are to do in any situation to which they apply, and for whom, therefore, any conflict of principles can only give rise to contradiction, the basic considerations, self-evident as they were taken to be by Prichard and Ross, have more or less weight in any case to which they apply, more or less stringency or force. For both thinkers, the resolution of such conflicts of basic considerations is to be achieved by a moral thinking that takes account of all of the morally relevant circumstances including the consequences of the actions under consideration.

It is also worth noting that while Prichard and Ross are intuitionists in all of the above three senses of the term, it would be a mistake to suppose that the adoption of intuitionism in the third sense of the term commits one to intuitionist theories as these have been traditionally understood. All that is implied by this third type of so-called intuitionism is that there is a plurality of principles and that there is 'no explicit method, no priority rules, for weighing these principles against one another'.[2] The key term is 'method'. For if by a 'method' is meant some rational procedure—of whatever sort this may be—that serves precisely and invariably to establish conclusions on which all rational persons must agree whenever any conflict of principles occurs, then it is not likely that any sound moral theory can avoid being intuitionist in this quite untraditional sense of the term. Even Rawls, who proposes the application of strict priority rules for the principles of justice which just institutions must satisfy, recognizes that in the actual non-ideal world in which we find ourselves there are conflicts of duty that arise in cases of justifiable civil disobedience and for which there can be no straightforward application of principles but only the weighing of competing considerations in a judicious manner.[3] Even in the case in which unjust or unfair social arrangements need to be modified in order to provide a better distribution of benefits and burdens, there may well be, minimal as it may be and outweighed by the resulting gain in the fairness with which others are treated, the unfairness to those whose plans for their future are predicated upon the special advantages they obtain from the existing and admittedly unfair arrangements.[4] In any case it should be observed that this proposed use of the term 'intuitionism' in no way commits one to those epistemological doctrines designated by the first and second uses of 'intuitionism' one or the other of which, historically, have been associated with ethical intuitionism. And, finally, the fact that a view may embody 'no explicit method, no priority rules, for weighing . . . principles or any other considerations against one another' does not entail that one must have recourse in cases of conflicting considerations to some esoteric intuition, 'gut feeling' or arbitrary fiat, unguided in any way by any rationale on the basis of which the conflict may be resolved. What is involved in this so-called 'intuitionism' is simply the rejection of the view that in morals, we can proceed *more geometrico* or, deductively, in any other way that is equally compelling, in securing the rational assent of all in every case in which conflicting moral considerations have application. The alternative to such a strong claim about the possibility of the resolution of moral disputes and differences, is *not* a weighing of conflicting considerations 'in regard to which we can only say that it seems to us more correct to balance them this way than that'.[5] For there is no correctness if all that is possible is seeming; and there is no seeming either if there is no conception of that correctness that seems to be present. Nor should we suppose that the only other alternative to the strong claim involved in the rejection of this so-called form of intuitionism is the supposition that all or some of us are endowed with mysterious faculties of intuition by means of which conflicts of principle or any other sorts of moral consideration may be infallibly resolved. For what can possibly count for or against the claim that one has this faculty, when those who claim to be endowed are unable to resolve their disputes concerning their findings? There may well be other possibilities. It may be that there are on occasion, rare as they may be, those terrible incidents in which the conflicts are of such a nature that there can be no morally viable solution; and for those tragically enmeshed in such incidents the reasonable attitude to take is neither agreement or disagreement with the course of action taken by such victims of circumstance, but pity, and admiration if they suffer their fate with dignity and nobility. And it may well be that even though there may be no rational procedure that is as compelling as a geometrical proof in securing assent to its conclusion, there remains nonetheless a rationale upon which in many cases of conflict reasonable men proceed. Aristotle remarked that 'it is the mark of an educated man to look for precision in each class of things just so far as the nature of the subject admits', and that 'it is evidently equally foolish to accept probable reasoning from a mathematician and to demand from a rhetorician scientific proofs'.[6] Similarly, in morals it may well be that however reasonably men may proceed to decide in cases of conflicts of moral considerations, they fail to achieve agreement but must nonetheless respect each other despite their differences and renounce as juvenile the demand for a method of resolving differences as effectively in morals as in mathematics. And, finally, when there is agreement achieved as indeed it is achieved in many or most of the incidents we face, the agreement may be due, not to principles for the application of principles, or for any other moral considerations, but to something quite different. I shall add comments on this point later on in order to supplement the brief remarks made earlier in Chapter I.[7] For the present it is important to recognize the alternatives to the strong position taken by Rawls concerning the existence of rational procedures for the resolution of conflicts of moral considerations, and that these do not involve those questionable epistemological doctrines traditionally associated with intuitionism. It would be less misleading, if one must have a label for any philosophical doctrine that rejects the strong claim made by Rawls for the resolution of these conflicts, to use the term 'pluralism', a term that he himself suggests as a possible alternative to the one he employs, to stand for the view that there is a plurality of moral considerations, but 'no explicit method' for weighing them against one another in any situation in which they apply. But it is essential that we look more closely at some of the important issues relevant to this talk about 'explicit method' to see whether or not there are considerations that may guide us in resolving these conflicts even if they do not qualify as the 'explicit methods' that Rawls has in mind.

II

Let us turn to the relation between rights and the goods to be achieved by benevolent action.

In his classic essay, 'Does Moral Philosophy Rest on a Mistake?' H. A. Prichard was led, for reasons that need not detain us here, to distinguish sharply between 'virtue and morality as co-ordinate and independent forms of goodness', between the goodness of a virtuous, e.g. benevolent, act and the goodness (which, characteristically, he takes to be moral in an excessively narrow, I believe, sense of this term) of a right act done from a sense of obligation.[8] Clearly, most of the instances Prichard mentions as cases of morally obligatory acts are just those which Kant would have described as being instances of perfect duties, and these as we noted earlier are in fact acts we ought to perform precisely because of the rights that are involved.[9] Now while Prichard does declare that 'we must sharply distinguish morality and virtue as independent, though related, species of goodness',[10] he does not attempt to spell out *what* the relation is, nor does he address himself to the question of what it is that we are to do when the claims of virtue and moral obligation are in conflict, as they are when we must choose between keeping a promise, thereby according a person his right, and performing a benevolent act towards someone who has no right to the benefit we are able to bestow upon him. The kinds of conflicts he does consider and for the resolution of which, apart from mentioning the need for thoughtfulness and the consideration of the consequences of our acts, he rests content with an appeal to a moral thinking in the actual situations in which the conflicts arise, are those in which one moral obligation conflicts with another. And we are left to wonder how it is possible to engage in any kind of moral thinking that would have as its object the determination of which consideration is the more compelling—according a person his right or providing some needed benefit to someone else—if virtue and morality are 'co-ordinate and independent forms of goodness'.

In the important essay of more recent date, 'Are There Any Natural Rights?' H. L. A. Hart also argues that the concept of a right belongs to a different 'branch' or 'sphere' of morality from that of good, on the ground that the former, but not the latter, involves the idea of the moral property of a person by virtue of which he is justified in limiting or restricting the freedom of others.[11] Hart is surely correct in emphasizing this important feature of the concept of a right, just as he is correct in insisting that it is altogether possible that there should be 'moralities' in which the concept of a right plays no role, that just as there might be a morality consisting wholly of a set of imperatives supposedly issued by some divinity or divinities, so it is altogether possible that there might be a morality whose prescriptions focused entirely upon some good or goods to be achieved by human action, perhaps human perfection, happiness or whatever.[12] But while correct in emphasizing in this and in other ways the distinctive ways in which rights, in contrast with goods and benefits, serve as grounds of right action, the remark that rights and goods belong to different spheres or branches of morality suggests, although certainly it does not imply and there is no reason to suppose that it was intended to endorse, the view that seems to have been entertained by H. A. Prichard that the moral constraints imposed by rights and those by the concern to promote the good, because different, are thereby independent and free wheeling with respect to each other in their service as reasons for right conduct. Hart's essay was written when insufficient attention was being paid to the distinctive and complex logic, to use the term then current, of the concept of rights, and when terms like 'obligation' and 'duty' were being used indiscriminately, conspicuously by Prichard and Ross, to mention only two among many writers, to cover those cases in which the obligations were, as Hart put it, 'owed' to particular individuals in addition to those cases in which benefits to be achieved or burdens to be diminished or removed serve as moral grounds for conduct. It is understandable, therefore, that Hart should emphasize the differences between the ways in which rights and goods operate as moral grounds for conduct while ignoring the issue of the manner in which these may be related and, accordingly, the rationale embodied in the reasonable ways in which conflict between the moral constraints of rights and benevolence may be resolved. At the same time it should be observed that the claim made by Hart that the existence of such special rights as those derived from promises or other relations or transactions between persons implies that 'there is at least one natural right, the equal right of all men to be free',[13] while it does not rule out the possibility of setting forth the details of a relation between such different sorts of moral consideration which might serve as a rational basis for the resolution of conflicts that may arise between them, does not itself indicate the direction in which such a development of moral theory may be undertaken.

III

Now to someone who is under an obligation there are, clearly, certain restrictions on the permissible scope of his conduct: he must abstain from certain performances and/or engage in others, whether or not it is to his advantage or liking that he do so. And this may be irksome. Indeed, it may appear only to further the interests of one who is already advantaged by an existing inequity in the distribution of the benefits and burdens that should be shared by all. If one considers how persons are severely deprived because of the accidents of birth, social and economic position, the talk about the rights of those who are affluent may well appear to be designed to insure that their special interests and advantages will be protected and that they will continue to be favored through the sheer accident of a fortune that is blind to need, merit or moral purpose of any kind. And to those in severely straightened circumstances, for whom whatever liberties they have must be narrowly channeled into the efforts they make barely to survive, the talk about the rights of man—to their property, their lives and their liberties—must appear to be hollow indeed when they are unable to count as their property the fruits of their own labor, live the kinds of lives worth living or enjoy any liberties except those of accepting their unfortunate lots and submitting to the dictates of others. It may appear, therefore, that the high-sounding phrases about the rights of man are simply designed to promote the security the privileged need in order that they may continue to enjoy their advantages, free from the jealous or arbitrary power of the sovereign and safe from the violence to which the impoverished may be inclined.

The short and easy way to deal with this sort of skepticism is to repeat the obvious: there are moral rights and these (in addition to or, minimally at least, these instead of the rights established by legal statutes or embodied in institutional arrangements) need to be respected. But what moral point can there be to the insistence upon honoring the rights of others, the meeting of one's obligations to them, if all that this does is to restrict one's own freedom and in no way contributes either to one's own good or even to that of the person to whom one is under a moral obligation? The admonition to respect the rights of others, the net effect of which is only to perpetuate the evil inherent in unjust social arrangements, can hardly be expected to be greeted with anything less than derision by those on the short end of the stick. And even where no issue of social injustice and deprivation is involved, what sense is there in the demand that rights be accorded and obligations be met and discharged?

Rights of whatever sort these happen to be may be asserted, demanded or exercised, with ulterior motives, even willfully or perversely, just as they may be accorded by those who are subject to coercive pressures and unable to press moral claims on their own behalf. There is no contradiction involved in saying that it would be wrong for someone to assert or exercise his right, or wrong for someone on some specific occasion and in the particular circumstances in which he finds himself to meet his obligation. Rights may be invoked with ulterior and questionable motives, just as, normally, they are employed in unobjectionable ways. Are we to suppose that we can somehow judge the moral propriety or impropriety involved in the given ways in which rights and obligations impose constraints upon conduct without regard to the goods and evils that befall those who are affected by these constraints?

If, as Prichard supposed, we must distinguish sharply as 'co-ordinate' but 'independent' the goodness of benevolent action from the moral goodness of the conscientious meeting of one's obligations, then if not actually implied there is surely suggested the view that in the latter case, in contrast with that of the former, the concern of the agent is not with the well-being either of the agent or of the persons being accorded their right but simply and solely with something quite different and independent of it, namely, some presumed moral attribute or relation in which the agent stands to others.[14] It looks, therefore, as if what is intended by the deontologist thesis expressed by Prichard that morality and virtue are somehow independent is that it would make perfectly good sense to talk about rights and obligations in complete conceptual independence of any consideration of the goods and evils, the benefits and burdens that are our human lot, that one can somehow understand the morality of according someone his right without any regard to the goods and evils that may befall him or anyone else.

Such a conception of the place of rights and obligations in morals may well strike one as being morally stuffy. The idea that rights and obligations are conceptually cut off from the goods and evils that can befall human beings will elicit the query, 'Why should we continue as we have in the past to attach any importance to rights and to obligations if these make no difference to the promotion of good and the avoidance of evil?' The short and easy reply to this, namely, that rights are rights, obligations are obligations, and as such are grounds for action—this following from the very meaning of the terms—is too fast. For why should we consider these grounds as important as we do? Further, what is the point of our talk about the morality of this or that act if there is no conceptual linkage with the fortunes of human beings, with the goods for which they strive and the evils they seek to avoid? And if there is no such point, why not undertake to revise our concepts, by ceasing to talk about rights at all (what can the point be of such talk if it is not that of protecting the interests and the fortunes of those who claim or assert them; and why indeed should we cater to persons engaged in this service to themselves?) Or, why not strip off from the conception of a right that normative feature that serves to render analytic the statement that rights are moral grounds for action, and this we can do simply by identifying the right that a person has with the entitlement derived from some sort institutional or social office? And why not then go on to advocate a new and a higher morality to replace the pointless one that we have repudiated, a new and softened morality that concerns itself with the joys and sorrows of human beings whatever our social or institutional relations with them might be? This indeed is the line taken by some who have recommended supplanting our common morality, with its stern and quasi-legal overtones of commandments and sanctions, by a morality of the heart, of love and affection for human beings. For, too often, the moralist's strident talk of rights and obligations, as if this could be understood in complete independence of any consideration of the joys and sorrows of human beings, has invited the repudiation of the morality for which such moralists speak and the recommendation that we follow a higher morality, one that bids us act not with an interest in so-called rights and obligations but with compassion for human beings, taking delight in their joys and striving in every way possible for us to relieve them of the heavy burdens they bear.

But is this conceptual sundering of goods and evils from rights and obligations even intelligible? In the essay to which I have referred Prichard speaks of obligations as 'involving' some sort of relation. The obligation to tell the truth involves, he declares, 'the fact that others trust us to speak the truth' which gives rise to the sense that communication of the truth is something owing by us to them, thereby implying, unless I seriously misunderstand him, that the obligation owed someone is one thing and the relation upon which it depends, is something else. What precisely we can say about the obligation—which, clearly, is the right viewed from the point of view of one with respect to whom a person has the right—other than that it involves or depends upon this relation, is something Prichard is unable to say, resorting at this point to a characteristic intuitionist stop: one simply grasps it by an immediate act of apprehension and in so doing understands perfectly and completely what is meant by 'an obligation' or 'a right'. But setting aside some of the obvious epistemological objections to this intuitionism, this conception of what is involved in the understanding of an obligation (or right) is radically defective. Instead of looking for certain objects which, supposedly, constitute the meanings of the substantives 'obligation' and 'right'—Prichard imagined that an obligation is a peculiar sort of an entity, the attribute of a person—we need to explore the ways in which these terms are linked together and each of them with other terms of our moral vocabulary in the sentences employed by us in the course of our moral communication with others. Writers of the recent past have employed various analogies between moral and other forms of discourse in order to dispel the fascination with the word–object picture of the meaning of a word—the'Fido'-Fido principle as Ryle once called it—according to which we need only turn our gaze from the word to the object in order to understand the meaning of the word. Some of the analogies proposed of the language of morals with that of games, ceremonies, commands, etc. have been useful in helping us to resist this tempting picture of the meaning of a word, although each of these analogies in turn has turned out to be something less than the open sesame to philosophical clarification it was first imagined to be.

What we have attempted to do, in our earlier discussions of the concept of rights and their correlative obligations, is to indicate the conceptual framework—the distinctive array of concepts—in which rights and obligations have their characteristic place, and the manner in which the latter function as grounds of action. To this end, attention has been called by way of reminders to what all of us already understand insofar as we are able to use the language of morals, until philosophical perplexity and bewilderment wreak their havoc by inducing in us a sense of estrangement from our own moral competence and our own moral understanding. We have remarked on how in particular sorts of cases a right may be claimed, asserted, demanded, acquired, waived, relinquished and forfeited, and the ways in which reasons of various sorts may be adduced for and against the claims that a person may be justified in exercising his right, or in according someone else his right. And we have explored the manner in which rights may be infringed or violated by those under obligation to those who, for whatever reasons, have rights with respect to them, and of the moral emotions and the moral burdens that, respectively, they must feel and bear. In short, the understanding of what it means to have a right, or to be under an obligation to someone else, is no simple matter like the possession of an attribute that can be apprehended by an act of intellection; it is a matter, rather, that involves mastery of a body of discourse by those able to employ it in the relevant practical affairs in which they are involved with each other.

All of this may seem to be idle philosophical drum-beating were it not for the unsettling nature of the query with which we are concerned here, namely, 'Can or can't we grasp the concept of rights in independence of the concept of a good or evil that may befall a human being?' Why not, and, in any case, how are we to go about providing a philosophically responsible answer?

It has been suggested by some writers that the concept of a right is, as it were, a kind of moral chain by which one person—the person under the obligation—is bound or tied to another who is thus able to control and restrict his freedom of action.[15] The figure is useful in a number of respects, conspicuously in emphasizing that the possession of a right by one person does impose restrictions on the permissible scope of action of anyone who, by virtue of that right, is under an obligation to him. It reminds us too that a person who has a right may or may not choose to exercise it; he may afford some slack in the chain that binds another to him, thus allowing him some freedom of action, or he may tighten the chain in choosing to exercise his right. Or, the chain he holds may slip from his grasp when, through misconduct of some relevant sort, he forfeits the right that he has. He may choose, indeed, to relinquish his right, when voluntarily he releases his end of the chain. And he may allow some slack in the chain without losing his grasp when he waives his right without relinquishing it. But this picture of the moral relation affords no hint of how it is that one person has come to be tied morally to another. Why, for example, does a promise bind the promiser to the promisee, confer a right upon the person to whom one has given his word? And the figure of a moral chain provides no hint of why it is that those morally tied to one another are reasonable in performing any of the aforementioned moves with respect to each other. Further, the picture provides no hint at all of the character of the damage—the moral damage—that, for example, a promiser may bring upon a promisee, when for whatever reason this may be, the former breaks the chain that binds him to the latter, wronging the latter in violating his right. Still less does this figure provide any hint of when and why it should be appropriate for a person wronged in this way to forgive someone who has transgressed against him, not as an act of mercy but because of his recognition of the wrongdoer's sense of guilt in the matter, his remorse and readiness to make amends and to do better in the future—matters that warrant and require the reciprocal response from the person who has been wronged, namely, a readiness dictated, not by generosity, but by the respect that he must feel towards someone now purged of his guilt, to resume his normal dealings with him with confidence and trust.

I mention these matters in order that we might have some comprehension of the complicated terrain we must cross and criss-cross, if we are to achieve anything like a perspicuous view of our subject matter and gain an understanding that resolves our philosophical perplexities about the issues with which we are concerned. For we need to see clearly how it is that the concept of a right is connected with the concept of human good and how, proceeding further, it is possible to provide some rationale for the reasonable decisions we make in adjudicating the competing claims of rights (and their correlative obligations) with other moral considerations including those pertaining to the benefits and burdens with which, reasonably, we are concerned in our conduct.

IV

The question we raised earlier is whether the concept of a right to be enjoyed or accorded can be divorced from that of a good to be achieved or a burden to be removed; and I shall begin with a consideration of the case of a promise by which the lives of persons are joined when a right is conferred and an obligation is assumed. This is only the beginning, for we shall need to explore other relations discussed in Chapter III in which as I argued the lives of persons are joined, in order to provide the necessary further development needed for our purpose. For although a promise is a paradigm case of a right conferring action, it is one that is not entered into by any and all persons, by total strangers as well as by those who conduct their lives with respect to each other in circumstances of mutual trust and understanding as in the case of friends and acquaintances between whom there exists a substantial measure of moral understanding. A promise is not lightly made nor does it succeed, i.e. it is not made and accepted with that mutual confidence between the parties concerned, if the verbal formula is employed when we deal with those altogether unfamiliar to us. In these peripheral cases, there can be no assurance that the promiser is as good as his word, that he will fashion his conduct in such a way that he will be constrained by reasons that are accepted and acceptable to the promisee. We are on guard when promises are made to us by those whom we have no reason to suppose will comport themselves in ways that are morally acceptable to us. In short, the promise as a transaction between persons presupposes a moral background of understanding that needs to be explored if the full story is to be told. Still, it may be useful to begin with the case of a promise, and to bring to focus now some of the conclusions reached in Chapter II, before going on with the development of a fuller account of the rationale that we need to elucidate.

It was argued in Chapter II that in central or nuclear cases of promises, the right of the promisee and the obligation of the promiser is possible only if there is a basic right that any person has, as moral agent, to go about his affairs in the pursuit of his interests. And it was argued that the infringement of this right by the failure, willfully or not, to meet his obligation is tantamount to subverting his moral status as an agent by bringing the line of conduct in which he is engaged, and on which the keeping of the promise depends for its success, to naught.

If this account is correct, the meeting of an obligation created by a promise cannot be the be-all and end-all of this moral performance. For there could not be the right that was being accorded by the meeting of the obligation, unless persons had concerns or interests and the right, as agents, to pursue these interests. This does not mean that the interest involved is an interest in oneself; for as in the case of a promise given to A by B to promote the well-being of C or to assist C in the realization of *his* ends, the interest of the recipient of the promise who thereby has the right in question is an interest in someone else who is in no way party to the promise transaction. In this case B's meeting of the obligation that he has to A consists in the benefit he confers upon C, whatever that benefit may be. In special cases the person assuming the obligation may serve as a surrogate for the person upon whom the right has been conferred. If I promise a friend that I will look after his son while he is away on an extended trip, I serve to some extent in the capacity of his father; and by promising as I do I assume some of his burdens and thereby provide my friend the peace of mind he needs in order satisfactorily to conduct his own affairs. Normally the promisee is the beneficiary of the promise-keeping action. In any case it is essential, if there is to be a right conferred by a promise, that persons have interests which merely as moral agents they are entitled to pursue. But these interests must be distinct from that moral interest that any agent has in being accorded his moral right. Unless this were true, the right that he has to pursue his interest would be the right that he has to promote his interest in the right that he has; and there would be no content to the right at all since there could be no intelligible answer to the question, 'What is it to which he has a right?' The right that persons have, merely as agents, must be the right to promote those interests they have as the specific human beings they are whatever their plans, projects, hopes and aspirations may be, interests distinct from that moral interest that, truistically, any moral agent has in being accorded his moral right.

The interests presupposed by but distinct from the moral interest we have are enormously varied. They are the interests that we have for ourselves and for others, whoever they may be, friend or stranger, those alive today or those who will follow in the immediate or distant future; they are the interests we have in planning as we do for the future in undertaking whatever our line of conduct may be. Now I remarked at the beginning of Chapter III that certain exclusions are intended in the claim made that a human being as an agent has the right to pursue his interests. The interest whatever it may be cannot be some passing fancy or idle whim or desire that is unconnected, in the broadest sense of this term, with some line of conduct in which the individual is engaged, for in that case there would be no point or purpose served by a promise, and whether or not independently of promises made agents have the right to satisfy some passing, idle desire I shall not here discuss; although it would appear that, for example, the right to wiggle one's ears (if one can) is that minimal notion of a right involved in saying that no one has the right to interfere, and it calls only for the abstention from interfering on the part of others. Further, it was expressly noted earlier that the right to pursue one's interests could not be construed in such a way as to include the morally absurd right to do the immoral. Shall we rule out, in addition, the right to proceed irrationally in the pursuit of one's interest?

The difficulty is that we want to allow for promises made and which do confer rights upon simple request, and sometimes without any reason being given for the solicitation of the promise, including the service to one's plans or projects of the promised action. Shall we say in such cases that we are unable to determine that a right has been conferred until we know that the promised action does reasonably advance the interests of the promisee? Surely not, although if we do not know that the promisee is rational, then in some cases at least we should hesitate to say that a right has been conferred, our ground being that no one has the right to proceed in an irrational manner. Promises are made by and to rational persons, but rational persons can be unreasonable, and we do not, I believe, want to say that it is only if the promisee is reasonable in thinking that the promised action is integral to the line of conduct he undertakes that he has a right conferred upon him. For in some of these cases the unreasonableness may not affect the issue of a right. If someone induces me to promise to give him a cashier's check rather than cash, where each will serve equally well, he may be unreasonable, but has he no right? I did promise him the cashier's check. We take it for granted that those to whom we make promises know what they are doing, but we should not suppose that whenever they do not, the promise is null and void. But render the example more extreme and unreasonableness becomes irrationality, and if irrationality infects the conduct of the person to whom the promise locution is addressed, the concepts of promise and right may well lose their grip.

Still, the question raised earlier concerning the connection between the concepts of a right and of good is clear enough if we recognize that the case of the unreasonable design of one's conduct to which a promise is relevant is a peripheral case, that the concept has to be understood as one that applies normally to cases of rational agents who are reasonable in the way they go about their affairs and in what they are interested. In such cases the conception of a right is linked not only with interests but with what does in fact serve that interest. But that which reasonably we require for the interests we have is precisely what we would consider good, good being that which in this way answers to our interests.[16] What is important, therefore, in the right that a person as agent has, to engage in his enterprises in general at least—this being the way the concept of his right is employed—is the idea of a good or goods in the pursuit of which he is engaged. Accordingly, it would make no sense to talk about rights and obligations without some presumed and, generally at least, actual good at issue.

This conclusion is reinforced if we consider still other ways in which the concept of a right is tied to other concepts, not extraneously, but essentially. For to understand what a right is, we need to understand that it may be claimed, asserted or demanded, exercised, waived, relinquished or forfeited, and the reasons that operate in each of these sorts of cases. So too with according a person his right or infringing it in any of a number of different sorts of ways. It is only in this way—by understanding how the concept of a right operates in a complex moral language in which the talk of rights goes on between persons engaged in activities that do or may affect each other, and not by an intuitive apprehension of some entity signified by the word 'right'—that we understand what it is to have a right. In short, we need, as we observed earlier, much more than the figure of a chain held by one person, by which he restricts the activities of someone else tied to that chain at the other end, in order to elucidate the concept of a right.

As we have just seen, the concept of good is implicated in the right of promisees. For that right rests upon a right that persons have as agents to pursue their interests, by reference to which what they need and seek to achieve are intelligible as benefits to be enjoyed and burdens to be removed, not necessarily but often for themselves. Were there nothing worthwhile to be obtained by the recipient of a promise with the help of the agency of the promiser, there would be no role played by the promise in the activities of promiser or promisee. The game of promising, in that case, would be an empty charade. And it is precisely because of the relevance of goods to be achieved and evils to be avoided, whether for promisees or for anyone else on whose behalf promises are solicited and/or made, that some of the sorts of items cited as reasons for claiming, exercising, waiving or relinquishing the rights of promisees are intelligible as reasons. And so too with some of the considerations adduced as reasons for according or infringing a promisee's rights. This is not to say that the fact that a person has a right is not in itself a reason or ground for claiming or exercising it, or the fact that a person would be meeting his obligation is not in itself a reason for keeping his word. Rather, it is to say that whatever right and obligation there is that operates as a ground in these cases does so because it implies that the person who has the right, the person to whom the obligation is owed, has a right to go about his affairs, if he is reasonable in the achievement of good and the remission of evil. Unless this were so, it would make no sense to cite the fact that a promised action is integral to a line of conduct in which a substantial good is to be realized makes the right in question (and its correlative obligation) a more compelling or stringent one than it would otherwise be, and therefore a good ground for claiming and exercising it rather than relinquishing it or waiving it. And it would make no good moral sense for the promisee, who decides because of unexpected and altered circumstances not to undertake the line of conduct the promised action was designed to support, thus severing the promised action from any good to be achieved, not to employ this fact in the way a responsible agent does by waiving or relinquishing the right he has. So too with one reason for waiving one's right (correlatively, one reason for infringing or denying someone his right), the fact, namely, that in the particular circumstances of the case, the burdens imposed upon someone else far outweigh the benefits to be achieved by the enjoyment or exercise of the right. Still less does this fact, that a consideration of the goods to be achieved and the evils to be avoided or remitted operates during the course of our deliberations about rights and obligations, establish that these—the rights and obligations as factors to be weighed in deciding what is to be done—exist *only* if it is beneficial to exercise the rights or to meet the obligations. Considerations of this sort establish, not that there are no rights and no obligations, but that the rights and obligations that remain may be insufficient in special cases fully to justify those relevant items of conduct by which rights are asserted and exercised and by which obligations are met and discharged.

Is there any simple way in which benefits and burdens are to be assessed in determining whether or not to claim one's right with a view to exercising it, or to accord another his right? Consider the difficulties involved in weighing the benefits and burdens of alternative programs of action. It is simple enough for me to decide whether to make do with a pleasant and inexpensive wine so that I might enjoy a not-to-be-repeated opportunity to relish a memorable but expensive delicacy for which the restaurant is celebrated, rather than dining on an undistinguished but pleasant dish and sipping a much more expensive wine I can easily enjoy on another occasion. Here my taste remains unaffected by my choice, and the latter is clear enough. But consider the following: Shall I forgo economic gain and give up a lucrative medical practice in one location in order, at some loss, to practice in a much more agreeable part of the country? Here, clearly, I must consider the problems involved in parting from old friends and forming new ones, the sacrifices involved in the loss of salary and, among other intangibles, the very difficult problem of determining the effects on me—my tastes and my interests—of the move I contemplate making. Here one needs good judgment not only about one's present interests and traits but also that rare ability to imagine with some accuracy the effects of the move one contemplates making upon one's interests and the very texture of one's life. But how much more difficult, where the decision affects someone else, and what is needed is not only imagination about oneself but about the interests, traits, life style and undertakings of someone else, where one must decide, in ways that will change the pattern of the lives of all concerned, whether or not to accord someone the right he has, or meet an obligation one has assumed. Instances of this sort may be uncommon but they do occur; and when they do, what is required is imagination and good judgment, a knowledge of relevant fact including a sensitivity to the interests of all concerned. But difficult or not as it may be to resolve the issue of good and bad, surely it is one of the relevant factors to be considered in determining whether or not to exercise one's right or to accord someone else his right. Indeed, Prichard's talk about the independent realms of obligation and virtue insofar as it suggests that the meeting of an obligation is the end-all and be-all of that moral action, opens the way to a kind of moral fanaticism: that one might be justified in standing on one's right or meeting one's obligation to someone, whatever the resulting benefits and burdens might be for anyone affected by one's action. It is moral folly to demand one's right, everything else being equal, at the cost of one's own ruin; and it is morally inexcusable to accord someone a right that serves no one's interest and, by that action, deny others the goods they urgently need, or not to relieve them of the heavy burdens under which they labor.

V

We need now to return to the question raised earlier concerning the relation between benevolence and the conscientious observance of the rights of agents in order to see more clearly the character of the relation between these distinct (Prichard's word is 'independent') matters. Why is it that one feels any sense of obligation towards those whose rights are connected, as indeed generally they are, with the interests they have and the goods with which they are concerned? That one is under an obligation and that by meeting it one benefits, generally at least, the person whose right one accords is one thing; but that this fact should be a matter of concern to one and impose effective constraints upon one during the course of one's own endeavors is something else again. For the sense that one is under an obligation is no mere intellectual exercise but one of practical concern to us. Why should this consideration move one as it does?

It will not do to cite simply the fact that one desires to benefit others or, following Hume, that one is naturally endowed with sympathy for others and is moved by the agreeable prospect of their good to assist them in achieving it. For neither the desire to benefit others nor the sympathetic pleasure at the prospect of their good fortune will account for the sense that we are under obligations to them, that we ought to accord them the rights they have against us. At best, they serve only to explain the benevolence with which we extend to them the help they need for the achievement of their purposes. Nor will it do to appeal to the autonomy or rationality of human beings as factors explanatory of the concern that we have for their rights; for why should it be the case that autonomy even provides the necessary support for the possession of rights let alone explain the sense that these rights are to be respected and accorded? If we are to understand how it is possible that, by promising, one could so conduct oneself over a period of time that one will be ready, at the appropriate time, to do the thing one promised to do and thereby contribute to the good of someone else, we need to look to those features of personhood which human beings exhibit in their dealings with others, not to occurrences and capacities like desire, sympathy or autonomy which individuals can exhibit independently of their transactions with each other. We need to attend to the manner in which segments of the lives of persons are joined when persons who are sensible of their obligations to one another conduct their lives with each other in such a way that during an extended period of time they remain mindful of the support they must give each other. Why then should there be this willingness to support the agency of another, the sense of obligation that colors a promiser's thought and action in such a way that he remains considerate of the other person and is prepared at the appropriate time to lend support to his endeavors and in this way contribute to his pursuit of his interests? Why should he, in the event he fails to keep his word, feel not regret at the thought of the other's frustration or sympathetic distress at the sight or thought of the other's plight he has brought to pass, but guilt and remorse for his own moral failure?

If, as some have suggested, a promise is a kind of bargain that is struck for the mutually advantageous exchange of benefits—A says that he will do x for B, if B will do y for A—the bargain need be only a conditional agreement. Each need not be concerned with the agency of the other, with his interests and with the achievement by him of some envisaged good; he need only be alert to the other's behavior in order to determine whether he has kept or is likely to keep his part of the bargain. And in the event he sees or foresees the other's failure to do so, he will have good reasons to break off an agreement that now is or will be null and void. In such cases there is not the involvement in the life of one person of the interests and concerns of the other, and there need be no remorse, no sense of guilt, and no moral damage that either person suffers or is likely to suffer from the other's default. This is not to say that an agreement *cannot* function in the way in which a promise does, but if it does, much more than such an agreement is needed. Specifically, what is needed is precisely that moral background required for the employment of promise-locutions so that they may serve as they do to provide the kind of formal notice given by promisers that they will undertake to support the agency of those to whom these locutions are addressed.

In his discussion of the obligation of promises Prichard came to a conclusion he advanced only with the greatest hesitation that promising 'can only exist between individuals between whom there has already been something which looks at first like an agreement to keep agreements'. He remarks that the agreement in question 'does not require the use of language' and expresses his puzzlement about this non-verbalized agreement by asking what this can possibly be since 'strictly speaking, (it) cannot be an agreement'.[17] There is something important in Prichard's query. Promises are given and received by those who are prepared to join their lives on the basis of a moral understanding that the endeavors of persons in which they pursue their interests and achieve the goods these define are not matters of indifference to them. Rather, such endeavors are matters of moral concern to them as the endeavors persons, as moral agents, are entitled to carry forward by their own efforts—and with the contributing support that those who have joined their lives with them are prepared to supply, failing which they are accountable to them for the moral damage they have perpetrated. Where such moral understanding is lacking, promises as in the case of those entered into between total strangers are viewed with suspicion. And this is why, pace Hume, promises are made and accepted by those united by the bonds of love and affection; for in such cases there is, conspicuously, that interest in others as agents and that concern to support their endeavors without which there could not be the rights conferred by bona fide promises.[18] In short, the agreement that operates as the logical substratum of promising is an agreement in the manner in which persons understand and conduct their affairs with each other when they show proper concern for each other as agents with the interests they have during the course of their endeavors, interests that define goods to be achieved and evils to be avoided.

To promise in good faith is to confer a right, to assume an obligation. This is possible only if one is concerned with the endeavors and interests of others and prepared to display that concern during some portion of one's life in which one is attentive to the obligation assumed and prepared to perform that act by which one accords another his right. One can, of course, fake this concern. Psychopaths who do not know the difference between right and wrong do something that superficially resembles this; they parrot but do not understand promise-locutions. For such psychopaths there can be no sense of the guilt incurred by the neglect of one's obligation since there is no sense of the moral damage as distinct from the injury, disappointment, pain or frustration that occurs as a result of the failure to perform the action described or referred to in the promise-locution. For such individuals the understanding of promising, because it is now divested of any moral import, degenerates into something like Rawls's so-called constitutive rule, i.e. that when one promises, one says something like 'I promise to do x' in appropriate circumstances (e.g. one says this in order to receive some benefit), one is to go on to do x. But that one is thereby morally required to do x is something else again, and why one is to conform to this rule, since one lacks any moral interest in other persons in the event that it does not serve one's purpose, is a matter for which the psychopath understandably cannot supply an answer. But if one does in fact fake the giving of a bona fide promise—this is not a matter of mere external appearances, for one knows what a promise is, but, morally flawed as persons sometimes are, one promises falsely—the faking trades on and is possible only if normally at least there are non-faking performances, i.e. promises that persons give each other and in good faith. Hence, if there are rights conferred by promises, it follows that those who promise, generally at least, are concerned with the endeavors of others and are prepared therefore to support them in their efforts to achieve their ends. And those who receive and accept promises, in good faith on their own part, must also be concerned with those who have offered such promises to them as the persons they are and who are entitled as such to engage in their own endeavors and achieve their own ends. And just as those who promise in good faith, and assume their moral burdens in doing so, must be prepared in unexpected and unusual circumstances to refuse to meet their obligations if the cost to the interests of persons, whoever they may be, is too great, so those who accept promises must be prepared, out of this same concern with the rights of agents to pursue their interests and achieve the goods these define, to waive and even to relinquish the rights conferred upon them. They too must recognize that in accepting promises their lives have been joined by those who have given them their words, and that they too must be prepared, to take due account of the interests that promisers themselves may have and the goods that these define, in deciding whether or not to claim or exercise the rights conferred upon them. To understand what a promise is, is to understand what is involved in receiving it as much as what is involved in offering it. If, then, there is promising, with the moral import it has for us, there must be the mutual concern of the parties to the transaction with each other as agents engaged in their endeavors during the course of which they pursue their interests and the goods these define. And since the goods and evils that befall others no less than oneself are among the desiderata of those who give or receive promises, the agreement implied by promising is, in part, an agreement in the way in which those involved in the transaction are, first, concerned with each other as persons in their efforts to achieve goods and avoid evils, and, second, are prepared to recognize the goods they seek and the evils they avoid as relevant considerations in deciding how best to bear the moral burdens assumed in the transaction of promising. *In part*, there is this agreement, but this is by no means the whole of the matter. For, as we noted earlier in the discussion of the rights and obligations that are distributed among the members of a family,[19] rights and obligations do not exist *in vacuo*; they exist only where there is a community of understanding of the complex array of moral concepts within which the concepts of a right and an obligation have their place, and, paradigmatically, when the setting appropriate for the enjoyment and exercise of rights is present. This is the moral agreement, the logical substratum that lies in the background of the full-blooded and central case of the transaction of promising.

Conspicuously, this substratum is displayed in the way in which the lives of persons are joined within the family when that social unit is as it should be. Here, strikingly, is that mutual concern with each other as persons, with interests and the goods that these define, the benevolence or good will towards those related to each other by their rights and obligations, and the mutual support that they provide one another in a variety of enterprises in which they are engaged. To a lesser extent this is true of those with whom we conduct our affairs outside the family in other sorts of social or institutional arrangements, but here again the moral rights and obligations are derived not from the character of the social arrangement or the institution but from the character of the lives of the persons involved during the course of which they display that concern with each other's benefits and burdens by supporting as they do each other's endeavors. This moral background is surely present in the relations of friends to one another, but even strangers have their rights with respect to us precisely to the extent that, however different their ways may be from ours—their interests, habits, customs, speech, race or allegiances—they are persons with whom in principle, however difficult it may be in practice, one can interact in those ways that are required as background conditions for the making and accepting of bona fide promises. We may be skeptical and properly so of the concern for us that a passing and total stranger may have, and hence on our guard against any promise he gives us, but, if he has rights against us and we obligations to him, then he and we share this trait, namely, a concern with others and the capacity to join one's lives with them.

It is not only, therefore, that rights and goods are conceptually linked, it is also that there could be no rights and no obligations we have to others unless the persons involved are able to join at least some segments of their lives with each other during the course of which they are mindful of each other's interests and concerned in some way to lighten each other's burdens and promote each other's good. It follows that benevolence—good will towards others—far from being independent of rights and obligations, is required of anyone who has rights or is bound to anyone who has them. There could not be the sense of obligation in the absence of a concern for others, no respect for the rights of anyone without an interest in his well-being, and no sense of guilt or feeling of remorse because of the violation of the right of anyone, without an involvement in his interests, a concern to promote his good. The idea that rights and obligations impose no requirement of good will towards others is incoherent. Far from it being the case that a consideration of the rights of persons occupies a separate moral domain from that of benevolence, it *depends* upon it; for in the absence of a concern with the well-being of others there could be no sense of the important role that the rights of persons, our own and those of others, play in our lives.

VI

Earlier I noted two sorts of skepticism concerning the talk of moral rights. The first is the skepticism of those sensitive to social injustice, who regard the talk of rights by those advantaged by the circumstances of birth, education, social or economic position, as self-serving. The second, abetted perhaps by this consideration, recommends a higher morality for human beings than the morality of rights, a commitment that goes beyond the protection that can be afforded by the appeal to rights and which emphasizes the joy that persons are to take in each other's happiness and the compassion needed to alleviate suffering.

I shall not here discuss the first of these skepticisms, although it is worth noting in passing that talk about the rights of others (indeed, the right that one has by virtue of a promise received the terms of which provide that the promiser assist someone in no way party to the proceedings) by no means is restricted in favor of those who are advantaged; such talk need not be self-serving in any way. It is, rather, the second of the two forms of skepticism to which I now turn. I argued that certain features of personhood must be stipulated as part of the moral background of promising, and we need to bring them to bear upon the sorts of dissatisfaction sometimes felt about the morality of rights as somehow too constricting and much too narrow for humane and enlightened human beings.

It was argued in Chapter II that the right of a promisee rests upon the right that he has as agent to go about his affairs in the pursuit of his interest, the promise being a formal assurance given by the promiser of his support of the promisee's agency by means of the action described in or referred to by the promise-locution. And it was argued in the proceeding section that what is implied by the moral transaction of promising is the good will of the parties concerned towards each other, the concern on both sides with the interests and the well-being of the other party. It was also remarked that this kind of mutual concern, in which persons are mindful and supportive of the endeavors of others, is exemplified most strikingly, although by no means exclusively, in the case of those whose lives are joined not briefly, as in the case of those involved in promise transactions, but during a major portion of their lives as members of a family. I want now to explore certain features of this situation in order to focus upon certain conceptual features of rights which may allay the fears often expressed that morality of rights somehow fetters our more generous and humane dispositions.

In a family that is as it should be, the lives of its adult members are so joined that they share many of their interests. Their lives are thus so intertwined that it becomes difficult for each to imagine what life would be like in the absence of the other. With the death of one there is not only the grief but also, for a time at least, the disorientation induced in the life of the survivor, who is at a loss to pursue interests in which the other was involved. What we need to look to more closely, however, is the concern of parents, not for each other, but for their children in order to understand, first, how interests enter into the special rights that young children, even infants, have, and the correlative obligations that parents have to them, and, second, how a child's sense of the rights of others normally is developed.

A. We should, I believe, maintain that even the very young infant does have rights against its parents, that the latter are responsible for its proper development, and that in attending as they do to its needs they are meeting their obligations to it. Yet the kind of explanations advanced earlier of the rights of promisees or of parents with respect to each other may well appear to be inapplicable to infants. Promisers support the agencies of promisees and this is equally true of husband and wife, each of whom, during the course of their life together, supports and helps sustain the agency of the other not only by furthering but in substantial measure by sharing the other's interests. But in the case of the very young infant there is little agency and hardly any line of conduct to be supported by a parent who cares for it; these appear to lie in the future. Nor does the young infant have interests, although clearly it does have needs and wants. And while there may be a sense of obligation that a parent has for its infant, there is nothing of this sort and no sense of the complex array of concepts which could even remotely be ascribed to an infant.

While nothing like the full array of concepts in which the concept of a right is enmeshed can be applied to the case of infants, are there no applicable features of the concept that warrant our talk about the rights of infants *vis-à-vis* their parents? The infant can take no interest and cannot be said to *have* any interest in many of the things that are good for it, e.g. the course of its future development and the steps that must now be taken to insure that this is properly managed; but it is *in* the infant's interests that parents act as they do when they plan and prepare for its proper development. But this, it would appear, relates only to interests the infant will acquire later on, when, no longer as an infant, but as a person who has interests of his own, he will then and only then pursue his interests and, as a being able to carry on with programs of action of his own, act in ways to which only then he will be entitled to act as the human being he will become. Hence, even if parents act as they do in the interest of an infant, the conceptual framework in which the concept of a right is embedded does not seem to apply to the infant, qua infant. If so, whatever right there is in the case of the infant would seem to be at best a future right, that when parents act *in* the interests of their offspring, they are engaged only in a complex exercise that is preliminary to the achievement by the latter of any moral right that it might have *vis-à-vis* its parents, that in acting as they do in promoting the latter's development they are not, strictly speaking, meeting their obligations to their infant. If this is true, however, it makes no sense to speak of the responsibilities of parents to their infant sons or daughters. For the notion of responsibility involves the notion of their accountability; but to whom are parents accountable? Unless it makes sense to speak of the rights of infants qua infants, they are not accountable to the latter, for they do not as yet have any moral rights against their parents; nor would it appear that they are accountable morally to anyone else acting in behalf of their children, for who could this be if it is not a parent? Those to whom parents would appear to be accountable can only be, on this view, the adults-to-be into which hopefully their infant children will develop. But since the implementation of the plans and projects that parents have for their children when they act in their interest is a matter that relates to them as they are before they have reached the moral status requisite for their possession of rights, the person who emerges from this process of development with rights of his own has no reason to complain, if this occurs because of the negligence of his parents, that they had failed to meet the obligations they had to him as young child—for qua young child or infant how could he have had any right against his parents? Shall we say then that parents have an obligation qua parents to that future person who later on comes into being with rights of his own? But suppose that for some reason or other no such moral metamorphosis occurs, to whom can parents be said to be accountable? And if there is no one—neither the young child nor anyone acting on behalf of him as a being with rights—what sense can there be in our familiar talk about responsible parental behavior towards their infants and young children? Clearly, the responsible behavior of a parent must be the behavior appropriate to the infant or child that consists in meeting a parent's obligation to that being who *is* infant or child, the behavior of one who accords his young offspring the rights that he has even as an infant or child, however insensible the latter may be of his moral status with respect to his parent, and however deficient he may be as agent with interests of his own.

How then is it possible that a parent is *now* under an obligation to an infant, that the latter *now* has rights against him? A parent, unlike a stranger who finds an infant abandoned on his doorstep, is under an obligation not only to attend to its immediate needs, but among many other things to plan and to provide for him, these being matters to which infants, qua infants, are entitled to receive from parents, not strangers. It will not answer our conceptual problem to invoke the moral consideration that parents, unlike strangers, have assumed an obligation towards an infant they bring into the world or adopt, and that no such commitments are made by a stranger who finds an abandoned infant on his doorstep. For our question is how it is possible for an infant, qua infant, who is devoid of any substantive agency of his own, who as infant *has* no interests of his own, who cannot possibly engage in any line of conduct for which any support could be given by anyone else, and who has no sense of any rights that he may have against anyone else, to have any such rights in his helpless and morally insensible condition?

Several points need to be made. First, the notion of what is *in* the latter's interest, as distinct from an interest that the latter may have, e.g. in some bright object or toy, does connect with the idea of some good, but in a different way from that in which it does in the latter case. A young child, even an infant, may reach for something it would not be reasonable to allow it to grasp. It does not follow, therefore, from the fact that it (or, for that matter, anyone else) is interested in x, that having x is good for it. But it does follow from the fact that it is in the interest of a child that, for example, it receives affection or training and an education of a certain sort that these are good for it to have. Our thought in such cases is that these items are among the things it needs for its development into a responsible being. Now, not all of the things that are in a person's interests, even when that person is not interested in those things because, perhaps, he lacks intelligence, foresight or good judgment, are the things that are bound up with his status simply as an infant, child or responsible person. What is in a person's interest may relate to some particular status or role he may happen to play in society, as a physician, teacher or employee. And parents, who decide that it is in an infant's interest that they plan a career for it, as physician, may be mistaken about its native talents and misguided by their parental ambition. But the education, for example, that is in an infant's or child's interests need not be tied to such specific roles that parents ambitious for their children have in mind. It need only be (a) the moral education required for its development into a responsible moral agent, and (b) the measures taken for the discovery, development and effective utilization of its talents in such a way that the adult to be will be able to develop interests suitable to his talents and enjoy the exercise of his rights as a human being. What in this way is now done in the child's interest is that to which the child is then and there entitled; and in acting in this way parents are acting responsibly, meeting the obligations they have then and there to the child who depends upon it for its support and guidance as it grows in maturity.

Second, some of the things parents do in the interest of their infants and children are in their future interest, some in their present interest. It may be in the future interest of the young child for a parent to establish a trust fund for his offspring to insure that funds will be available to him at some future date, but it is in his present interest that a parent responds to the early glimmerings of an infant's agency by bestowing upon it the love and affection it requires for its proper development.[20] And it is in the infant's present interest that parents supply it with what it needs for its immediate and continued survival; for even an infant, as I shall argue in the next chapter, is, qua human being, entitled to life itself as well as to the many things necessary for its growth and development into a responsible moral agent. But while the full story cannot now be told, something needs to be said now in order to make good the claim that there are enough conceptual features present even in the case of the infant to render intelligible our familiar talk of the rights of infants *vis-à-vis* their parents, of the obligations the latter have to them.

Third, parents, like strangers, may be indifferent to these rights that any infant has as the human being he is, just as they may be indifferent to the special rights that an infant has against them, rights to whatever it is that parents can provide in order that it may enjoy the goods, present and future, that are ingredient in the course of a life that is worthy of a human being. But here, as in the case of promises or the relations of husband and wife, we need to attend to those features present in the relations of those who are not indifferent but concerned with what is morally required of them, in order to ascertain whether or not the structure in which the concept of such a special right has its place is exemplified in the relation of parent to infant to a degree sufficient to justify us in ascribing any right to the latter which he has then and there against his parent.

Now despite the striking dissimilarities that obtain between infants and those to whom unhesitatingly we do ascribe special rights, the lives of parents and infants are nonetheless joined in ways that compensate for the deficiencies in the agency, interests and understanding of infants. An infant, and less and less so as it begins its development very soon after birth, is largely passive. It is, at first, completely dependent upon its parents for the most elementary of its needs without which its survival is impossible. It has few if any interests, but even here there is agency and there are interests and understanding that sustain its life. Here the interests that parents have when they act in the interests of their young infants who cannot have any idea of the progress they are to make in their development, of what is needed for this purpose, or even of what they now need in order to survive, are interests that parents supply when they act in the interests of their offspring. These are surrogate interests, as it were, which parents supply on behalf of and in support of their offspring. So it is with the agency of parents when they act as they do in the present interests of infants far too young to have these interests on their own part or to do anything on their own to further them. This is an agency that is supportive of what is in the interest of a being with which parents have joined their lives and to which, even at a very early age there are the responses, diffuse and undiscriminating as they may be—and less and less so as maturation proceeds—that the very young infant makes to the ministrations of the parents who care for it. Indeed, just as the parents provide surrogate interests and agency for the infants in support of their development, so they contribute their own understanding and their own moral response when, acting on behalf of the moral interests of their infants, they claim the moral, no less than the legal, rights that their offspring have. And parents, not their children, are accountable and in some cases liable for the damage or injury the latter may cause others. Despite, therefore, a young infant's lack of agency, of interests that *he* may be said to have, of understanding of and response to his moral relation to his parents and others, and of moral responsibility itself, his life is joined with that of his parents at first mainly by what *they* do in making him an important part of their own lives.

Parents, acting on behalf of their infant offspring in making up these deficiencies supply out of their own resources surrogate interests, agency, moral understanding and moral response, when in various ways they act on behalf of them, i.e. in their interest. Generally, as the course of the development of an infant proceeds during the years—the end result of which is the emergence of a being with interests, agency, moral understanding and moral competence of his own—the contributions that parents make in the form of the surrogate agency, interest and moral understanding and competence that they supply in remedying these deficiencies, decreases. But in the course of the life of a family that is as it should be and in which the lives of parents and children are joined, so that more and more common interests are shared and each takes pride and pleasure in the achievements of the other, there remains a high level of agency, interests, understanding and moral response that can be attributed to both parents and their offspring even though these, in the case of the latter and in decreasing measure as they develop, are surrogates supplied by parents.

But while this is our response to the first of the two issues raised earlier on page 147, it is by no means the whole story. For, if a promise is a paradigm case in which a special right is conferred and an obligation is assumed—if this is the model to be employed in elucidating the special rights of infants against their parents—then, antecedently to the ways in which interests are involved when parents meet their obligations to their infant children, the latter must be supposed to have a status as human beings with the right that goes with that status to pursue the interests they have. But in the case of young infants the requisite moral background appears to be missing; we have, rather, a moral blank, as it were, no agency and no interests and no line of conduct in which they could engage, the defeating of which would be the moral damage they would suffer when negligent and indifferent parents fail to join their lives with them and supply out of their own resources, the interests, agency and understanding their infants lack. What is missing in the account given above of the ways in which parents join their lives with their young children, supplying surrogate interests, agency and understanding when they act in their interests, and in this way giving substance to the moral relation in which they stand to them, is the status of even the young infant as the human being it is with the moral right that any human being has, without which, it would appear, there could not be the special right of the infant that it has against its parents. Is it possible to attribute to those newly born infants anything like the status of human beings with rights qua human beings? And if not, how could *they* be said to possess any special rights that *they* have against their parents?

I shall not now pursue the matter further, but defer consideration of it until such time as we have explored the topic of human rights and considered in that connection the relevant features of the concept of a person, a concept we apply not only to morally mature adults and young children, but also even to young infants.[21] I turn, therefore, to the second of the two issues raised on page 147.

B. In order to deal with the question concerning the development of a child's sense of others as persons who have rights, we need to comment on certain other features of the relation between parent and child. The concern here is not to advance speculative hypotheses about the psychology of the moral development of children but to remind ourselves of features of the concept of moral personhood central to our account of rights, in order to prepare the way for comments concerning the rationale of the moral decisions to be made given competing moral considerations.

Conspicuously in the family the lives of persons are bound tightly by the love that persons have for each other, the joys and delights they take in each other's good fortunes and achievements, the admiration, emulation and even idealization of others by which efforts are encouraged and burdens are lightened—in short, by a whole range of natural affections that facilitate the characteristic ways in which the lives of husband and wife, siblings, and parents and children are united. The infant too young to have any clear sense of the fact is the beneficiary of the love of its parents who, even before its birth, have planned and prepared for it and made it part of their own lives; but it begins at an early age to respond, as it becomes increasingly aware of it, to the love it receives from its parents with its own natural affections towards them. These stirrings of the feelings of the very young child for its parents, and for its older siblings too, mark the beginnings of its concerns for other human beings. Without these affections and the personal attachment to others within the family, it is deprived of the means that facilitates its sense of others outside the family circle with whom it may join its life in its dealings with them.

The child who is rejected by his parents, who senses their indifference to him as a growing human being with the interests of a person of his age may be rendered incapable of forming attachments to others. In such cases the relations with others become self-centered, the dominant interest being in having others cater to his own private interests. Such persons may enjoy the admiration and good will of their fellows but be unable to reciprocate these feelings. In the absence of any affection that bind them to others, there can be no pangs of guilt when they misuse their fellows or any remorse that they feel when they are aware of the damage they inflict upon them. Instead of guilt and remorse the estranged person feels fear and insecurity lest others respond in kind and thwart his own endeavors. Instead of moral indignation, he feels hatred for those who stand in his way.

This is not to say that this is the inevitable aftermath of the denial of the love a child normally receives from its parents. Human nature is resilient, and often fantasy and the close attachments that young children form with others of their own age can alleviate the handicaps imposed upon them by cold and indifferent parents. Nor should it be thought that parental love is sufficient to bring to pass a child's sense of a person as a being with whom close ties may be established outside the family circle. Tribalism is a danger and it may occur in a social unit as small as the family where the love of its members for one another may occur only at the cost of its isolation from the society of which it is a part. The point is, rather, that the love a child receives from its parents, and the love with which it responds to them, serves as a basis for the child's proper moral development, essential to which is its sense of persons as beings with whom it can join its own life and to whom it owes the help and assistance they need from it during the course of its dealings with them.

The love the young child receives from its parents and siblings, and to which it responds, shows itself first in its propensity to deal with them, not generously or benevolently (that belongs to a later stage of its development when it becomes sensible of the interests of others and defers pursuing its own out of good will towards them), but trustingly and openly in the delight it takes in its play with them. And as it grows and its own developing interests come into conflict with those of others, the child loving and admiring its parents seeks to emulate them in the ways in which they deal with conflicts of this sort. It depends upon its parents for their counsel and pays heed to their admonitions, among others to regard its friends and acquaintances as beings who, like themselves, love and are loved, are capable of joys and sorrows and are prepared to conduct themselves with kindness towards and consideration for others. The child comes, therefore, to appreciate those outside the family circle as persons like those within it and towards whom feelings like those which it has towards its siblings are appropriate. It comes to form ties of friendship that very often match in closeness of attachment the relations it has with its siblings. But even where the circle of those with whom it carries on its affairs include its fellows at school or on the playground, and towards whom its feelings are a good deal less than the warm feelings of love and affection it has for any of the members of its own family, there remains a willingness to adjust its interests to those of its fellows out of a concern with them as the human beings they are.

There is, of course, a good deal more that needs to be said in spelling out the details of the child's moral development. It needs for example to surmount the shock of its disappointment with those who fail to reciprocate with the concern and the trust that it extends to them, and to contrive despite such rebuffs to reckon with their interests and to display a willingness to resume its dealing with them. And where the child itself is at fault because of its preoccupation with its own immediate ends, and where, too, its own jealousies and envy of others mar its relations with outsiders, it needs the guidance and counsel of those upon whom it relies implicitly—its parents—to help it mend its ways. For here, too, its fault, like that of others who on occasion fail to display any concern with its own interests, is sometimes exhibited during the course of its relations with its siblings; and the corrective measures that it comes to adopt as appropriate to such incidents in which outsiders are involved are measures of the same sort as those that are employed for its dealings with those who are inside the family circle. The developing child, in all of these cases, troubled as its affairs may be on occasion and recognizing as it does the consideration it must give those within the family, learns that those outside the family also need to be given consideration; for it learns that they are beings towards whom others are bound by love and affection; it learns that they are beings with whom it is possible to engage in various forms of transaction on the basis of mutual confidence, and therefore that their interests, and generally the interests of persons with whom they may have dealings of any sort, are not to be ignored as a matter of indifference to it. Whether or not the relations of morally maturing children with their friends, acquaintances, and even strangers, are marked by love and affection, their concern with each other as persons whose interests they may not ignore but must keep in mind in their traffic with them is a natural outgrowth of that concern with others first displayed to those in their own families.

The point is that the love and affection that members of a family feel towards one another disposes them to regard each other, not merely as the psychological subjects of good or bad experiences, but as persons with whom, as the agents they are, they are to deal with each other with the mutual understanding of the support they provide one another during the course of their dealings with each other. The love and affection that unites the members of a family into a group of human beings living with one another serves not merely to establish relations of sympathy so that each may respond with feelings of delight and distress for the good and bad fortunes of others; it serves in addition to convey a sense of each other as persons to be dealt with morally in ways that are supportive of their endeavors. It is this sense of what it is to be a human being that is carried over by the growing child during the course of its dealings with those outside the family circle and towards whom a good deal less than that warmth of feeling it has towards its parents and siblings is possible. For it comes to see others—friends, acquaintances and even strangers—as human beings with whom, as with its parents and siblings, it is possible for it to carry on its affairs with that same mutual understanding. It is this same love and affection that binds parents and child which enables the child to accept, not resent, the admonitions, guidance, and, when it misbehaves, the disapproval and even the punishment that parents administer, to make amends out of a sense of guilt and to be penitent for the wrongs it may have committed. It is this same love and affection that makes possible the normal moral development of children as they acquire a sense of others as persons to whom they owe the consideration they give them during the course of their endeavors. In short, it is this same love and affection that enables the child to acquire and to apply in its dealings with others the complex array of moral concepts, the shared understanding of which operates as the background of the consideration they give to the interests of others and the goods and evils that may befall them.

It is in line with this thought that we need to understand some, perhaps not all, of the features in certain cases of self-sacrifice. Parents who deny themselves many of the good things in life in order to cater to what they consider to be in the interests of their children may be unwise in the judgment they make as to what is good for them; or they may be misled by an excessive zeal and benevolence in supposing that, in providing their children with the benefits they themselves can ill afford to lose, the good fortune they thus enable their children to enjoy is in fact sufficiently great to justify the sacrifices they make; or, they may be mistaken—perhaps even foolishly so—in supposing that the sacrifices they make for their children will not be wasted upon them. But the concern of parents, wise or foolish as it may be, is commendable for the concern they show for children, and is a further development, even when it is misplaced, of that propensity of theirs as parents who, in acting in the interests of their children, meet their obligations to them. For parents who willingly give up material advantages in order to advantage their children do so out of the love for them with which, in their own thinking at least, they act as parents should, as much so as when they nursed and cared for them as infants. And those who like Father Damien travel to far-off places in order to nurse and care for those who are helpless victims of natural misfortune do so out of a sense that they are their brothers' keepers no matter who and where they might be.

It is often said about such cases that the mere fact that they represent themselves as doing what they are morally obliged to do, while refraining from asserting this about others who are unmoved to follow their example, shows that they themselves recognize that what they are doing goes above and beyond the call of moral duty. But this conclusion appears to be not only invalid but untrue. On the interpretation given, Father Damien is really being untruthful in representing his self-sacrifice as conscientious conduct. Yet there is no reason to accept this conclusion unless one rejects as absurd the plain import of his words, namely, that he unlike others is morally bound to act as he does. For what was being claimed by Father Damien is that his own case differs from that of others in a way that made it appropriate for him to think of himself as acting out of a sense of obligation to the far-off lepers. How is this possible? The answer it seems to me is two-fold. First, Father Damien thinks of others as having special obligations by virtue of the special ways in which they have joined their lives with one another, e.g. as husbands, parents, or whatever. Second, he takes his own case to be different from that of others because of his priestly vows to treat all human beings alike as children of God in whose interest he must act selflessly, as God's intermediary, in order to relieve them of their suffering, as much so as any parent is obliged to do for the children in his household. It would be a silly misrepresentation of Father Damien's attitude to suppose that in going off to Molokai Island he merely took himself to be doing what anyone else would or should do. And it would be equally absurd to suppose that in acting as the father of his flock of lepers he was being condescending towards those for whom he was devoting his life. It is rather that he considered himself to be doing, with respect to those far removed from the circle of the family in Belgium in which he grew up as a child, the kind of thing his father had done for him, namely, of acting in the interests of those unable to fend for themselves. What this does imply is the extraordinary concern of a Father Damien for any human being, a concern he recognized to be distinctive in his case, in which the love and affection he felt for any human being was of that special order commonly reserved by parents for their own children, who share their joys and sorrows yet feel keenly their own responsibility for their misdeeds and even their misfortunes. It is one of the marks of the saint that he takes himself to be under an obligation to *any* human being, whoever and wherever he may be, of just that sort that parents have to their children. For him the line between special and human rights has disappeared.

Whether or not one subscribes to the religious underpinnings of the conviction of a Father Damien, that all persons are equally children of God and for this reason are entitled to receive from him, as God's intermediary, the assistance they need in order that they may live their lives with as much freedom from misery and suffering as a helping hand can provide, what is important in the example of Father Damien is his conception of human beings, alien as they might appear to those with whom he was familiar in his native country, as beings to be given, not merely humane treatment, but the kind of treatment that any father would give his children as a matter of their entitlement. This is a conception of human beings that involves a radical extension, and no mere development with its normal change in the diminished affection for others, of that sense of others first acquired within the bounds of the family.

In his Riddell Memorial Lectures, Sir Walter Moberly described what he labelled the 'developed Christian' (and perhaps saintly) conscience of a person who, along with an extraordinary compassion for any human being, feels an overwhelming sense of responsibility, as his brother's keeper, for the misdeeds and the misfortunes of others, a

sense of responsibility (that) is, in quality, more shattering than the secularist's because he must answer, not only to his peers, but to Almighty God. (For) towards the offenses of other people, even when they are under his authority, his attitude is different. He looks beyond the offense to the essential man, made in God's image; and even in judging the offense he is pitiful and eager to make all possible allowances. . . . The responsibility of which he is chiefly conscious is his own responsibility for doing something to put things right. Above all, his attitude towards the offender is never fundamentally hostile. Even when his indignation is most fierce he will remember that he is not dealing with an enemy but with an erring brother. The whole transaction is within the family.[22]

VII

Philosophers are often moved, when they consider the many different sorts of moral constraints, to exclaim in despair that these are an ill-assorted and unrelated heap of obligations. How is it possible for any rational person to cope with this bewildering array of apparently unconnected moral considerations? Unless we can somehow order them in some serial relation that establishes relations of precedence, it would appear to be impossible to determine rationally how we are to act when faced by competing moral considerations. And yet it is manifestly absurd to suppose that promising, for example, always takes precedence over (or is preceded in importance by) truthfulness, truth-telling, life-saving, parent or children-caring, or whatever. Are there then deeper principles obscured from our common view to which we need to turn in order to make sense of the heap of moral constraints? The history of moral philosophy is strewn with the wreckage of various attempts to formulate first principles hidden from our common moral understanding. The problem is not like that of the grammarian or linguist of formulating rules or principles in order to bring into clear focus the regularities embodied in a language. For in our enlightened moral practice, in which we are sensitive to other human beings, there are no such comparable regularities to be discovered in the ways in which, on particular occasions, given moral considerations take precedence over others, regularities which would provide the data for generalization in the form of priority rules; we need only reflect for a moment in order to provide decisive counterexamples to any proposed set of ordering relations. Indeed, there are those rare cases in which persons are tragically enmeshed in circumstances from which it is not possible for them to extricate themselves and for whom we can only feel, not approval or disapproval for what they do, but admiration, when they endure their tragic fate nobly, and pity—and for ourselves perhaps a sense of relief that we are spared the moral agony that is their lot. And there are also those more frequent cases in which the choices and decisions made are not clear-cut and concerning which reasonable men may adopt different stances while maintaining their self-respect along with a respect for those whose choices and decisions differ from their own.

If we focus our attention simply on the acts of persons and ignore the moral relations in which they stand to one another, then here as in the case of the traditional problem of the obligation of promises, the inevitable result of this preoccupation is bewilderment. It is small wonder that the catalogue of possible constraints, when these are viewed completely out of context, in a moral vacuum, leave us confused and bewildered, when they happen, as on occasion they do, to support alternative courses of action. There is a good reason for doing x—one ought, after all, to care for one's parents—and there is a good reason for doing y—one ought, after all, to keep one's promises; but if this is all one has to go on, heaven only knows what one is to do. But the lesson to be learned from this is not that there *must* be universally quantified first principles together with priority rules for their application so that one might proceed *more geometrico* and without any moral reflection to resolve our problems. Once more we need to be reminded that there is much more to morality than what it is that we are duty-bound to do, that the moral constraints expressed in our familiar precepts, even when they point to alternative lines of conduct, are constraints imposed upon agents who are concerned to deal with each other as moral agents.

Anything like an adequate account of the manner in which competing moral constraints may be assessed by reasonable and responsible agents, as they take due account of each other's rights, obligations and the goods defined by their interests, must await a fuller treatment of the topic of human rights. For, as I shall argue later, there are human rights that call not merely for non-interferences or abstentions on the part of others, but performances not because of some special relation in which one stands to others but merely because of their status as human beings. It will be argued that such human rights are fundamental and must play a special role in our deliberations when they are brought into conflict with other considerations. For in those cases in which the rights of human beings, as such, are violated, persons are treated as if they are not members of the moral community of persons with whom others can deal on the basis of a shared moral understanding. The overriding requirement imposed upon any person, to serve the moral community of which he is a member, dictates that he take whatever steps are necessary to provide the appropriate setting within which such morally ostracized persons can enjoy the rights they have as human beings, on terms of moral equality with anyone else, so that they may conduct their affairs with whomever it may be with the dignity that is appropriate to their normative status, joining their lives with others, and entering into various moral relations with them.

My present concern, however, is to discuss the rationale of the decisions we must make with respect to those to whom we are bound by the special moral relations constituted by our special rights and obligations. And here the story that needs to be told, at least in broad outline, is how it is that we are to conduct ourselves given our sense of what is involved in such rights and obligations.

We need to be reminded here of the logical substratum of, or background conditions requisite for, the existence of such rights, a paradigm case of which is the right conferred by a promise.[23] For here what is required on the part of promiser and promisee is the mutual concern of the parties, who have joined their lives by means of the promise transaction with each other as persons who are engaged in the pursuit of interests that define the goods and evils they seek to achieve and avoid respectively, in consequence of which they are prepared to recognize these goods and evils as relevant considerations in deciding how best to bear the moral burdens they have assumed with respect to each other. Further, as members of the moral community of persons, there is a common understanding of the complex array of moral concepts within which the moral concept of a promise as a right conferring and obligation assuming transaction has its place. And finally, insofar as both parties involved are not only able but willing to join their lives with each other, as mutually acknowledged members of the moral community, the setting appropriate for the enjoyment by both parties of the rights they have as human beings must be present.

Paramount in the concerns of both parties involved in this and in any other moral relation in which, without truncation, the complex array of related moral concepts has application, is the preservation of the moral community by which they are bound to one another: the respect that each has for the rights of the other, the continued willingness of each to join his life with the other, and the common understanding of the moral relevance of considerations, including the goods and evils that may befall either (and anyone else affected by the way in which each conducts himself with respect to the other) to the way in which each bears his moral burden and adopts his moral stance towards the other. What is of overriding importance in the moral relations of persons who have special rights (and their correlative obligations to one another) is the preservation and, where it is weakened or threatened by the moral fault of either party, the restoration of these conditions of moral community in which they may join their lives. It is for this reason that explanations are offered for not according someone his right where doing so is purchasing a minor good for that person at the expense of a major evil suffered by someone else. It is for this reason, too, that rights should be waived and even relinquished, namely, the concern to avoid imposing such heavy burdens upon others that the display of unreasonableness renders others chary in the future about any dealings with him lest, unreasonably, he stand on or demand his rights, whatever the costs and consequences may be. It is for this reason too—the overriding concern with others as the possessors of rights and with whom we can, confidently, join our lives during the course of our transactions with one another—that when those who have done us moral injury by wrongfully infringing our rights, are remorseful and properly penitent, we owe them our forgiveness. And it is for this same reason that, when rights conflict with rights, or with any other type of moral consideration that may unexpectedly intrude, the measures we need to adopt, whether in order to maintain our good moral relations with others or to restore them when we have been thoughtless or otherwise morally at fault, will need to be tailored to the particular traits and temperaments of those with whom we are concerned. What we must do when we are dealing with A whose traits, temperament and knowledge of us differs markedly from B's, may understandably call for different measures from those that are required when, in exactly the same circumstances, we are involved with B, in order to insure that good moral relations will be maintained or restored. Finally, morality is not geometry; there are no proofs and none which insure that all reasonable men will agree. How great must be one's own burden if it is to outweigh the benefit to be provided someone by according him his right? The query rests on a misconception, for necessarily there is no sharp line to be drawn between right and wrong answers, but a band or spectrum like a twilight zone, with no clear line that separates it on the one side from the light of moral good and on the other from the darkness of moral evil. And this means that reasonable persons can and in some cases may be expected to differ from one another in the moral stances they adopt towards those whose rights they respect, at the same time that they continue, despite their differences, to appreciate each other's moral integrity. The threat posed by fanaticism, which characteristically restricts the domain of persons to be respected for their integrity to those persons who fully endorse our every conviction, is as destructive of the moral community of persons as religious fanaticism is of the community of spirits which religion itself professes to promote.

NOTES

[1] *A Theory of Justice*, p. 34.
[2] Loc. cit.
[3] Loc. cit., p. 364.
[4] In a recent case in the State of California in which the state legislature after extensive debate and as the result of public pressure voted to rescind a statute conferring excessively large retirement benefits upon public officials leaving public office, it was argued by one member of the legislature that the proposal to rescind would be unfair to those who had entered public office and in doing so had counted on the handsome retirement benefits provided by law in compensation for the losses in income they suffered by giving up lucrative business practices.
[5] Loc. cit., p. 39.
[6] *Nicomachean Ethics*, bk. I, ch. 3, translated by W. D. Ross.

[7] Cf. pp. 15–18.

[8] Cf. p. 12 of *Moral Obligation*, Oxford, 1949, in which this essay is reprinted.

[9] Cf. ch. I, p. 3.

[10] Loc. cit., p. 11.

[11] The essay, reprinted in a number of collections of essays, first appeared in *The Philosophical Review*, vol. LXIV, no. 2, April 1955, pp. 175–91.

[12] Ibid., p. 176.

[13] Ibid., p. 175.

[14] Prichard does declare that 'where obligations conflict, the decision of what we ought to do turns not on the question "which of the alternative courses of action will originate the greater good?" but on the question "which is the greater obligation?"' (op. cit., p. 8). And he goes on to say that 'when, or rather so far as, we act from a sense of obligation, we have no purpose or end' thereby seeming to deny that any consideration of the goods and evils that can be produced by according a person his right (correlatively, meeting one's obligation to him) is relevant to the determination of whether or not we ought to perform that act.

[15] H. L. A. Hart employs this figure in order to question the legitimacy of speaking about duties to oneself. See his essay, 'Are There Any Natural Rights?'

[16] See Paul Ziff, *Semantic Analysis*, Cornell University Press, Ithaca. N. Y., 1960, and the discussion by Rawls in *A Theory of Justice*, pp. 399–404.

[17] 'The Obligation to Keep a Promise', by H. A. Prichard in *Moral Obligation* (Oxford, The Clarendon Press, 1949), p. 179.

[18] Promises *are* exchanged between husbands and wives and between friends, although often at least the assurances of future performances upon which the successful agencies of those to whom they are given are dependent, and understood by both parties to be dependent, are given not by the use of the familiar promise-locutions, with their air of formality and moral solemnity, but by the use of sentences which in different circumstances serve only to express the speaker's intentions. Nevertheless, the moral force of such assurances is precisely the same as that of those conveyed by familiar promise-locutions. 'Don't worry, I'll do x'; 'I *am* going to do x', etc. often serve as effectively as 'I promise to do x' to confer a right upon the addressee.

[19] Cf. ch. III.

[20] Later in this chapter I shall discuss the moral importance for the developing child of the love and affection parents provide for their children.

[21] See pp. 220–3.

[22] The Riddell Memorial Lectures at the University of Durham, Twenty-first Series, were first published in 1951 by the University of Oxford Press, London, under the title *Responsibility*. The quotation above appears on p. 35 of the reprinting of the Lectures by Fortress Press in 1965, under the title *Legal Responsibility and Moral Responsibility*.

[23] See pp. 142–5 above.

VI
Human Rights

In this chapter I shall explore, to begin with, certain features of human rights, and, following this, the relation between human and special moral rights. I shall then consider the various candidates for the title of human rights, the much-discussed problem of the basis of such rights and, finally, a number of apparent counter-examples to the view advanced here. Among these are the cases of infants to whom we do ascribe human rights even though qua infants they lack many of the attributes of persons as moral agents.

I

Let me begin by setting forth a number of the distinctive features of human rights.

(a) It was argued earlier that the rights and obligations of those who engage in promise transactions, or in any other way in which the lives of persons are joined, are possible only if those involved have, as a basic or human right, the right to conduct their own affairs in the pursuit of their interests. It is this right, as I argued in Chapter II, that explains how it is that a right is conferred by means of a promise and why it is that the breaking of a promise does moral damage to the promisee. Both promiser and promisee understand that the agency of the latter will be supported by the former's performance of the promised action, and hence that the omission of the promised action is as effective a way of subverting the right of the promisee to pursue his own endeavors as it would be for one to interfere with another's endeavors by acts of commission. The respect, therefore, for the right of a promisee to the performance of the promised action is a respect that occurs only if there is a respect for the right of a promisee as moral agent. Without this right that promisees or anyone else capable of entering into promise transactions have qua moral agent, there could be no right that anyone has qua promisee. And the same conclusion applies to other cases in which there are special rights and obligations. For the mutual understanding of the support that persons provide for the agency of others need not be conveyed by a formal declaration as in the case of a promise, but are clear enough to the parties involved as they join their lives with one another, within the family circle or in the course of their traffic with one another in a wide variety of other circumstances. In all of these cases it is this basic right of persons to pursue their interests that is fundamental.

(b) This basic right, unlike the special rights to which it is basic, is inalienable. That is to say, the right of a person to go about his own affairs in the pursuit of his interests, since it is a right that he has as the moral agent he is, is a right that cannot be waived, relinquished, transferred or forfeited. Conceivably, one could cease to be a person, while remaining alive, by taking some drug that transforms one into some monster; but in that state, while one ceases to have the right, one has also ceased to be a person. And one can, of course, utter some such verbal formula as 'Don't consider me as a moral being'; but this cannot serve to waive my right even though it may succeed as the improper solicitation it is. So too with relinquishing, transferring and forfeiting the right one has qua person—one may do moral violence to oneself as person, and others may do moral violence to ourselves; but if there is a right that one has qua person it is logically impossible for anyone, oneself, or anyone else, to do anything that would deprive one of this moral possession without depriving one of one's status as a person.

Complaints are made on occasion that persons are deprived of their rights including, allegedly, their human rights, but it would hardly do to infer from this that their rights may be taken away from them and that they cease to have them as in the case, for example, of the disbarment of a lawyer by which he ceases to have certain rights as an officer of the court. For the complaint that persons are deprived of their human rights when, for example, they are subjected to forced indenture by their employers, is a complaint that their rights have been violated and implies, clearly, that they have rights they are unjustly prevented from exercising. If one were deprived of one's rights in the sense in which one would be deprived of things in one's physical possession by having them taken away, one would no longer have the *rights*, and there would be no grounds for the complaint. So it is with the denial of a person's right—this does not consist in denying that he has the right but, rather, in denying him, by withholding from him, that to which he has the right or the means or opportunity for its exercise. And if, rightly, a person is punished and confined in order that he might purge himself of his guilt, what he loses through his improper conduct, i.e. forfeits, is not his right qua person to engage in the pursuit of his interests, but certain opportunities to exercise the right that he has. It may be objected that a person who has a right has the right to exercise that right. But what does this mean? A person has a right to believe that someone he sees leaving on a trip will not keep the engagement he has made to meet him later that day; but 'having a right to believe' means nothing more than having good reason to believe. Does saying that if one has a right, one has a right to exercise it, amount to anything more than voicing the logical truism that if one has a right one has good reason or ground for doing what is involved in exercising it? If it means anything more than this, it is not clear what it is. Certainly it cannot mean that if one has a right one has a sufficient reason for exercising it, since this would beg the very point at issue. It would imply that punishment, by which a person expiates his guilt during the course of which he may not and cannot proceed as persons normally do with their affairs, is wrong. The criminal upon whom the punishment is imposed may not himself recognize when he is sentenced that there is good reason for imposing the punishment upon him, but if punishment is successful in making the criminal repent, *he* will then have good reason for having submitted to it. In such cases the right even of the criminal to pursue his interests is infringed; but to say that it is violated implies the point at issue, namely, that it is an unjustified or wrongful infringement of his right. But justified punishment is not a self-contradictory notion; neither is the idea of justified punishment by which a person is prevented from exercising his right.[1] If one is jailed for a misdemeanor on election day and unable to vote, it does not follow that one is deprived of one's right to vote although one is rendered incapable of voting; being deprived of the right to vote is quite a different matter.

(c) The infringement of a right, justified or unjustified as it may be, does moral injury to the person. If, for example, punishment is justified, the moral damage incurred by the person who is punished, which consists in the fact that he is prevented from going about his normal affairs in the pursuit of his various interests, is outweighed by other considerations, sometimes, hopefully, by the fact that he will be purged of his guilt and be made better by being punished. However, a wrongful denial of a moral right does moral damage, Period. Unlike justified punishment it calls for the remedy and rectification it itself cannot provide. But the wrongful denial of a human right traditionally has been considered to be of quite a different order of magnitude from that of the violation of a special right such as that of a promisee.

Now I have argued that in the case of special moral rights the moral damage resulting from their violation consists in the fact that these endeavors which depend for their success upon the support to which the agents are entitled by their special rights are just as effectively subverted as they would be by willful interferences with conduct to which any agent, as such, has a right.

Here someone might object as follows: 'Your account of the right of a promise, by connecting it as you do with his right as agent to proceed with a line of conduct in which he pursues his interests and achieves his good, is inconsistent with the traditional view that there is a vast difference between the violation of a special right such as that of a promisee and the denial of a human right. For on your account to violate the special right of a promisee is to violate his right qua person or human being. It follows that the violation of the special right is an attack on his status as a human being. If, on the other hand, the important difference between the violation of a special right and that of a human right is to be maintained, your account of the special right must be abandoned; and even though the violation of the latter right may bring to collapse a line of conduct in which etc., etc., what is also wrong about it is that it is the breaking of a promise and as such the violation of a right.' Have special rights been conflated with human rights on the account presented here?

One could of course point to cases of the violation of human rights, as in the case of serfs or slaves, which involve not non-performances by those guilty of the injustice, but performances. And one could point to the contrasting and typical case in which the violation of the special right conferred by a promise involves a non-performance, i.e. the failure of the person obliged to perform as promised. Yet this is hardly enough by way of reply to the objection raised, since the violation of the right of a promisee may involve a performance, as in the special case in which a person promises, not to do such-and-such—where normally he might well be expected to do the thing in question—but, acting true to form does the very things he promised not to do. And, implied, as I shall argue later in this chapter, by the right of a person to pursue his interests, is the right he has to life itself; but there are cases in which one would violate his right to life by a non-performance, if deliberately one failed to give him the help he needs to preserve his life. There are, however, more decisive considerations that may be adduced in reply to the objection, to which I now turn.

1. Why does a promisee, A, have the special right to a performance by B, the promiser? We need, clearly, to cite special circumstances that apply to A and B and which do not exist where only the right of agents to go about their affairs is involved. The following facts apply in central or nuclear cases:

(a) B's promised act is one that A himself is unable to supply out of his own resources as an agent. This covers the quite special cases in which the act is one of abstention, e.g. B promises to abstain from doing such-and-such, an act which normally he would be expected to do in the appropriate circumstances.

(b) B's promised act is one that A requires for the success of some presumed course of action on which he is bent.

(c) In engaging in some presumed course of action A is assured that B will perform the needed act of commission or omission.

(d) A understands, when B uses the promise-locution, and B understands that A understands this to be the case, that A can depend upon B's performance, as much so as he can on any of his own performances during the course of the line of conduct on which he is bent.

(e) B recognizes that the performance promised, one that will support A during his endeavor, is one with regard to which he is not being merely helpful to A but one in which he is functioning as a surrogate for A in doing what A on his own is unable to ensure. This is what is meant by saying that the use of the promise-locution is designed to provide the assurance to the promisee that henceforth he may regard the promised action as one that is as much a *fait accompli* as any act that he himself is able to perform. And the promiser for his part now views the promised act as tied to the respect that he has for the promisee as an agent entitled to go about his affairs: he will feel obliged to perform the act if and only if he feels obliged to accord A his right as agent to go about his affairs. The promised act is regarded, therefore, on all fours with any act the promisee is entitled to perform on his own behalf in the course of the exercise of his own agency. Accordingly, if the promisee has a right to the promised act, it follows that he has a right to perform those acts through the exercise of his own agency as he pursues his interests.

The converse does not hold, namely, that if persons have this basic or human right as agents, they have any given special rights. It is only if the specific circumstances arise in which promises are made and accepted, or in which in other ways persons live and interact with each other, that special rights occur.

Neither is it true that the act to which A has a right is an act to which *he* in the ordinary course of events has a human right. That act is not A's act at all, but B's. B's promised act is one to which he, B, has a right as agent to do or not do as he, B, chooses; but B's act is not one to which A, merely because of A's status as a moral agent, has any right at all. In the absence of the promise, A would have no right to B's act, however helpful it may be to his endeavors. For it is only by virtue of what is mutually understood by both A and B, concerning the way in which B will view the promised act and his own role as agent with respect to the agency of A, that A has a special right to B's performance. Far from it being the case that special rights are conflated with human rights, the account given implies that any act to which an agent has a special right cannot be an act to which he has a right merely as a moral agent.

But does it follow from this account that, in the special circumstances of a promise transaction, a violation of A's special right to B's performance is a violation of A's human right to engage in his endeavors? For B's performance is essential to the success of the enterprise in which A engages, given the assurance B conveys by means of his promise; and, by failing to perform as he promised he would, B subverts A's agency in that instance. It would seem to follow, therefore, that the violation of A's special right is also the violation of a human right, and that, accordingly, there is no substance on our account to the traditional view that the denial of a human right is a much more serious matter than the denial of a special right since unlike the latter it strikes at the heart of the normative status of persons as human beings. To put it bluntly, haven't we cheapened the moral coin by involving every violation of a special right in the violation of human rights?

Once more we need to proceed with caution. To begin with, B's violation of the special right of A to B's performance does morally damage A, but the involvement of A's human right to engage in the pursuit of his interests serves only to explain the fact that moral damage has occurred. For on the account given, the violation of A's right, in the circumstances in which A proceeds with his affairs as much assured by the promise of B's performance as he is of any performance of his own, is as effective a way of subverting *that* instance of A's agency as it would be for some third person to intrude into A's affairs and prevent A from succeeding in his endeavors. How else except by bringing to naught A's agency, *in that given enterprise* in which A engages on the assurance provided by B's promise, is it even intelligible that A suffers any moral injury? What makes the injury *moral* injury is the fact that the injury suffered is the injury suffered as *moral* agent. And what is peculiar to one's status as moral agent is the fact that one has the right to carry on with one's own affairs in accordance with one's interests. It is, therefore, a strength, not a weakness of this account that according to it the violation of a special right implies, in the way in which it does, the violation of a human right.

Here we must emphasize that the violation that occurs is the violation of the human right *only* with respect to that specific line of conduct chosen by our agent; it is not, as we have described it, that sweeping violation of the human right that consists in depriving him of the right he has to engage in *any* enterprise of his own choosing. The violation of a person's human right is a much more serious matter; it is in effect to deal with him as if he did not count morally in our traffic with him.

2. Consider a case in which a person's special right has been violated—a line of conduct in which he has engaged, for the success of which the promised act was essential, has been brought to collapse. But although morally damaged he remains a moral agent to be dealt with in accordance with his status as the possessor of the right that any agent has, and, because he has been morally damaged, he is entitled by that fact alone to respond in ways that are reserved only for him and because of his distinctive moral authority as the person damaged. This is true even in the case in which, because of unusual circumstances, the infringement is necessary and the best that could have been done in those circumstances.

To deal with an individual as the possessor of a right is not merely to consider him as a being capable of enjoying goods and suffering evils or as a being who visits these upon others. It is to regard him as one to be respected for the rights that he has in consequence of which one is able to join one's life with his and conduct one's self with him on the basis of a shared moral understanding. Morality imposes the requirement upon all moral agents to preserve and promote—not impair—the moral relations made possible by their rights as agents. Accordingly, even if in the particular circumstances of one's dealings with a person one is fully justified in infringing his right as the least of all possible evils, one owes him an explanation in order to assure him of one's continued respect for him as an agent. And it is he, if his own endeavors have been adversely affected so that he has been morally damaged, who is entitled to remedy or restitution, if this is possible in the given case, and it is he who must give his assent to these efforts to rectify matters, failing which any effort on the part of the person responsible for the moral damage is unavailing. This is not to say that there are no reasonable constraints upon what the person who has suffered the damage may demand; there must be, if the rectification is to avoid depending upon the arbitrary and capricious will of the person who has suffered the damage. The point is that while there are moral burdens imposed upon both transgressor and the one who has been transgressed, the latter is entitled not only to disapprove, as spectators may do, but to ask for and receive restitution or redress for a loss that has been suffered. In any case, he and he alone can forgive the transgressor, doing so reasonably—this being the moral burden he must bear—if there are suitable demonstrations of remorse for the guilt incurred. As Locke put it, 'He who has suffered the damage has a right to demand in his own name, and he alone can remit.'[2]

As possessors of rights as agents, persons possess, therefore, moral authority in their dealings with one another. One can submit to the maltreatments one receives at the hands of others, as animals do; but this is not to assert ourselves as persons. Such assertion of oneself as a person with rights may be irritating to others, and it may even be dangerous. But unless it takes some appropriate form by which it is made clear to those who have infringed our rights that an infringement has indeed occurred, that remedy is called for, and, if wrongfully done, that the guilt incurred must be purged, one not only submits to the blows one receives from others but fails to maintain one's own integrity as a moral agent. With the moral authority of a person as a being with rights, there is the implied requirement of integrity imposed upon us, that we conduct ourselves with dignity and in ways appropriate to our status as beings with rights on terms of equality, qua moral agents, with others, asserting ourselves as persons by holding them to account for their transgressions against us.

It is this integrity of ourselves as moral agents that we can and must maintain when, as on occasion it happens, the special rights that we have against others are violated by the misconduct of others. In such incidents we may be indignant and outraged by the violations of our rights and the resulting subversions of our agencies in those endeavors in which we were engaged. Yet we remain nonetheless persons with the entitlements that any person has even in the eyes of those who have transgressed against us. However grudgingly and even resentfully they do so, they acknowledge at least tacitly the distinctive position of moral authority that we, as the morally injured parties, have with respect to them: the fact that our role goes beyond that of spectator who may disapprove of their misconduct but cannot, as we can, hold them to account, demanding of them the explanations that might, as we see it, reduce the degree of their fault even when they do not serve to eliminate it, laying claim to restitution or redress, and by our very act of holding them to account inviting the suitable demonstrations on their part of those pangs of remorse that serve to purge them of their guilt and that justify us—those morally damaged but not morally demeaned—in forgiving them.

But contrast the violation of the special rights we enjoy with the violations of a human right and the deprivations that these imply. In the former cases the rights we enjoy are rights we have *vis-à-vis* those whose lives have been joined with our own and with whom there is mutual regard for each other as moral agents. In such cases we enjoy a moral authority with respect to them, to waive or relinquish our rights and, when as on occasion it happens that they are wanting in their regard for the special rights we enjoy, to assert ourselves with dignity and self-respect as the moral agents that we are. But in the latter cases the consequences are far more serious. The possession of a special right implies the possession of a right that persons have as agents; and in the absence of the mutual acknowledgment of the right of persons as agents there could not be the rights and obligations by which the lives of persons are joined. The violation of the right of a person as agent—not as it happens when a special right is violated by bringing to collapse some specific line of his conduct, but rather by denying him or depriving him of any such right at all—is therefore to foreclose the possibility of joining one's life with his, of standing in any moral relations with him that is defined by a right and its correlative obligation. It is therefore to consider him devoid of that status as a person with whom, for example, it is possible to engage even in a promise transaction. For promises, as we have seen, cannot occur in a moral vacuum. And we cannot join our lives in any other way with those whom we cannot respect as the possessors of rights qua moral agents and who in turn are incapable of any sense of obligation to us. For the person who is deprived of his right to conduct his life in the pursuit of his interests, there can be only the hope that others will deal with him kindly or generously, even if they regard him as one who, being outside the moral pale, they cannot morally damage or demean, however much they may hurt.

It may be objected, however, that the contrast just drawn between the violation of a special right and the violation of a human right is all in black and white, without any of the intermediate shades of gray. In our present society there are violations of the right of persons as moral agents which do not involve, in the way in which this is true of slavery, the total banishment of persons from the moral community. And, second, are there not human rights that go beyond that basic right of persons, upon which we have dwelt at length? If there are a number of such human rights, the deprivation of human rights may be the deprivation of some but not all human rights; and if this so the deprivation may not involve that total ostracism from the moral community of persons.

In the next sections I shall pursue these issues, discussing first the possibility of intermediate cases in the violation of our human right and, then, the catalogue of human rights.

II

(a) Not every violation of a human right is tantamount to treating persons as slaves, as if like animals in the field they were subject to no moral constraints of any sort but only to the inducements to accept their lots which are provided by the comforts and conveniences supplied by their masters or to the fears of what they might suffer if they do not obey them. Even the blacks and 'coloreds' of present-day South Africa are treated by the ruling whites as if they had certain minimal moral sensibilities which enable them to impose certain constraints upon their supposedly inferior and baser natures. The moral apartheid of which the present policy in South Africa is symptomatic is, rather, the removal of these oppressed groups from the circle of the morally elect, those privileged morally by their moral rights to enjoy a moral authority and to conduct themselves on terms of moral equality with others in their privileged group. And the white, who endorses this policy of the ostracism of black and coloreds from the circle of the morally elect and who has treated them badly, may like Hobbes's sovereign echo the words of David after having sent Uriah to his death, 'To thee only have I sinned.' [3]

(b) But we need not restrict the denial of human rights to outcast groups who, like the South African black and the American Indian, have been relegated to their ghettos or reservations. Understandably, such social outcasts are filled with resentment when they compare the degradation they must endure with the advantages that others enjoy, often at their expense. But where the violation or denial of our basic rights has as its moral victims, not the members of a group of social outcasts but a sub-class of the in-group itself, its victims may be long unaware of the moral injury they suffer. This has been particularly true in the case of women whose status relative to that of men as an inferior group has been sanctioned by our social practices and institutions and by our very language in which the masculine gender has been employed with unfailing consistency to refer to those whose roles range all the way from the heads of small social units to the very *deity* himself (how else are we to refer to that being?). It is only in relatively recent times, given the long history of our civilization, that many women have come to resent the position of subservience to which they have been relegated by the male-dominated society of which they are members, and, with it, the idea that the right that women have to pursue their interests is the 'right' they have to assist, serve and cater to the more important endeavors that are reserved for men only. The unjust restriction imposed upon the endeavors of women is a violation of that right that they have to pursue the interests that go beyond those social roles to which they have been restricted by custom and tradition; and this injustice goes far beyond the collapsing of some specific line of conduct, as in the case of the breaking of a promise or the violation of some special right. For in this case there is a wide-ranging restriction or interference with those varying endeavors in which women do have an interest, which social taboos, customs and practices of various sorts have imposed upon women, thus impairing in these many ways and respects their very moral agency and subjecting them, as women recently have complained, to the treatment of them not as persons but often as sex objects—to bring children into the world, rear them, and to cater to the needs, at home, of their husbands. In these roles women may be thought to have rights—although often at least, the male chauvinist's conception of women is that they have duties to perform that go with their station, but hardly any rights *vis-à-vis* their husbands—but these rights, if any, are often restricted to the household, perhaps in the kitchen but not in the bedroom.

There is, therefore, a broad spectrum of cases in which a basic right may be violated or denied, ranging from those that are dramatized by ghettos, reservations or native quarters, through those intermediate cases one can observe among members of one's own society, as in the case of women but by no means confined to them; shading off without any clear-cut line of division to those relations between specific persons in which, as the saying goes, one person treats the other like a dishrag; and finally to those relatively infrequent incidents in the relations between persons who, except for their moral lapses, respect each other as persons, when one violates some specific right that another person has against him. Where, then, do we draw the line between a violation of a human and a special right?—But why should we draw any line at all? Here as in any other instances in which one finds a spectrum of intermediate cases lying between the extremities and which shade off without sharp breaks from one typical case to another, we ought not to attempt to draw sharp lines. Rather, we should recognize, first, how these cases vary and, second, how in differing degrees and respects the moral damage incurred, even when it is accepted by those who suffer it, may involve, on the part of those responsible, attitudes and conduct that, to a greater or less degree, deprive persons from the consideration that is their due.

III

I have dwelt at length upon the basic or human right of agents to engage in their affairs in the pursuit of their interests; and I have argued for the central importance of this right on a number of issues.

But given the catalogues of items that have been called natural or human rights—rights that go far beyond the liberty of agents to engage in the conduct of their own affairs—it may be suspected that I have perhaps placed undue emphasis upon the right selected for special attention and that it will not, by itself, yield the results the traditional theory of natural or human rights was designed to secure. If there are a number of human rights, the deprivation of one such right may not be the deprivation of others; hence, even if this right is not merely one that is violated on some occasions but one that persons are prevented from enjoying on any occasion, it does not follow that the deprivation of a single human right, specifically the right upon which attention has been focussed, is in effect casting those affected out of the moral community.

There is an even more important consideration. I have argued that, for example, promisees have their special rights only if they have the right as persons or moral agents to pursue their interests; and I generalized from this to other cases in which individuals are morally related by special rights and obligations during the course of their dealings with one another. But if there are other human rights in addition to this basic right, it might be thought that this generalization from the case of the special right of promisees is too hasty. In any case, writers in the past have provided us with different catalogues of human rights which need to be examined.

John Locke offers as candidates for the title of natural rights the rights to life, liberty and property.[4] The authors of the Declaration of Independence in 1776 altered the list somewhat to include, but not to restrict them to, the rights to life, liberty and the pursuit of happiness, thus avoiding some of the troublesome features in Locke's concept of property, not the least of which is his attempt to gobble up under this term anything that a person has or that can be said to be 'his', including his life and his liberty. The authors of the Declaration of the Rights of Man and of Citizens, endorsed by the French National Assembly in 1789 and prefixed to the French Constitution in 1791, listed the following as 'sacred' human rights: liberty, property, security, and resistance of oppression. Once more we have variations in the listings, but not without echoes of Locke's original compilation. Much more recently, in 1948, the General Assembly of the United Nations was not content with the rights to life, liberty, property and security of persons, but in a generous mood included as human rights a wide variety of items including among other things the right to rest, leisure and periodic holidays with pay! And in a less impassioned way it has been argued that persons have a right to punishment.[5] Still other writers have mentioned the right that persons have to just institutions or to institutions that protect their goods and interests.[6]

One reaction to this plethora of claimants to the title of human right is that they are all pretenders and that the thesis that there are any human rights at all should be viewed with skepticism. But this hardly follows; in any case the philosophical jibes and sallies of Bentham among others that the doctrine is nothing less than nonsense upon stilts are in fact premised upon their own misconceptions of what Locke among others have intended, or upon the sheer historical accident that the doctrine of human rights has been associated with philosophically indefensible views concerning the state of nature, consent or property.[7] Yet how shall we proceed in an effort to determine which ones among the various claimants are genuine?

We can, I believe, usefully begin by setting aside a number of spurious items for several reasons, and if we do this we shall notice an interesting clustering among those that remain to be considered.

Now some of the so-called human rights relate to specific or special institutional matters and cannot therefore be ascribed to human beings merely as human beings and whatever the specific form their activities may take in their social roles or institutional offices. This is clearly true of the right to property. When Locke attempts to sever the conceptual connection of property with legal statutes by ascribing the right to property to men in the state of nature, the concept of property has been so far emasculated that to say that an object is someone's property borders on saying that it is at his hand or in his physical possession. As for the right to periodic holidays with pay, this involves a right that occurs only within some social arrangement in which compensation is provided employees in exchange for their labor. So too with other alleged human rights in the statement endorsed by the Assembly of the United Nations: the right of citizenship, freedom of assembly, participation in public service and the affairs of government, social security, technical and professional education, participation in the cultural, artistic and scientific affairs of one's community, and so on. All of these are rights which persons have not qua persons, but qua members of various sorts of social institutions or insofar as they

interact with one another within specific sorts of social arrangements. To say that these are human rights would imply that they are
in some way fundamental to or implied by the rights of persons
within specific sorts of social circumstance; but far from being
necessary for such specific or special rights these rights are in fact a
sub-class of such rights. Indeed, in a number of countries many or
most of them are legal rights conferred upon persons by statutes.
This is not to say that there are not good moral reasons for establishing such legal rights or that the violation or denial of such rights is of
no moral concern. For if there are human rights, then given the
circumstances of human life—the technological and scientific
achievements, the necessity for political and other forms of social
organization of considerable degrees of complexity—it is essential
that persons be made secure in the enjoyment of these so-called
human rights if they are to be accorded the respect for the actual
human rights they have. Put in another way, if there are human
rights, then given these complexities of the circumstances of human
life, it is morally required that other rights—the right to vote, participate in social service, technical and professional education,
etc.—be established by statutes. For unless human rights are thus
implemented, persons may be said to have rights as persons but such
radically curtailed opportunities to exercise and enjoy them as to
reduce such declarations to mere rhetoric. It is understandable, therefore, that these special legal, social and institutional rights, which are
not as such human rights at all but which are relevant to their
enjoyment, should have been thought to be rights that are bound up
with our nature or status simply as human beings.[8]

Still other rights are suspect as candidates for the title of human
rights for quite different reasons. Some appear to be not so much
rights distinct from other rights mentioned in the several catalogues
of human rights as analytic consequences of the possession of these
rights. The 'right' asserted in the United Nations' document to
effectively remedy the violation of rights is not itself a right distinct
from the rights that are violated; it is, rather, a conceptual feature of
any right that if it is violated, the transgressor owes the person
morally damaged remedy, restitution or whatever it is that may be
appropriate in the given case. So too with the French Assembly's
'right' of persons to resist oppression. This too is a logical consequence of the possession of a right, this time the right of persons to
conduct their own affairs with dignity and as they themselves

choose. For the so-called right to resist the oppressive incursions by others into one's own affairs is not a right but a moral requirement imposed upon any person, since the alternative to this way in which one maintains one's integrity as a person is submission to the efforts of oppressors to demean one by destroying one's freedom.

The claim that the guilty have the human right to punishment, and that they may demand on this basis to be punished, needs careful consideration. Some have supposed that it is as intuitively self-evident that a guilty person ought to be punished as that a promiser ought to keep his word, but even if this were true it would not follow that a question of a right is at issue in both cases. For how would the commission of an offense confer a right upon the offender? The answer given is that the guilty person is morally blemished, and that he ought to be purged of this condition by being made properly remorseful and penitent through punishment. We owe it to him as a moral agent to remove the moral flaw which issued in the crime; and punishment, so this thinking goes, is the respect we pay the guilty who, as moral agents, are entitled to the purgation punishment is designed to provide. Such a view is in sharp contrast with those advanced by some would-be social reformers who seek to dispense with punishment and substitute for it therapy, social reform, or reconditioning on the premise that the criminal is ill, the victim of his society, or the product of his environment. On such views, persons are regarded not as agents, but as patients, and their behavior not as actions they perform but as unavoidable end products of the forces that operate within them. Understandable, however, as a salutary protest against views in which there is no room for the respect we owe persons, even offenders, the claim that there is a human right to punishment does have its own peculiar difficulties.

To begin with, the idea of a right to punishment is the idea of something one may demand as one's right; but to demand one's punishment as a matter of one's right may well demonstrate that one has no moral need for, and ought not to be given, the punishment for which one clamors. For one who cries out for the punishment he deserves as a matter of his right is already suffering the pangs of remorse and displaying that contrition of heart and repentance that punishment itself is designed to secure but which in that instance is sheer suffering that serves no useful purpose.

One reply is that the penitent himself feels the need for punishment.[9] He is distressed and remorseful but demands the punishment in order to expiate his guilt, without which he cannot, in good conscience, resume his former place with others in the moral community of persons. No doubt there are such instances, and they are not pathological. For the individual, blemished as he is, would be dishonest with others, were he to live with them as he did before the blemish was revealed in his offense, and dishonest with himself were he to adopt the usual methods of concealing the moral flaw from himself. For such a person there is the need to suffer the punishment and only in this way to do the penance that is required. Remorse is not enough. What is required is the constant reminder of the fault manifested in the misdeed in order that the individual may attain that moral rectification within himself that is the expiation of his guilt.

Even where the above account of the matter holds good, the guilty person's efforts to undo the damage he has caused others and to rectify matters within himself must be matched by a willingness on the part of others to help him, if need be, to reduce the severity of the punishment or to curtail it, and to forgive him, lest he suffer unduly and needlessly. But not all cases of guilt are to be dealt with in this manner. If a child, say, voluntarily confesses to some minor misdeed and in this way shows that he will not repeat the offense, should his parent automatically impose the punishment, even if he cries out for it? And for many offenses the flaws and blemishes are relatively minor; they are not those radically askew conformations of character in the self, on account of which, once it is dismayed to learn of their existence, that self feels the need to undergo those protracted periods of penitential suffering that only punishment can sustain. In many cases the remorse suffered is punishment enough; and even if the offender should cry out for punishment as a matter of his right, that would be, in our eyes, a quite mistaken and morbid sense on his part of the nature and degree of his fault. It is therefore a mistake in my opinion to maintain that persons have the right as human beings to punishment for their crimes. It is enough to say that, in some cases, they ought to be punished, perhaps on the ground that they may be made better for the punishment they receive, and in others they ought to be forgiven on the ground that the remorse they have suffered is punishment enough, and, in itself, a quite effective expiation of their guilt.

What lurks in the background of all of the spurious candidates for the title of human right is the conception of a person for whom respect as moral agent is due. If such respect is to be accorded persons, it can be argued, plausibly, that there should be institutional arrangements that enable them to acquire title to some property through their labor. And Locke's talk about property in the state of nature and the right that men have to it in the absence of any social relations of any sort has this sound point, that the forcible removal from the physical possession and use by a person of some object to which no one has any title at all would be to treat him in the way we treat animals when we remove objects from their grasp without any sort of compunction. Again, if persons have the right as agents to engage in the pursuit of their interests and, hopefully, in the achievement of their goods and their happiness, it is particularly important that there be established the special institutional rights with which the General Assembly of the United Nations was concerned in order to provide the members of our complex modern societies with the abilities and opportunities to pursue their interests. So it is with the alleged right to institutions that protect the goods and interests of persons; what is of central importance here is the right of persons to pursue their interests and achieve their good, and the alleged right to protective institutions is not so much a right, let alone a human right, as a matter of what ought to be established in consequence of the right that any person qua person has to pursue his interests. So too with those alleged rights that, on closer inspection, turn out to be not rights distinct from this basic human right, but analytic consequences of the right. And finally, what is important in the claim that there is a human right to punishment is the insight that punishment properly and legitimately administered needs to be contrasted with: the *lex talionis* of primitive society; punishment conceived as confinement for the protection of society; punishment as deterrence (including the morally objectionable practice of imposing unusually severe penalties upon one or more persons in order to deter others, thus balancing the damage inflicted upon the former by gains with respect to the latter); punishment as character reformation (an impossible goal given the familiar conditions of imprisonment); punishment as therapy; or punishment as conditioning—none of which involve the idea that punishment serves to purge those upon whom it is imposed of their guilt and by thus redeeming them enables them once more to join their lives with others. Punishment as the means adopted to purge persons of their guilt is, in fact, a mark of the respect we have for those to whom it is applied, for even the guilty who need to be punished in order to be redeemed are to be respected for the rights that they have. They have the right as moral agents to conduct their own affairs in the pursuit of their interests even though when confined in accordance with the terms of their punishment they are denied during that time the opportunity freely to exercise it. For they have not forfeited this right even though it has been infringed, since they continue to be human beings, and, in compensation for the moral injury suffered by the infringement of their right through the punishment they receive, benefit by being purged of their guilt and restored to good standing in the moral community.

I shall not attempt to examine the credentials of all of the very many candidates for the title of human right. Some of these have been elevated mistakenly to the status of rights in order to underline their importance or desirability, as in the case of the so-called right to happiness or to punishment. Others are analytic consequences of the right that persons do in fact have to conduct their own affairs as they choose; for it is this right, and not a right distinct from it, that justifies resistance to oppression, the demand for redress and relief from the interferences of others or the rectification of social practices and institutions that permit and perpetuate the violation of this right. Still others are rights established by statutes, contracts and legal rulings which insure that in the complex circumstances of modern life this human right will be preserved, as in the case of the rights of persons to vote, or to receive the education they need in order to participate effectively in the institutions of government and in the enjoyment of the cultural and economic life of their society. And there remain, finally, rights implied by this fundamental right of any agent to fashion his own life, pursue his interests and thereby enjoy his goods, namely, the right to life itself and for the young the right to a moral education without which they cannot achieve moral agency. This central right that persons qua persons have is, therefore, the right upon which in earlier discussions we have focussed our attention. It is in terms of it as a matter of logical consequence that we have the right to life and to the moral education that prepares the young for membership in the moral community. And it is this same right that needs to be borne in mind in whatever provisions are deemed necessary for the structure of our economic, educational and political institutions if the conditions of social justice are to be achieved and maintained.

There are, of course, important implications of our basic human right together with the implied rights to life and to moral education for individual and social action. These will be discussed in the next chapter. For the present, however, let us turn to the much-discussed question of the basis of human rights. What is there about persons that renders intelligible the possession of such rights?

IV

Locke, and following his lead, the authors of the Declaration of Independence, declared that God had endowed men with certain natural or inalienable rights. In a similar but muted vein the French Assembly declared 'in the presence of the Supreme Being' that there are certain '*sacred* rights of men and of citizens'. The United Nations' statement, however, scrupulously avoids all mention of God, and with few exceptions more recent writers have followed suit. But even if the origin of natural or human rights is to be ascribed to the agency of God, this would be intelligible only if in endowing men with rights God also endowed men with a nature suitable to the possession of those rights. For we do not ascribe rights to animals unless we attribute human characteristics to them; and it makes no sense to suppose that there could be two classes of human beings identical in every relevant respect but only one of them the possessor of rights. What is there, then, about the nature of persons that renders it intelligible that they have human rights?

The question may conjure up the picture of fixed Aristotelian essences and, in the case of man, an essence from which human rights are somehow deducible. But, fixed or not, is there a set of characteristics constitutive of personhood such that the possession of rights follows logically from the possession of at least some of these characteristics? Here we have once more the old problem of how it is possible to deduce this matter of morality—the possession of any human right—from the matter of fact about certain entities that they have at least some of the features of personhood. Indeed, the problem is even more acute than that raised by G. E. Moore concerning the derivation of value properties from the so-called natural properties of things. A thing that is good, philosophers say, possesses the attribute of goodness in addition to those good-making attributes of pleasantness, or whatever; but the possession of a right is not like the possession of an attribute. Persons are good or bad, or, as philosophers put it, they possess the attributes of goodness or badness. But while persons possess rights, we cannot, in similar fashion, say that they possess the attribute or attributes of rights. No doubt if someone has a right then we can say that he has the attribute of having a right; but having or possessing a right is not like having or possessing an attribute. Rather, it is one's moral property; but how this—one's moral property or possession—can possibly be deduced from a set of characteristics constitutive of personhood is at least difficult to fathom, especially so if we consider the fact that these characteristics would seem to be characteristics which an individual has by himself whereas rights are the sorts of things an individual has against others. One might, of course, attempt to widen the use of 'characteristic' so as to apply it to relations as well. But how it would be possible to deduce the possession of the moral relation that consists in one person having a right against someone else, without including that very right among the characteristics upon which the alleged deduction is based, it seems impossible to understand. Of course, *A has a right against B* is deducible from *B is under an obligation to A*; but the deduction is trivial; the two propositions are in fact logically equivalent. We can deduce the occurrence of rights from nothing less than what involves the occurrence of rights. And if the sense in which human rights are based or rationally grounded in the nature of persons is that their occurrence or possession is deducible from certain facts about persons, then nothing less than the ascriptions of those rights or their equivalents can serve as deductive premises and in this sense a rational ground.

In what sense human rights can be said to be based upon or grounded in the nature of human beings is a matter, therefore, of crucial importance. It may be useful at this point, by way of a preliminary exercise, to consider a number of attempts that have been made to locate the basis or ground of human rights in certain facts about or features of human beings.

Is the fact that persons are capable of feeling pleasure or pain an adequate basis for the ascription of fundamental rights to persons? Surely not, since this is also true of animals, yet we do not ascribe rights to them unless we anthropomorphize them. Nor will the fact that we feel sympathy for others even if, mistakenly, we thought that it is directed only at human beings, help us here; it is no accident that there is no room in Hume's moral theory for moral rights as distinct from legal rights that are established by statutes in order to promote the happiness of mankind. Besides, we consider ourselves to be the possessors of rights, but it makes no sense to say that each of us sympathizes with himself when pleased or distressed.

Nor will it do to suppose that it is on account of their rationality—a matter often supposed to be characteristic of human beings but not of animals—that persons have rights. For rationality is compatible not only with immorality but with amorality as well, the lack of any sense of the distinction between right and wrong and any sense of the rights of others. One can imagine beings who are able to think—form concepts, make inferences on the basis of empirical evidence and draw conclusions concerning the relations of ideas—yet are so far different from the rest of us in the considerations that move them to act as they do that, however much they might resemble us, we would treat them not as human beings or in no way members with us of the community of moral agents, but as a race of beings apart with whom we could not carry on our affairs in the way that human beings can with each other. Alternatively, if by 'rationality' is meant that reasonableness that characterizes persons with whom we are able to join our lives, the appeal to rationality, if indeed it manages to avoid circularity by tacitly invoking in the reasonableness of moral agents a sense of the rights of agents and of one's own obligations to them, is at least unhelpful since it leaves undisclosed those characteristics of persons which are ingredient in their reasonableness and upon which in some sense their rights as moral agents are founded.[10]

A more familiar line takes as central and necessary for the possession of rights the autonomy of persons, their ability to organize their own activities, choose and decide for themselves how best to go about their affairs. In one respect this requirement is too broad, in another too narrow. Too broad, since it would apply not only to morally responsible persons to whom we should not hesitate to ascribe rights, but to intelligent sociopaths choosing and deciding for themselves in complete indifference to the moral interests of others. It could apply, imaginably, to strange creatures from another planet acting in ways that made little or no sense to us and to whom, as in the case of the sociopath, the ascription of rights would be at best problematic. Too narrow, since we do ascribe rights even to those unable or unwilling to plan, choose and decide and act for themselves: the pathetically submissive wife who accepts the choices and decisions on a wide range of matters of interest to her which her husband legislates for her; the slave who is content with a life he himself plays no role in fashioning; and the young child. For most of the rest of us there is more or less autonomy—those for whom the acceptance of orthodoxy, in whatever area this may be, is an easy alternative to a disturbing insecurity threatened by any attempted self-criticism and self-reliance; and those suffering some degree of mental incapacity, for whatever reason this may be, to choose and decide and act autonomously—yet we do not think that there are degrees to which persons as persons have rights. Certainly we prize autonomy; it is, clearly, a desideratum of any sound program of moral education. The autonomy of persons as we know them is a moral achievement; but unless we reserve rights as the special privilege of morally admirable persons, it cannot be the quality that invests moral agents deficient in autonomy with their basic rights as human beings.

It may be objected, however, that human beings—the most submissive persons who are content with their lowly stations, even the most downtrodden of slaves—does have some measure of autonomy, and that restricted as the range of the choices and decisions may be that he makes for himself in the areas and the social stratum to which he is confined, he has nonetheless a degree of autonomy that animals do not have, but enough to warrant our ascribing rights to him. But why should the fact that he is able to make a range of choices and decisions not possible for the contented cows in the field warrant our ascribing any rights to him? The acquiescing wife of a domineering husband from whom all of the interests that she might have as a person in her own right have been washed out, may decide for herself how to go about her tasks in nursing her children, preparing meals or cleaning the house; but why should this invest her with rights that she has as a human being, rights that she has on terms of equality with anyone else including a domineering husband who is indifferent to her? Is it that she does have needs in common with other human beings and, like all other persons, a capacity for the enjoyment of human goods and happiness? But from the mere capacity to enjoy such goods we cannot infer a right to them or even a right to engage in those activities by which these may be secured; animals too are capable of their rudimentary delights and satisfactions and they too on occasion are in need, but when we deal kindly and humanely with them it will hardly do to support our conviction that we are dealing with them properly—as indeed we ought to—on the ground that they have any moral rights in the matter. And if all that warrants our consideration of the state of our poor housewife is that she has unfulfilled needs and unattained goods, we do not have a foundation strong enough to support the complex conceptual framework in which the concept of a right is embedded. What is there about her status as a person, over and above the existence of unsatisfied needs and unattained goods and well-being, that causes us to think not merely that her lot needs improvement but that her rights as a person have been violated, that she has not only suffered but that she has suffered damage to her moral status as a person? For there is much more in this example than unkind, ungenerous, unsympathetic, unfair or cruel treatment; there is the degradation of a human being.

One suggestion, inspired by Kant, is that human beings have intrinsic worth, that this intrinsic worth is not shared by animals or things, and that it is the source or ground of the rights of human beings. We respect persons because of their intrinsic worth, not because of the value they have in serving the interests of others; and when we degrade them by violating their human rights, we treat them in the way in which we treat things by failing to respect them for their intrinsic worth and the human rights that go with it.

Undeniably, the talk about the intrinsic value of human beings, the sanctity of human life, or the worth of the individual has been effective in rallying men and women to the cause of human rights by reminding all of the distinctive moral status of human beings and the need to accord them the treatment that is their due. Our problem, however, is not the moral question whether human beings as such have rights, but the philosophical question of the ground of the rights that they do in fact have, and which need to be respected in any treatment that is to be given them. Here the standards are conceptual, not moral; and the answer to which we now need to attend must be appraised on its intellectual merits. Does the appeal to intrinsic worth and the respect for persons solve our philosophical problem?

We need, clearly, to understand what is meant by 'respect' and 'intrinsic worth'. In each case, however, we are faced by a dilemma.

Consider the first. If by 'respect' we mean the respect that is appropriate only to those we hold in high esteem, then it cannot serve to explain our ascription of human rights even to those who are unworthy of our respect: the very many human beings who fall far short in the excellences for which we hold the few in high regard.

But if by 'respect' is meant something other than what is commonly meant by this term—something applicable even to the morally disreputable whom we do not, as we should say, respect at all—we are threatened with circularity; for then it is difficult to understand what is meant by 'respecting a person', even one who is morally blemished, if this is not an ellipsis for 'respecting the rights a person has'. Kant himself seems to avoid the dilemma, appearances to the contrary notwithstanding. He does say, 'Respect is a tribute we cannot refuse to pay merit whether we will or not; we can indeed outwardly withhold it, but we cannot help feeling it inwardly.' And this remark invites the criticism that Kant, as Vlastos put it, 'tends to conflate the value of persons as ends in themselves and on this ground the objects of respect with that of their merit'.[11] But this interpretation rests on the special features of the example chosen by Kant, namely, that of a morally estimable person, in order to illustrate the point that respect for such a person is a matter we cannot withhold because of what in such a man is conspicuously (but not exclusively) present. For Kant goes on to remark that the respect we have for a person is really for the moral law to which morally worthy persons are manifestly obedient. Unfortunately, the moral law, which embodies the requirement of rationality, which Kant takes to be lawfulness in one's willing, provides no room for rights as the moral property of agents. Kant's ethics is an ethics of the duties of agents as rational beings; and despite his eloquent espousal of the popular doctrine of inalienable rights in his essay *Perpetual Peace*, there is *au fond* no place for that doctrine in his own moral theory. Accordingly, Kant avoids the dilemma we have posed precisely because the concept of the respect for persons is not designed by him to provide any ground or basis for human rights.

Can we avoid the dilemma posed above by appealing to the intrinsic worth of persons? Is it this worth of the individual which provides an adequate ground for the fundamental rights of persons? But if both the morally worthy and the unworthy person equally possess intrinsic worth—for how else can these rights be ascribed equally to all human beings?—we are threatened once more with circularity: the intrinsic worth of persons is their status as beings endowed with rights and as such the objects of our moral interests. For what else can be meant by 'the intrinsic worth of persons'? Kant's remarks are unhelpful here, not only because he does not introduce the notion of the intrinsic worth of persons as a ground of human rights, but also because of the obscurity of his talk about persons in respect of their rationality as ends in themselves. One suggestion, by Vlastos, is that we need to translate 'A's human worth' into 'the worth of A's well-being and freedom' on the ground that these 'are aspects of his individual existence as unique and unrepeatable as is that existence itself'.[12] But how this provides the ground of equal rights is not clear. For the 'aspects of his individual existence' that are 'unique and unrepeatable' and that constitute *his* well-being and *his* freedom rather than the well-being and freedom of someone else would seem to be just that well-being and just that freedom that he does in fact have, restricted or curtailed as these may happen to be; but the freedom and the well-being, if these are matters of one's right, may and usually do go far beyond that which happens to be the lot of many if not most individuals. Shall we say then that it is the *capacity* of well-being and freedom that are bound up with a person's individual existence, that persons are equal in this capacity and that this constitutes the ground of equal human rights? But something is surely missing here, as Vlastos himself recognizes; for we cannot move merely from equality of capacity for, to equality of the right to, well-being and happiness.[13] But neither can this move be facilitated, as Vlastos believes it can, by adding the additional premise that one person's well-being and freedom are as valuable as those of anyone else.[14] At best it would show that, so far, we have as good reason to promote A's well-being and freedom as we have to promote B's, namely, that in either case we would be promoting something of value. And so far, too, there would be no reason to prefer one distribution of well-being and freedom between A and B over any other, between giving A and B equal portions and giving all to A and none to B. For value is value, wherever and whosesoever it may be. But if both A and B equally have a right to these items of value, then it makes a good deal of difference how we distribute them. Plainly, value-talk no more implies or entails rights-talk than does capacity-talk. The conceptual ramifications of the concept of rights go far beyond those involved in the concepts of value or capacity. And it does not help us to be told that a person's well-being and freedom are aspects of his individual existence, aspects that are unique and unrepeatable. For if this means anything more than the tautology that the well-being and freedom of a person are *his* (mis-leadingly expressed by saying that no two persons could have the same well-being, freedom, or anything else, but only something similar),[15] it is too obscure to assist us in seeing how it is that the worth of a person provides any ground for his rights.

Despite the inherent difficulties in all of this talk about respect and worth, there remains something which needs to be brought to the surface. For all persons are alike in being members of the moral community; and, morally flawed as any person may be, he is, as a member of that community, the reasonable object of the moral interest of everyone else.

V

It will be recalled that in examining past efforts to explain the obligation of promises we remarked on an important source of their failure: the attempt to explain the complex features of the moral relation constituted by the right conferred and the obligation assumed by means of a promise, in terms of what is done by or happens to the promiser, as if by closer attention to the promiser alone one could discover somehow the moral network that connects the thoughts and actions of promiser and promisee. There is a similar source of failure in the proposals examined in the preceding section concerning the fundamental rights of persons. For all of them, in one way or another, and except upon pain of circularity in the explanations they offer, attempt to found such rights upon features or endowments that individuals have in their own right, as it were, features that serve as their admission tickets to the moral community. If we look for admission tickets of this sort, it is not surprising that we shall be as perplexed here, as philosophers have been when they focussed their attention upon what promisers do or upon what happens to them when they addressed themselves to the obligation of promises. It is not, therefore, by reference to some sort of attribute that constitutes the essence of human beings, to their rationality, autonomy, uniqueness or to the actual or potential realization of value in the experience of individuals—matters that pertain to their endowments merely as individuals—that it is possible to comprehend how it is that each person has that moral status as the possessor of human rights. The rights that all human beings have in common cannot be explained simply by distributing among all of the members of the human race features that each has as individual and in independence of any relation in which he stands to others.

Let us consider, first, what is meant by saying that persons are on terms of equality as members of the moral community. Surely it is not that they have some attribute or endowment simply and solely as individuals and equally with respect to everyone else; for if we look for such attributes or endowments we shall find none. Nor does it mean that, whatever the sorts of things there may be that constitute well-being (the variety of goods that are enjoyed or prized by human beings), that persons have a right to them, or that they ought to be given equal portions of such goods. We are concerned with persons, not in some never-never ideal land in which all of the differences between persons—in a variety of morally relevant respects—have been erased, but persons as we find them in the actual circumstances found here on earth. Persons are more or less responsible and conscientious in their moral concern for others and hence more or less likely to enjoy those goods made possible by the close ties of friendship and by cooperative activity—the warmth of love and affection and the variety of goods promoted for those who engage in cooperative activities that require for their success the maintenance of trust between the participants. Persons are more or less flawed and deserving of the punishment they ought to have and need for the expiation of their guilt, and hence more or less properly saddled with those burdens and those denials of goods that constitute their punishment. Persons, because of their particular circumstances, are more or less in need of protection in one form or another in order to preserve at least a tolerable, but never equal, degree of security, given the conditions in some blighted urban quarters which bring to mind Hobbes' account of the state of nature. Persons are more or less capable of enjoying the values of inquiry, aesthetic creation and appreciation, and participation in the cultural activities of their society; it would be absurd, therefore, to propose that everyone be allotted an equal portion of these goods. And so it goes. The moral equality that consists in the fact that persons are equally members of the moral community does not imply that everyone should be given, least of all that he is entitled to, an equal portion of any human good.

Neither does this moral equality imply that persons are capable of enjoying the same goods. For given the differences in the natural endowments and capacities of persons, the circumstances of their birth, social position, economic status and education, along with other accidental factors of various sorts, understandably there are enormous variations in interests and in the kinds of good defined by them. The pursuit of interests to which persons are entitled cannot preclude inequalities in the distribution of benefits and burdens; and neither can it insure that persons will have the same interests and enjoy the same goods.

What does follow from the fact that all persons equally have the right to pursue their interests is that any person, even the most advantaged and the most powerful in the influence he exerts over others, is accountable to the lowliest and most disadvantaged for any infringement or violation of the latter's rights as a human being. It is this moral authority that anyone has with respect to anyone else, high or low, who may act in any way that adversely affects the exercise of those rights, to call upon him if need be to respect and accord him these rights and, if these are denied, to demand redress for the damage he has suffered in being subjected to treatment as if he were not a full-fledged moral agent, in respect of which anyone is on terms of equality with anyone else and in this sense equally a member of the moral community of persons. Failing to exercise this authority in ways appropriate to the circumstances of the case, anyone who is wronged submits to or acquiesces in the treatment he receives as if he were an inferior sort of being. What we label the dignity of a person is not a matter pertaining to some precious internal quality of his nature as a human being—his rationality or his autonomy—but that sense he displays of his own status as a being who is authorized by his rights to conduct himself in the expectation that his rights will be honored by others, but who is prepared in the event this does not happen to assert the moral authority he has by virtue of his rights. When rights are violated, this assertion of one's authority may spill over into resentment and, depending upon the form of the transgression, into violence that may be destructive of dignity itself. But violence may take very many different forms. It may show no moral restraints of any sort, not even the respect for the rights of others including the right to life itself. Yet it may also be the violation of discriminatory practices and it may brook the violence to which those determined to preserve such practices are prone. It may involve violating statutes and executive orders of those occupying posts of civil authority. In one way or another it may be disruptive of familiar patterns of life, and, depending upon the responses made to such disruptions, the protests, demonstrations or any other forms of self-assertion will involve violence of one kind or another. Violence in itself is not a good; but in given circumstances and in some of its forms there may be no reasonable alternative. Certainly, the laws of the land, popular declarations to the contrary notwithstanding, are not sacrosanct; the most effective and the only possible way of voiding bad legislation may be to violate the law openly and dramatically in order to subject it to judicial review rather than meekly to abide by it in the often vain hope that legislators will come to their senses and rescind it by their own voluntary action. Some form of protest in the effort to obtain recognition of one's right and redress for one's grievances is essential if the dignity of those who have been morally damaged is to be secured. For it would be unworthy of oneself as a person with rights, who as such is on terms of moral equality with anyone else, willingly and submissively to accept the degradation to which he is subjected. It would be wronging oneself if under these circumstances one made no effort when suitable occasions arise to assert oneself as a moral agent, i.e. to assert one's moral authority as the possessor of rights. For this authority imposes upon those who have been denied their rights the requirement that, if need be, they take risks and in any case exert themselves in calling to account those who have cast them outside the moral pale. This is not a task that can be delegated to others, for to rely upon others to act for them is to put themselves in the position of children who act as they do under the direction of others who alone are presumed to be morally mature and qualified to speak to their rights. And those who are oppressed are not like those who lack some skill and need instruction in order to acquire it so that they might perform those tasks for which it is essential. Those who are oppressed, unless they are insensible of their own moral plight, suffer the oppression under which they labor, resent the moral damage they suffer, and, given the opportunity, are able to conduct themselves as others do in their moral dealings with human beings. They are, therefore, moral agents on terms of equality with others as members of the moral community. And they can maintain their own self-respect and achieve dignity in their dealings with others only by acting on their own behalf and calling for the righting of the wrongs they have suffered. They may and usually do need the help of others; but that help cannot serve as substitute for the assertion by them of their own moral status.[16]

Now to assert oneself as a moral agent is to present oneself in such a way that one will be dealt with in ways appropriate to one's status as moral agent. But how is such a result achieved? Is it that one displays one's suffering and solicits the sympathy of those moved to make this response? Sympathy, as Hume once noted, is much too variable and uncertain a motive to account, by itself, for a common conviction reached by persons who vary greatly in the warmth of their feelings and in their proximity to those protesting the mal-treatment they receive. Besides, even if one were persuaded to subscribe to something like Hume's ingenious but bizarre picture of the mechanism of human nature and his ad hoc stipulation that the moral sentiment engendered by sympathy is one that occurs when and only when one adopts a general point of view that cancels out the variability and uncertainties of our personal feelings, this would explain at best the disposition to relieve those protesting the denial of their rights of their suffering and to adopt whatever measures are needed in order to afford them humane treatment. But it would not have the least tendency to explain the fact that we respond as we do by recognizing their rights and dealing with them, not as we do by comforting those in pain, but by according them their rights. For the response that is appropriate to those who protest in reasonable ways the degradation to which they have been subjected is not the kind of response we make to those who suffer—'Patience. You'll feel better soon.' It is, rather, the recognition that they have been deprived of their rights, and not merely of goods and comforts that make life pleasant or tolerable. It would appear, therefore, that in asserting oneself as a moral agent one is not merely if at all soliciting sympathy but showing something about oneself in order to obtain recognition of one's status as an agent and to receive the treatment appropriate to that status.

But what is it that the person protesting the denial of his human rights shows about himself which provides some sort of basis for these rights? To be sure he shows that like his oppressors he has, in the words of Shylock, 'hands, organs, dimensions, senses, affections, passions', that contrary to the opinion of those who seek to preserve the status quo he is not animal-like in his natural ferocity and rendered tractable and kept in his subservient role only by fear and the threat of the lash. But how do the items to which Shylock refers show that he has rights and is on terms of moral equality with his oppressors? The point of Shylock's recitation is the cry for ven-geance against those who have abused him in the past, not the demand for the redress of his moral grievances. What then are the facts about himself that someone, who asserts himself as a moral agent and demands his rights on terms of equality with his oppressors, displays about himself, facts that warrant the claim that qua human being he has rights and as such is a full-fledged member of the moral community of persons? For surely it cannot be that in asserting oneself as a moral agent one shows that one has rights unless one shows something about oneself that justifies this moral conclusion, any more than one can show that something is good or right unless one calls attention to certain facts or features which render compelling the conclusion that the thing in question is good or right.

Yet this is our perplexity: How can the morally dispossessed, in asserting themselves as the moral agents they are, make plain even to those who had been unwilling or unable, because of ignorance, stupidity, indifference, insensitivity, lack of imagination or whatever, that they have rights? A right is not some hidden talisman that can be brought out into public view so that even those whose vision is blurred can dimly make out its outline by means of its inner light. But if, on the other hand, one makes clear that one has a right only by presenting or displaying certain relevant facts—for a right is not some sort of object that can be made visible to the eye of a beholder—how can any facts, short of the fact that one has a right, render the moral conclusion compelling? For the facts one presents or displays about oneself seem to be far too fragmentary to support the moral conclusion, that one has been deprived of one's rights and that redress for the moral wrongs suffered is mandatory. What then *are* the facts one displays and how do they bear upon this moral conclusion?

VI

There were, of course, certain facts even about the blacks of America several generations ago who for one reason or another submitted, often through fear, to the variety of injustices they suffered which deprived them of any hope of enjoying that moral equality to which they were entitled by their rights as human beings. They had interests that any human being has in food, clothing and shelter; and they were concerned to enjoy a measure of the elementary goods defined by these interests. And, like whites, they experienced a wide range of feelings and emotions, including those involved in their dealings with one another, during the course of which they displayed love and affection for each other within the circle of their family and close friends, pride in their culture and heritage and in each other's minor achievements which they often concealed from the view of some outsiders who might be offended by their attempts to raise themselves above their 'proper' station or who might be amused at the sight of what they took to be sub-humans mimicking the behavior and aspirations of human beings. And the subservience they showed towards privileged whites in their posture, style of discourse and the very forms of address they reserved for them, were, as DuBois and others have observed, forms of protective coloration by which they could appear to cater, with concealed amusement and contempt, to the pretensions to superiority of their masters.

To a superficial observer the fragmentary glimpses of the lives of such social and moral outcasts might not have seemed sufficient to warrant ascribing to them the moral equality that was theirs, much as it might induce sympathy and a desire to relieve them of the burdens under which they labored. Rights are not often apparent unless they are manifested by those who have them, in appropriate forms of behavior, in their demeanor towards others, and in what they say and do in their dealings with them. And they are not likely to be manifested in these various ways by those who live under the fears and threats to which they are exposed if they provide any evidence that they are sensible of their rights. It is understandable, therefore, that under these circumstances, the moral resentment of those who have been deprived of their rights should spill over into rage and those extreme forms of violence which serve only to buttress the conviction of those who have degraded them by treating them as if they were less than human and incapable of any moral feelings. But there have been those members of outcast groups who have provided evidence of their moral status as human beings, who have asserted their rights and made good their claim to moral equality. But what is the evidence they have provided and how does that evidence make good their claim? If we look for facts or features that are hidden and concealed in the examples of those who have made good their claims to their status as moral agents, we shall be disappointed. For what they have shown lies open before us, not so much in what they claim for and say about themselves as in what they reveal about themselves when, like Douglass, DuBois, King and their followers, they address themselves to the evils inherent in the institutions and practices of their times, when they endeavor to awaken the conscience of those undisturbed by and even party to measures that have degraded human beings, and when in various ways they arouse those who have submitted to these indignities to a recognition of their status as persons with rights. In short, what such persons show about themselves, by the example they provide others through their own demeanor, conduct and speech, is that they are as fully qualified as any others to employ the language of morals, to apply the concept of rights along with the conceptual structure in which it is embedded, during the course of their transactions with others.

But how can what they show in this way about themselves provide a 'basis' for the fundamental rights that they have and share equally with others, since what they show is nothing less than more of the very same thing for which a ground is needed, namely, that they are in fact moral agents and as such the possessors of the very rights for which a ground, presumably, is required. But the answer is, first, the general observation that at some point all explanations must come to rest, and, second, that in the present instance the explanation cannot be given in terms of mysterious and hidden phenomena of human life—for if the ground were hidden from view, how would it be possible to ascribe rights as all of us do to those with whom we have only the most casual dealings?—but in those general and familiar features of the lives of persons which are accessible to all of us: the fact that they have interests in the pursuit of which they seek to achieve a variety of goods for themselves and for others; the fact that these interests are intelligible to us and that they and the goods they define are in large measure similar to our own; the fact that their lives like our own are bound by love and affection with those of others within the circle of their own family and friends; the fact that like ourselves they are beings who carry on their affairs with others to whom they are not bound by love and affection but with whose well-being they are concerned, adjusting their desires and their concerns to theirs, and in joining their lives with them give them the support they need and require for the successful pursuit of their endeavors. The philosophical understanding of the rights of human beings must come to rest on nothing less, and on nothing else than, this enormously complicated and moral form of human life itself; in order to spell it out we would need to describe and comment on the most familiar of the endlessly varied and complicated ways in which in thoughts, actions, and feelings persons reveal themselves as the moral beings they are. Instead of looking for a basis for human rights, we need to see more clearly and in its rich and complex detail just what it is for persons to have the rights they have as human beings. It is here that all explanations come to an end.

Another objection: The elucidation of the so-called basis of the rights of human beings may fit the case of a Frederick Douglass who as a participant in the language-game of morality was far more sophisticated and competent than the white supremacists of his time. He was aware, even more clearly than many of the abolitionists of his day, of the implications of the possession of rights and of the authority conferred by it. But surely no such competence can be ascribed to those black contemporaries of his who submitted meekly and even willingly in their servile roles, and who thereby appeared to lend credence to the old dictum of Aristotle that some 'are by nature slaves, and for these . . . the condition of slavery is both beneficial and just'.[17] A number of observations, in reply to this objection, are pertinent.

(a) In some communities, a person is required to give appropriate notice to others of his legal rights and immunities in order to preserve them; but it is not the case that moral rights need to be asserted in order to be retained. Must one, however, be aware at least of the fact that one *has* rights in order to possess or retain them? To assert that awareness is a necessary condition of the possession of rights is to lay down too strong a condition, either in law or morals. Children, for example, possess legal and moral rights even before they are aware of them. Further, those who are bound by the close ties of love and affection seldom think of their rights against each other. And whatever may be true of sinners—that generally but not invariably they are aware of their rights and of the obligations that are correlative with them—the saint is notable for his love of and compassion for others and for his apparent oblivion to any rights that *he* might have against them.

Is it possible for someone to be insensible of his fundamental rights as a human being? Although such rights are inalienable, they are not inviolable by oneself or by others. And if, willingly, one sells oneself into slavery and even assents to Aristotle's dictum, this shows, not that one has no human rights, but that human beings are as capable of self-debasement as they are of self-destruction.

(b) Nor is it the case that the character of their lives is so far different from ours that we are unable to understand them, and they us, in any circumstance in which we may be brought together with them. However strange they may appear to us, they are not like unfamiliar beasts or imaginary creatures from another planet whose desires, interests and endeavors are so radically different from our own that however humanely we try to deal with them, given our sense that they like us are capable of pleasure or pain, we are unable to predict how they are likely to deal with us in any situation in which we are involved with them, and must, therefore, in order to protect ourselves, live in complete isolation from them. For however benighted our morally disenfranchised human beings are, they display attributes like our own. They, like us, are concerned with the interests of others; and they, like us, are concerned to achieve certain familiar goods for others no less than for themselves. They display moral feelings familiar to us in their dealings with one another and those close attachments to others which we display towards those whom we love, and who, loving us, encourage and help to sustain us in our endeavors. And however much we live apart from them, this is not that complete isolation appropriate to beings with whom moral communication is impossible, whose ways are so far different from our own that we can make no sense of what they do.

(c) The kind of case with which we are concerned is radically unlike that of the infant whose moral comprehension, including the sense of what is involved in the possession of rights, lies in the future. For in our example, as in the case of many in our own society today whose moral thinking like that of Polemarchus in the *Republic* is a reflection of the imperfect morality of the time, there is a substantial degree of moral understanding which serves as a basis upon which the exhortations, reminders and instructions of a moral leader can build a better moral understanding. Moral education is not conditioning or indoctrination which have as their object the establishment of predetermined and unthinking patterns of response to others. And while such education can transform the moral thinking of those who have willingly accepted their moral ostracism, it can also dispel the comfortable illusions of those who regard themselves as morally privileged. In both cases the progress achieved, and often by the same example and teaching of an enlightened moral leader, rests upon a common basis of moral understanding that often goes unnoticed by oppressed and oppressor alike. The question is whether or not that basis, imperfect as it may be, is sufficient to support the ascription of rights to those who in varying ways show something less than the moral understanding of those who are sensitive to their own rights and the rights of others, whoever they may be.

The present issue is not unlike the one that arises in instances of the use of promise-locutions by children before they are fully aware of all that is involved in the moral performance of promising in those central or nuclear cases to which the full panoply of related concepts applies. At a very early stage in the development of its comprehension, a child plays the game in which it imitates its elders, saying 'I promise . . .' and then going on to do . . . for reasons it does not yet understand except that this is the way the game is played. It expects others with whom it engages in its play to do the same when they utter these operative words; and in line with this expectation it proceeds as it does with its affairs, just as it does on the basis of any of its expectations that arise during the course of other games it plays with its fellows, complaining here as elsewhere when its expectation has been defeated that there has been an impropriety—for this too it has observed as the 'proper' response of adults to what they call the breaking of the promises they have received. So far, however, there is nothing in the giving and receiving of promises that involves any understanding of the moral import of such performances, that rights are conferred and obligations are assumed, that failure to perform the so-called promised act is a violation of a right with all of its moral consequences. But with a growing moral understanding a child soon comes to appreciate that the defeating of the expectation created by the use of a promise-locution is unlike the defeating of the expectation that occurs in baseball when the batter, having swung at and missed the ball three times, will leave the batter's box and allow play to resume in accordance with the rules of the game. Not doing what one had said one promised to do, a child soon learns, is something more serious than such unacceptable play behavior; it learns that it is wrong and wrong not merely because it is unsporting or unfair, but wrong in a much more important way. And here one can imagine a variety of intermediate cases in which the breaking of a promise is viewed in increasingly serious ways as morally wrong because in some sense or other harmful, that the wrongdoer is the object of some form of appropriate emotion for a failure that is at least regrettable, certainly shameful, and perhaps even more serious because of its impact on the person to whom the promise was given. But, short of the emergence of the clear realization on the part of one growing in moral maturity and understanding that in using a promise-locution one is conferring a right and assuming an obligation, that in so doing there are moral requirements imposed upon both the person employing the locution and the person to whom it is addressed, at what point shall one say that in using the promise-locution one has not been playing the game of imitating adults, but promising? The answer, surely, is that there is no point at which a sharp line can be drawn that would mark off non-promises from promises. As a child develops in moral maturity it learns to distinguish different sorts of cases from one another, and peripheral cases from those central or nuclear cases to which the full array of concepts, in which the concept of a promise is embedded, applies without any truncation. Must we then wait until the child completes and perfects its moral understanding before we can say about any of its promisings so-called that in uttering promise-locutions it assumes obligations and confers rights? In our account of promises in Chapter II, central or nuclear cases of promises were described as those in which rights are conferred and obligations assumed; our present question is whether the stronger condition is required that those who engage in central or nuclear transactions of promising must be aware of this fact. And the answer to this question is, surely, that no such condition is needed, or even possible. For the realization that a right is conferred implies as a matter antecedent to it the existence of the right. Besides, the condition would imply that no right is conferred by a promise made by those so morally ossified that they believe that a promise must be kept whatever the costs may be. For even in the case of those who take such an absurdly rigid view there are enough features of our central case to warrant our view that in promising they do confer rights and assume obligations. Here we need only attend to the way in which a promise functions generally at least even in the lives of such benighted persons: The promised act is important for the success of the promisee's endeavors, who proceeds with his line of conduct given the assurance provided by means of the promise-locution. And the promiser, however imperfect his own understanding of the moral import of his promise may be, is mindful during the course of his pursuit of his own interests of how he is to contribute to the support of the agency of the promisee, the assurance of which he has conveyed by means of his promise. The lives of both are joined in such a way that there is the moral relation constituted by the right that one has against the other.

Similarly, the question with which we are concerned in the instances of those who willingly submit to the will of those who morally ostracize them is not whether they recognize that they have human rights, but whether the character of their lives warrants our thinking that they are moral agents and that they are the possessors of fundamental human rights. We need to ask whether there is enough moral understanding that they show in the ways they conduct their affairs with one another, upon which moral leaders can build in awakening in them the sense that they are moral agents and as such on terms of moral equality with those who have sought to keep them outside the moral pale.

Do they exhibit any sense of what they owe each other when they provide each other with the help they need in their endeavors: the members of their family groups, their friends and neighbors and those with whom they labor? Do they have interests in common with those outside their group—their self-styled superiors—and do they share with the latter certain basic goods which they seek to achieve for themselves and for others? Does each of them exhibit a concern for the well-being of others, a readiness to adjust his desires and his endeavors in accordance with those of others? Do they show moral emotions that are appropriate to the situation in which their concerns and interests, and those of others, are affected by what they and others do, or fail to do: moral indignation and resentment, remorse, shame and guilt? Do they make amends or perhaps seek forgiveness for what we would describe as misconduct? These are some of the sorts of items the presence of which in the lives of our moral outcasts shows that they are sufficiently like ourselves in the moral understanding we have to warrant our thinking of them as moral agents who are on terms of equality with all others, whatever their view of their own status may be. The fact that it may occur neither to the oppressed nor to the oppressor that they have so much in common, and hence that they can enter into various sorts of moral relations with each other as equals, each being accountable to the other, is testimony only to the extent to which the myopic view that human beings take of themselves and each other can obscure the most familiar and morally the most important facts about them. It is one of the functions of a Douglass who, like others, has suffered the moral damage of being read out of the moral community to focus attention upon these commonplace matters in order that those who, like him, have been dealt with as inferior beings may recognize their own status as persons with rights and take the necessary steps to gain the dignity that befits them as members of the moral community.

Moral education generally, whether it proceeds from an imperfect understanding of what is involved in a promise or from an imperfect understanding of ourselves or of others as persons endowed with human rights, begins with some initial basis of understanding and draws attention to matters which for one reason or another are ignored or obscured from view but which, once due attention is paid to them, renders compelling the moral advance that takes place. For in the course of moral development there is not only the discovery of matters of fact to which previously at best only passing attention has been paid, but important changes in moral concepts. Where at an earlier stage of development a promise may be viewed merely as a device for the useful exchange of benefits and burdens and their breach as a matter of regret and the occasion for disapproval because of the resulting unfairness (ironically, a view of the import of promises not infrequently shared by moral philosophers), a closer inspection of the role of a promise in the support it provides for the endeavors of a promisee transforms our conception of that breach from the unfair withholding of a benefit to the damage inflicted upon another agent. And the further consideration that the person who suffers the damage is a human being who, like oneself, is to be treated not merely as one who, like inferior beings, experiences pleasure and pain, frustration and delight, and with regard to whom one ought to feel shame for the damage one inflicts upon him, but as one with whom one can carry on one's affairs in ways similar to those with whom one deals within the circle of our family, friends and acquaintances, as one with whom one may join one's life, transforms our conception of the appropriate ways of dealing with him. There develops, therefore, a fuller grasp of what is involved in promising, that the breach of a promise is no mere occasion for regret or shame, but the kind of emotion—a sense of guilt and remorse—that is in order whenever we subvert the endeavors of others.

In moral development generally there is this characteristic interplay between the increased awareness of facts about ourselves and others, and the change in our moral concepts, the end result of which is the mastery of the complex language of morals. One of the functions of a Douglass, with respect to oppressed and oppressors alike, is to call attention to those commonplace matters of fact about both groups, which are easily missed because the various pressures that operate in a divided society, pressures that give rise to those striking differences that obscure these facts and dull our sensibilities to others—the differences in social status, economic roles, habits, dress and even in the forms of speech that are employed. But the force of the moral instruction provided by the example, reminders and exhortations of a Douglass also has its effects in the increasing moral sophistication that results from attention to these matters of human fact. Here we need to bear in mind that this moral instruction is imparted to persons of widely varied degrees of moral understanding. At one extreme, the moral thinking of members of an oppressed group, like that of children whose moral development is in progress, is apt to reflect their condition of extreme dependence upon the admonitions and the authority of others—in the case of a morally ostracized group upon those who represent themselves as the spokesmen of a comforting deity upon whom they depend for the promise of a better existence than the one that is possible for them in their earthly circumstances, and in the case of children upon the authority of their parents upon whom they are completely dependent for their care and guidance. In such extreme circumstances, as in the case of those who are developing an increased understanding of the moral import of a promise, the attention to relevant facts about their lives and their relations to others enables them to acquire the moral concepts to be employed by them in their dealings with one another as responsible moral agents. At the other extreme there is a far greater moral sophistication, and the reminders provided by the example and instruction of a Douglass, for oppressor and oppressed, serves only to alert them to what had gone unrecognized by both, that all of them are equally moral agents. At some point, no doubt, the interplay between attention to matter of fact and conceptual growth ceases, so that the reminders of a moral leader serve only to widen the sphere of application of the concepts that have already been acquired and mastered. But for many whatever their social station may be and even as adults, there continues to be this interplay between reminders of the most commonplace facts about ourselves and others, and growth in the grasp of moral concepts. Many are not only deficient in moral excellence but also in moral understanding itself when, to consider only one instance, they do not understand that there are moral burdens that go hand in hand with moral rights, and that these cannot be treated as if they were like banknotes that are payable on demand.

VII

There are other cases in which we ascribe basic rights to human beings which appear to pose much more serious problems than those we have considered so far. The case of the very young infant and child is one of these, for here at first only in the most embryonic way if at all do we find those features of the lives of persons to whom in an altogether unproblematic manner we do in fact ascribe human rights. But for reasons that will become apparent later, after the ground has been laid in the discussion of certain other hard cases, I shall postpone the discussion of this case until later, at the very end of this chapter.[18]

It is not possible, within the limitations of this work, to discuss all of the indefinitely many sorts of cases in which those general features encountered normally in human beings are more or less absent but in which we are more or less inclined to ascribe human rights to individuals. And there are those cases of animals, in particular our household pets and even certain higher forms of animal life, e.g. dolphins and chimpanzees, to whom some are inclined to ascribe rights but who appear to lack certain of the distinctive features of human beings the presence of which, on our account, provides the appropriate conceptual place for the presence of human rights. Yet while we cannot examine every possible apparent counter-example to the view presented earlier in this chapter, it will be useful to consider a few selected cases that may indicate at least some of the general considerations that need to be kept in mind in dealing with alleged counter-examples.

At the outset it should be observed that any account would be in serious error if it attempted to provide a set of necessary and sufficient conditions for the possession of a human right. Persons vary enormously, not only in their moral excellence and in their grasp of moral concepts, but in ever so many different respects: in their intelligence, their powers of judgment and imagination, their sensitivities to and concerns with the interests of others, their ability to restrain and modify their own desires in the light of the interests, desires and endeavors of others with whom they have dealings, their ambitions and the goods they seek to achieve for themselves or for others, the extent to which they join their lives with those of others, and in their varying degrees of mental and physical health some substantial measure of which is required if persons are to have that degree of understanding of themselves and of others, and those capacities and skills all of which are essential for the intelligent intercourse of persons. In each of these and in indefinitely other respects, there are enormous variations encountered in human beings, from the high end of the scale down to the vanishing point; yet without regard to such differences we ascribe rights to human beings, to those who are handsomely endowed by nature and nurture and to those singularly deficient, mentally and physically.

It is possible, however, to adopt the approach employed by us in our account of promises in order to deal with most of these variations. We may take as central those cases in which these features are present at least to the degree encountered in normal human beings, by virtue of which it is possible for them to conduct their lives with one another in ways in which intelligent and responsible persons do. Other cases in which deficiencies exist, despite their differences from the normal cases, are sufficiently similar to the latter to enable us to count them as persons with whom, albeit in more restricted ways, it is possible for those normally endowed to conduct themselves with such individuals, attending to their interests and the goods they seek to achieve and receiving in return a like treatment during the course of their commerce with them. The young child, the neurotic, the physically handicapped, even those whom we count as irresponsible in their dealings with others, and in whom we are understandably reluctant to repose much confidence that they will behave properly with us in circumstances in which their own interests are affected, not to mention those of limited intelligence and lack of imagination, who are thereby unable accurately to assess the impact of their conduct upon the well-being of others, are nevertheless sufficiently like us in their mode of life to permit us to carry on with them, on the basis of mutual understanding, some measure of our normal human activities. However different from us such individuals are, they are beings who have some measure of understanding of us and enough interest in our own well-being, to enable us to join our lives with them in many of our activities. They are not like strange creatures we do not understand or beings so deprived of human traits that they are insensible of the support we give their agency by the manner in which we deal with them and who fail to respond to us a like manner in their own limited ways. If, then, we take as our starting point the normal person, these deviant individuals can be seen as sufficiently similar to warrant our thinking of them as moral agents endowed with rights. It is understandable, therefore, that some are prepared to regard even their household pets, different as they are from any of the members of their family in their appearance, aptitudes and the range of activities in which they enter into with them, as beings who have rights. Whether or not such anthropomorphizing of animals is justified, the point remains that where we attribute to individuals even to a limited degree those features present in normal agents, we do ascribe rights to them. And the fact that children and even those of subnormal intelligence, to consider only two classes of cases, may be unable to assert their rights as human beings, to hold accountable to them those who deprive them of these rights, or in other respects to demonstrate by what they say and do that they have our understanding of relevant moral concepts during the course of their dealings with others, does not show that they are not human and without any of the rights that human beings have. A promise binds even when it may lack some of the features present in central cases, and a human being may be subnormal mentally or physically and yet sufficiently like the rest of us to warrant our treating him as a person with the rights that go with his moral status as a person.

There are, however, extreme cases, but while it is not possible here to discuss even most of them, three types of cases come readily to mind and need to be discussed in order to focus upon certain important features of our concept of personhood: those of psychopaths and sociopaths, the cases of terminally ill persons in a coma, and those of very young infants, to all of whom we have at least some inclination to ascribe the basic rights of human beings.

A

We have some inclination to ascribe rights to sociopaths and psychopaths. Such persons, however, are so disoriented with respect to their social groups or those individuals with whom they work and live that, however much they may damage or distress others with whom they are involved, they feel no regret, remorse or guilt because of the hurt they inflict on others. They appear to recognize that others are pained, distressed or grief-stricken when, brushing aside the latter's interests, concerns, hopes and aspirations, they indulge their fancies, satisfy their own desires, or rationally proceed to optimize their private goods. They engage in the so–called 'practice of promising', understanding by this a conventionalized and mutually useful form of transaction governed by a certain constitutive rule in order to exchange benefits and burdens, a kind of barter in which performances are the commodities and bargains are struck by those who engage in this practice. But, lacking that interest in the well-being of others that is implied, as we have seen, by the sense a person has of his obligations to them, such persons feel no remorse or guilt or even regret for anything they do that brings distress to others when they ride roughshod over them as they pursue their own private satisfactions. The remorse we feel, for example, is testimony to the lasting concern we have with the good of those to whom we are morally bound, since without that concern we should not be distressed, as indeed remorseful persons are by their own misconduct. Sociopaths and psychopaths do have certain sorts of feelings towards others; they can and do feel affection for certain individuals. If they lacked all of the feelings that attract persons to one another, they would be monsters incapable of entering into any sort of personal relations with anyone else. The trouble in their case is not that they suffer a sense of isolation from one another in ways that would make any cooperative activity impossible, even that cooperative activity involved in receiving instruction from others in learning a language, acquiring a skill, or mastering the conventions of one's social group, in games, business, politics or whatever. It is, rather, that they are incapable of forming lasting attachments that can survive the pressures of their moods, desires, whims, hankerings or their interest in their own private satisfactions. The desire they may have for the well-being of those to whom they are attracted and for whom they feel affection is not that lasting concern that normal people have and which is implied by the sense of obligation they have to others or the remorse they feel when they realize that they have damaged them. Not infrequently, they are the products of a childhood in which they were deprived of the love and affection of their parents or of those assigned to care for them.[19] Such persons are the loners of our society who are incapable of those feelings, attitudes and emotions by which normal persons are bound to one another.

For what would they understand by 'love' or 'loyalty'? The poet's line, 'Love is not love which alters when it alteration finds', is no mere hyperbole. Neither should it be taken simply as a normative remark. For it is also a conceptual comment, namely, that love is the kind of emotion that survives many of the changes that take place in the lover and the loved. Love is not some internal condition that comes and goes like passing fancies, whims, moods and desires any more than it can be turned on and off with each tick of the clock. And so too with one's loyalty to a person or to one's group which is not loyalty but something else again, perhaps sentimental feeling, self-indulgence or whatever, if it cannot withstand the force of a number of contingent psychological factors. The disorientation of the sociopath or the psychopath from society and from other persons is their disengagement in their thoughts and feelings from the interests and concerns of other individuals and the social groups of which they are members, so much so that the very terms we employ to mark some of the most familiar of the emotions and attitudes we have, apply in their case at best only problematically and then only in an attenuated fashion.

This disengagement from others is not alienation. The person who feels alienated from others is distressed by his condition and unable or unwilling to join his life with others because their interests and aspirations are or appear to be foreign to his own. He is prepared and anxious to form close attachments and, typically, he develops intensely close relations with those who are similarly disposed and have strong loyalties to groups and devotions to causes, often at considerable peril to his own well-being. The condition of our abnormal individuals is that they are untouched by the feelings, interests and well-being of others. They recognize that others may suffer as the result of what they do, but they do not feel impelled to justify their conduct, since this is not even a matter that occasions any regret. They learn that others, who break their promises and fail to make good the assurances they give, utter remarks that soothe those whom they hurt, but they feel no need to redeem themselves in their eyes. And, given their sense of what it is that others do, they themselves will do only if it should please them for whatever passing interest they may have in the matter. But this is not a matter that concerns them, and often at least they go on with their affairs without bothering to say anything about their destructive conduct. The point is that they feel none of the moral emotions, have no sense of any moral constraints, and are unable to join their lives with others in such a way that they are mindful of the agency of others during the course of their own conduct. Whatever associations they may have with others are unstable and transitory, subject to the whims of their desires; for the interests of others are not a matter of concern to them should they stand in the way of what they are disposed to do.

Still, such individuals, different as they are from us in these ways, can be and often are pleasant and interesting companions, until, of course, their aberrations are manifest; and those who are lulled by their good company during such balmy periods can and do form close attachments to them. Indeed, the sense of obligation to such persons can survive the grievous disappointments that occur when their aberrant condition manifests itself. Psychopaths and sociopaths may be incapable of the natural and moral feelings and emotions of normal individuals, but they are often at least the objects of these natural and moral feelings of normal persons who feel sufficiently committed to them to help and protect them. And one might argue that society itself has certain minimal obligations to them as it does to any of its members, so that, whether or not our pathological individuals have any sense of obligation, feel any moral emotions or have any moral understanding of what is involved in their relations to normal persons, they nevertheless do have rights. For society, their parents, friends and other protectors can and do act on their behalf, as much so as the parents or courts can and do act on behalf of infants devoid of moral feelings or sensibilities of any kind. Further, such pathological individuals share with us many of our psychological traits. They are intelligent human beings, often quite talented and interested as we are in a number of the goods that human beings seek to gain for themselves.

The case for the status of psychopaths and sociopaths as persons with rights might appear to be even stronger than that of the young infant whose rights are actual and present but whose agency, interests and human attributes such as those that are exhibited even by our abnormal beings lie in the future. But there is a vast difference even with respect to morally relevant present features between these cases, even though neither exhibits that moral understanding that would enable them to assert or claim a right and react with moral feelings and emotions to those who might injure them. And this difference is shown in the quite different ways in which the parent of an infant and the parent of a psychopath act when they are mindful of the interest of the one who concerns them. For the parent in his role with respect to the infant supplies in what he now does for it interests and agency of which the infant is itself insensible and incapable respectively. That is to say, it is the parent who is sensible of what lies in the interest of the child, including what lies in his interests as a being who will develop into a moral agent with those human features characteristic of normal persons, and who now plans and takes such measures as are necessary for this development. The parent of an infant makes good from his own resources as a moral agent those features of the developed moral agent that are lacking in the infant's condition. But in the case of the parent of a psychopath there is, if he is aware of the condition of his offspring, no such contribution that he makes. For if he is responsible and mindful of the pathological condition of his offspring, he will seek to protect others from the ravages they suffer when it happens that, because there are no constraints of love, loyalty or morality itself, such individuals lash out violently to indulge their fancies or satisfy their desires at the expense of others. And he will seek to protect his pathological offspring from the violence that this may provoke in return by making clear to all concerned something the psychopath does not understand since he has no moral sensibilities, namely, that his offspring is not responsible for what he does. It is protection that the parent of the psychopath provides, not those programs of action supplied by the parent of a young infant which are in the interests, including the moral interest, of the infant. And if those who befriend and love the psychopath act as they do in ignorance of his condition, they are in error in supposing that it is even possible to establish normal moral relations with him and that their commitment to him is of the same order as that which they can make to others.

Do sociopaths and psychopaths have the fundamental rights of any moral agent? An affirmative answer would imply that they are on terms of moral equality with any other human being. A negative answer would seem to put them apart from all towards whom we ought to give any moral consideration. Aristotle declared that the man who does not repent is a different sort of man and deserves a name of his own, in order to indicate that he is to be treated differently. In the case of the abnormal individuals we have been considering we do have special names. But whether we are inclined to give an affirmative or negative answer to our question, what is important is not the answer in itself, but the reservations and qualifications in which these answers must be hedged. For what is of the utmost importance in this situation is the recognition of the highly unusual features of the case of a psychopath or sociopath, how far different these are from those of a normal central case of a human being—a moral agent—and hence how far different is the character of the moral relations *we* can enter into with him, i.e. the moral posture possible for us to adopt towards him. Indeed, our posture will vary with different cases, some being far more prone to violence than others, and unpredictably so. But the more extreme their condition, the more we are moved to regard them as different sorts of beings with whom even the transitory and precarious associations some of us have with certain psychopaths and sociopaths are impossible; and then, unhappily for us and them, they must be institutionalized in order to protect others and even themselves from harm. Yet even in such extreme cases there are moral constraints to which we are subject in the ways in which we conduct ourselves with them. To be sure, there are certain moral constraints imposed upon us in our relations with animals in the field. It would be reprehensible for us wantonly to shoot at animals in the field simply in order to test or demonstrate our marksmanship. But our moral concern with even extreme psychopaths or sociopaths goes further. They are not only members of our species, but beings with whom their parents and their friends and associates may have concerned themselves and even reposed their hopes in. And the interests they have and the goods they aspire to achieve, which we share with them, are distinctively human. So there is some warrant for the ascription of moral rights to them, minimally the right we may respect if only by caring for them as we do in the home and in institutions, even though in extreme cases they are utterly devoid of any moral responsibility and any moral feelings, emotions, or propensities. Besides this, there are other matters that may determine the moral stance we take towards them: compassion, perhaps gratitude for what they may have meant to those who had planned for and lived with them before their pathological condition had come to light, and pity for them as they now are. For the human being who is so far different from the rest of us that he must be placed in an institution, is an object of sorrow and pity, and all the more so the more his state is like that of an animal; yet we do not pity animals because they are animals.

B

So far we have been concerned with the fact of extreme variability in the state of human beings. We need to turn now to a quite different sort of apparent counter-example to our account of fundamental human rights, this time in order to call attention to an important and often neglected feature of our concept of a person.

Consider the case of someone lying in a hospital bed in a coma, in the very last stage of a terminal illness. We regard such an individual as a person. It is Mr. Smith who lies there, not a cat or dog whose life, many of us at least, would not hesitate to terminate. Yet Mr. Smith who lies there is incapable of any agency. Nor is he conscious in any way or capable of regaining consciousness. Yet we treat him as a person, who has rights to which we respond as we do when we continue to care for and watch over him as we await his death.

If we think of the person as a self whose experiences are related by memory and connected somehow with the body, there is no longer the person, Mr. Smith, who lies there on a bed, but only the bodily remains, with its lingering biological functions. And while out of respect for the memory of Mr. Smith, we should no more throw that body out on the rubbish heap, as our primitive forebears would have done, any more than we should do so when that body is pronounced dead by medical officers, we should have no reason on this view of the nature of personhood to think that there is any person there with any rights at all. But then why should we not think of persons in the same way when they lie asleep or lapse into an extended unconsciousness when, for example, they are dealt a sharp blow on the head by a thug or suffer injury in an automobile accident? Is it that we believe or hope that they will awaken or regain consciousness, continue with their normal mode of life, and resume their traffic with us? But suppose this does not happen: the man asleep suffers a heart attack and dies in his sleep, or the man who has lost consciousness never recovers it and dies as the result of his injury. Are we to say then, that we were mistaken in supposing that it was a person who was asleep or a person who was unconscious, and hence that our supposition that he had any moral right to life itself or to the care and treatment we gave him was mistaken? One might invoke the conception of a person as an immaterial substance or soul whose immaterial mental functions remain, hovering somehow outside the body and waiting perhaps to resume connection with the body, in the way in which some primitives imagine this to be the case. And if we accepted this picture of the person we might then think of the body as a kind of vessel for the soul, to be cared for and protected in the expectation or hope that the person who remains as a spirit or soul will resume his residence in the body. But unless we accept this picture of what exists when the person is asleep or unconscious, why should we think that there now is a person there, asleep or unconscious, who is a subject, and to whom rights may be ascribed? In any case, even if it should come to pass that he awakens or regains his consciousness and memories, it does not follow that while asleep or unconscious there is a person with rights, but only and hopefully that there will be one. Sometimes it is suggested by those who hold this view of the nature of personhood that we can employ the analogy of a rope that consists of fibers, one laid over the other, none running the length of the rope, and all held together by the lapping of fiber upon fiber; here the lapping of one fiber upon another is the analogue of connections of experiences by means of memory. But even if one should move along in the direction in which a rope is laid out, find a break, and then the beginning of another rope which at that time sends fibers back which join with and overlap the fibers of the rope that had come to an end—so that one could now say that the two ropes had been joined to form one rope—it would remain the case that there was a period of time during which there had been a gap separating the two ropes, a gap in which there was no rope at all. But short of committing oneself to some form of identity thesis of the relation of mind and body, we should have to say, on the view suggested, that when consciousness ceases, there ceases to be a person with rights. And this would hold true not only in the case in which there is coma before death, unconsciousness because of anaesthesia or a blow on the head, but also in sleep before awakening. Yet all of these conclusions, for many or most of us, seem unacceptable.

A full discussion of the nature of personhood is impossible within the limits of this work; but it may be worthwhile to mention two matters that are immediately relevant to the problem we have raised.

(1) Our concept of a person is the concept of a being whose life extends over a period of time and who undergoes various changes during the course of which he learns to apply to himself and to others terms which describe his feelings, emotions, attitudes and conduct in ways which involve an essential reference to the past. He now feels grief or remorse or regret or guilt; and these necessarily relate to what is past but which are reflected in his present state of mind. He is *now* depressed or dejected, but the depression or dejection is often at least over something that has happened in the past. He now redresses grievances, atones for and purges himself of the guilt he incurred by

what he did long ago. He rewards those who have helped him. He is grateful to those who have displayed kindness and generosity towards him and now displays his gratitude in appropriate forms of conduct. He has a sense of obligation to those who have joined their lives with his and supported him in his endeavors, plans and projects which have now borne fruit in the goods he enjoys. He forgives those who have trespassed against him or is merciful to those who even now do not even regret having damaged him in the past. And so it goes. These are moral feelings, attitudes and actions which relate to the past as much as they pertain to a present stage of his life. No doubt memory is involved in all of these; but what binds the present to the past are no more present images of the past but those feelings, emotions, attitudes, moods, dispositions and actions which give their significance to the events in the present by relating them to earlier incidents in our lives. The conception of personhood as a temporarily ordered sequence of experience connected by memories is an impossibly anemic view of what is involved in the lives of persons. Locke, for whom the criterion of identity of self is memory, distinguishes the self from the person which he takes to be a being who is concerned and accountable, concerned about and accountable for as much that lies in the past as that which occurs in the present.

(2) The essential references to the past in the items mentioned above also involve essential reference to other persons. Our concept of a person is not merely the concept of a being who is the subject of experiences but of one who in the broadest and etymological sense of that term is, to use Locke's term, forensic. Whatever counts for this individual being Mr. Smith will involve not only his present state of mind or his memories but matters pertaining to his relations with other persons. If in addition to a person's memories we look for his identity in a lifeline with its different stages during the course of its history, we shall need to include in that history the ways in which at different times his lifeline intersects and parallels, in extraordinarily complicated ways, the lifelines of those with whom he has had various sorts of dealings and in many cases supported or received support from them in thought and action over an extended period of time. And if we think of a person as a peculiar complex of the mental and the physical, and, finding a break in the mental because of deep sleep or unconsciousness or coma, we then look for his identity in the lifeline of the events in his body, then we are faced with the following dilemma: Either we ignore completely those relations with others

that count for his being the person he continues to be even during such gaps in consciousness, or, since most of the events in his body are irrelevant (e.g. the outset and disappearance of dandruff or toothache), we shall have to attend to relevant bodily events including those bodily events which, so one might speculate, occur whenever persons engage in their various forms of traffic with one another. But even if this speculation could be made good and the relevant bodily events and states identified, this could be done only by employing our present criteria for the identity of persons, and we should still continue for all ordinary purposes to use them.

Here then lies Mr. Smith, lying in deep sleep, devoid of consciousness, a person like ourselves in those relevant features of his life which establish him as a moral agent with fundamental rights, even though at this time he is devoid of consciousness, and we are not. And we should not retract our view that he does—now—have rights even if it should happen a few moments from now that he is struck dead by a heart attack and never regains his senses. So our statement that he is a person, with rights, is not the predictive statement that he will awaken and exhibit those features that establish him as a person with rights. Neither is it the statement that he is capable of awakening and displaying these features of personhood, for even if an autopsy should reveal that at the time he was suffering the onset of the attack and in that condition was incapable of regaining consciousness, we should not on that account change our minds. Neither are we merely, if at all, subscribing to a contrary-to-fact conditional in ascribing rights to him, namely, that if he were to awaken—something later events showed not to be possible in view of his physical condition at the time we ascribed rights to him—he would display those relevant features of personhood that warrant the ascription of rights. Mr. Smith lying there asleep is someone who has made and received unfulfilled promises, he is father of x, husband of y, stands in this or that moral relation to still other persons, who even now have rights against him and obligations to him. Even if he were a total stranger about whom none of these details are known, we see a person lying there asleep whose life we take to be like our own, not in respect of his immediately present condition but in those features extending back into his past life which establish him, as much as they do each of us, as a moral agent with rights. For it is these features in earlier phases of the life he now lives, even asleep, that are relevant and decisive.

So too when Mr. Smith lies before us, still under anaesthesia in the recovery room of a hospital or unconscious in an automobile wreck, even with our uncertainty that he will ever regain his senses and resume his mode of life with us or with others. And in the extreme case in which he now lies in a coma during the terminal phase of his life, those who observe him, saddened as they are by his present condition, observe a father or a loved one, to whom even now they remain as they have been in the past when he was alive and well—with whom they conducted their lives in ways in which he supported them in their endeavors, and they his—under those obligations which they had and continue to have to their father or loved one. They continue to care for and watch over him now as they do, not out of respect for his memory, for he is still alive, but for what he continues to be as long as he lives, a person to whom they remain bound by their moral relation with him and which they respect only if in these extreme circumstances they treat him as a person, not as some animal whose demise they might hasten without any moral compunction. Even if, observing Mr. Smith lying in a coma before he expires, we have no such special moral relations with him—he is not *our* father nor is he one with whom *we* have had any relations in the past—he remains as he was, a being whose life, which extends back into the past and cannot be restricted to its present segment, resembles that of our own. The past in his life is no more irrelevant to his status as a person with rights than the past in our lives is irrelevant to our present status and to the rights and obligations that bind us to others. Devoid as he may now be of all capacity for agency or understanding of his own moral status or medical condition, he remains, as long as he lives, a human being who as the possessor of rights merits treatment quite different from that which we owe animals with whom no such moral relations of any kind may be possible.

It may be objected that, since so many of the features present in the normal case are missing in the case of our man in a coma, the very rights he has are pale shadows of rights that normal persons have; and hence that we should say that he has whatever rights he has only to a greatly diminished degree. But promises, too, may be deviant; but the mere fact that they are deviant does not show that the rights they confer are rights in some reduced degree but rather that the moral burdens assumed by promiser and promisee are appropriately affected. That is to say, the unusual character of the circumstances in which a person makes a promise bears on the question of the nature of the moral requirements imposed upon both parties, unless of course these circumstances are such as to render the promise morally self-defeating or null. And in the same way, the rights of our Mr. Smith in a terminal state of coma are rights that he has—as parent, promisee, or whatever—even though his present circumstances are such that he can do nothing in respect of his right and all that we can do, in respecting the right that he has as a human being, is to accord him the right that he has to life itself by continuing to give him medical attention.

Our case of the person lying in a coma to whom nevertheless we ascribe rights is of course unusual and extreme. But our sense of the reality of the past that is conserved in those moral relations we have to him, as indeed they are in those cases in which we ourselves are morally related to others, support our sense that even in his extreme condition, he is a person to whom others are bound by virtue of his rights as a human being. There may be little that remains in his present condition of those features of moral agents like ourselves in the central sorts of cases in which, as responsible persons, we are mindful of the moral burdens that go with our rights and the authority that goes with their possession. Yet his life, like our own, cannot be compressed into the narrow band of the present but involves the earlier stages of his life in which these features were fully evident and which need to be borne in mind in any categorical assertion we now make about him.[20] Unless this is done, any moral claim we make about anyone with whom we are presently concerned is subject to defeat by the momentary flickering out of his consciousness.

C

It was argued in the preceding chapter that in the case of a young infant the deficiencies in its agency, moral understanding and interests are remedied by the surrogate agencies, understanding and interests of its parents who join their lives with and care for it during the early stages of its development. The infant's life qua infant is confined almost totally within the family circle. It responds as it does to an environment limited to the circumstances provided through the ministrations of its parents; but it lacks those features of moral agents which would enable it, on its own, to join its life with those outside the family, some or many of the features of which are required, on the account advanced earlier, for the possession of human rights. But if the possession of special rights implies the possession of basic human rights—for how else would it be possible to understand how the concept of a right is embedded in the complex structure of related moral concepts?—we are faced with a dilemma: Either we must abandon the claim that infants do in fact have moral rights against their parents and any rights as human being, or we must abandon the view for which we have argued that human rights are possible only for those beings who exhibit features that enable them to join their lives with any human being within or without the family circle: parent, friend, casual acquaintance or total stranger.

It is an old and familiar idea that, devoid as the infant is of the requisite features of moral agents, it has the potentiality to acquire them. But it is not enough merely to say that infants have this potentiality, or that this is present. For how can this potentiality, present as it may be, confer present and no mere potential or future rights upon the infant? What, indeed, is meant by a present potentiality? The contingent matter of fact that some time in the future it will come to have those features of moral agency that will enable it in the future to join its life with others in the ways in which morally mature agents do? But if this is all that is intended, it does not follow that there is anything in its *present* condition to warrant our ascribing moral agency and rights to it now, any more than the fact that it is true of a person that he will later acquire the skills of a bicycle rider establishes that he is now a bicycle rider. The problem with this talk about present potentiality is that it leaves us at a loss to understand what the difference is that the presence of a potentiality makes to the *present* condition of the infant. The present condition of the infant, we are told, is somehow big with its future moral agency, but unless we invoke entelechies and impute them to the present state of infants, we seem to be at a loss to make out a plausible case, given our account of the basic rights of moral agents, for the possession by infants of any of their rights. And even present entelechies cannot be the bearers of rights, unless in some way we invest them with the status of persons—but how is this possible?

We remarked in the preceding subsection that we do rightly ascribe rights to persons even though, in the present segments of their lives, they have lost all capacity for entering into any moral relations with others. We argued that we cannot identify such persons with their status in present segments of their lives. Our concept of a person, however much in such cases to which it applies and in which the features of normal paradigmatic cases may now be absent, is the concept of a being who lives a life of which the present is only one segment. The status of a being to whom we apply our concept of personhood is determined not only by his condition during the present segment of his life, but also by the character of his life in the past. In a similar way, we cannot identify the status of a member of the human species with that status which he may happen to have in the present without regard to the future. For in addition to the moral concepts we apply to human beings which involve an essential reference to the past, there are the broad range of concepts involved in any present exercise of intelligence in proceeding as agents do in their endeavors, concepts which involve an essential reference to the future; for the future segments of the life of an agent, like those in his past, are part of the life he lives and are involved in his status as a person. Persons act prudently, with foresight and determination in carrying out their plans and projects, yet these involve a reference to eventualities in the future even though they operate in the present thoughts and actions of agents.

Now we think of the acquisition of a skill like that involved in riding a bicycle as a matter that not only lies wholly in the future of an infant but as one that is dependent upon a variety of quite contingent factors which may or may not come to pass in its life in the future. But we do not as parents, when we nurse and care for an infant during the course of its development, acting as we do in the interest of its moral development and education, regard the gradual appearance in the future life of the infant, of its moral agency and understanding, as a matter that is as contingent as the acquisition of those capacities, traits and skills that are dependent upon the particular accidents of circumstances, opportunities and fortune in the way in which this is true of bicycle riding. We think of the infant as a developing being, the later segments of its life in which its moral agency gradually makes its appearance being not merely temporal successors of its present segment, but as ensuing in accordance with its nature given the conditions of nurture supplied for it by its parents. The concept of an infant, in short, is the concept of a being in whom these changes may take place, in accordance with the expectations of those who act on its behalf and in its interests, as a matter of its natural development as a human being. It might be thought that this is only a definitional matter so that just as, by definition, we apply the word 'combustible' only to things that are naturally capable of undergoing combustion, given the necessary application of heat, so we apply the term 'infant' only to those beings who are capable of undergoing transformation into responsible moral agents, given the necessary application of the suitable conditions of their nurture. Yet this analogy is at best only superficial; for a combustible remains a combustible even if it never burns, whereas the idea of an infant that continues unchanged in its condition throughout a period in which normally substantial development takes place, strikes one as being peculiar so much so that it would be as misleading to apply the term 'infant' to such an imaginable creature as it would be to those striking cases of deviant beings brought out of the womb and into the world for which special terms are employed in order to make clear how far they deviate from the paradigm cases to which we apply the term 'infant'. However it is that this is so, the concept of an infant that we employ is the concept of a human being *in* its infancy. The conception of an infant connects, therefore, as essentially with the life of a human being, with respect to which infancy is only one segment, as much so as present phenomena of human life such as purpose, intention and prudence, etc. connect essentially with the future phases and conditions of human beings. An infant that dies before any substantial development takes place is not merely a being whose life has been cut short in the way in which this is true of adults whose lives are terminated before middle or old age has set in, it is a being that is deprived of the life of a human being by whatever accident of disease or misfortune that has brought about its early demise.

In ascertaining, therefore, the moral status of an infant we need to take account not only of its condition in the infant segment of its life, but in those subsequent segments in which, as the result of the ministrations of its parents or of any others who substitute for them, the development in some substantial measure of the agency and understanding of persons takes place. It is, then, by virtue of the future in the case of infants, just as it is by virtue of the past of those now incapacitated by an enduring lack of consciousness that precedes their death, that we count them as persons despite the radical deficiencies with respect to features requisite for the possession of rights of such human beings—persons—during their then present segments of their lives.

VIII

Given the nature of our human existence—the extraordinarily varied conditions and situations of the members of our species—we should be prepared for indefinitely many different sorts of cases which pose problems, practical or theoretical, when we consider how far they depart from those central sorts of cases to which the full and complicated array of concepts, in which the concept of rights is embedded, apply unproblematically and without truncation. At what stage in the history of the development of a fertilized human ovum shall we say that we have a human being with rights? The practical necessity of making a legal judgment cannot be resolved by the philosophical reminder that there may be no sharp line that can be drawn to mark off personhood from non-personhood. Decisions must be made, and so lines must be drawn, with all due respect to the necessity of weighing this fact in determining the degrees of fault and liability. And there are other cases as well in which we are faced with a spectrum of cases, where mental and bodily abnormality defeat any effort to draw a sharp line between the human and non-human. Nature does not present us with persons cast from certain fixed molds, and non-persons from still others; and decisions in our practical affairs and in our legal judgments must be made, by courts and administrators, among others, whether in this or that extreme and deviant case, an individual is to receive the treatment accorded normal human beings. But however imperative it may be for some practical purposes to make decisions of this sort, we ought to resist the temptation to give a flat-out answer to the question that might be posed about every borderline case whether or not there is a being who counts morally as a person with rights. For the features relevant to the ascription of rights may be far too removed from those present in normal cases to warrant any substantive appeal to rights in justifying the moral stance we adopt towards some of these unfortunates; yet there will be enough, independently of any consideration of rights, fully to justify us in the moral treatment we give them. For we shall be able to deal responsibly with such extreme cases though we may not be accountable to these unfortunates nor, since they are so far removed from us in their mode of life, to anyone who could reasonably be thought to act in their interests.

NOTES

[1] There are many sorts of reasons for 'punishing' criminals; indeed, the term 'punishment' covers a nest of varying but related concepts. In the remarks made above, I have concerned myself with punishment understood simply as those measures designed to purge criminals of their guilt. But there are many other reasons for confining wrongdoers. But confinement, whether or not it serves or is even designed to serve the purpose of restoring, through atonement, expiation, or rehabilitation in any other way, does limit the freedom and abridge the right even a wrongdoer has as a human being.

[2] *Second Treatise of Civil Government*, ch. II.

[3] Cf. *The Leviathan*, pt. 2, ch. 21, p. 112 of the Everyman's edition.

[4] *The Second Treatise of Civil Government*, ch. II.

[5] Cf. Herbert Morris, 'Persons and Punishment', *The Monist*, 52, no. 4 (October 1968), reprinted in among other volumes, *Human Rights*, ed. A. I. Melden, Wadsworth Publishing Co., Belmont, CA, 1970.

[6] Cf. Stuart M. Brown, Jr., 'Inalienable Rights', *The Philosophical Review*, vol. 64, no. 2 (April 1955), pp. 192–211.

[7] See my introductory essay in *Human Rights*, Wadsworth Publishing Company, Belmont, CA, 1970.

[8] More on this matter—the appeal to human rights in support of individual and social programs of action in a complex modern society—in the next chapter.

[9] I am indebted to Prof. D. Z. Phillips for referring me to this way of dealing with the paradox, by Simone Weil, whose view on this matter is discussed sympathetically by Peter Winch, in *Ethics and Action*, pp. 197 ff. and later on pp. 219 ff.

[10] It is the fact that the rationality involved in the Moral Law, as Kant sees it, is formal and as such far removed from the reasonableness that marks the thought and action of responsible agents that accounts for one's shock in reading H. J. Paton's endorsement of Kant's view in *The Categorical Imperative*, Hutchinson's University Library, London, 1946, 'It is fundamentally immoral to regard killing as a special privilege of my own from which other men are excluded.' (p. 70) As if the immorality of killing a person can be dealt with on all fours with arbitrarily making an exception for oneself by

walking on a lawn from which pedestrians are barred for good utilitarian reasons!

[11] Cf. 'Justice and Equality' by Gregory Vlastos in *Social Justice*, ed. by R. B. Brandt, Prentice-Hall, Inc., Englewood Cliffs, 1962. The parenthetical remark is mine. The passage quoted is from the *Critique of Practical Reason*, tr. by L. W. Beck, University of Chicago Press, Chicago, Ill., 1949, p. 185.

[12] Loc. cit.

[13] In a footnote that appears only in the reprinting of his essay in *Human Rights*, ed. A. I. Melden, Wadsworth Publishing Co., Belmont, California, 1970, p. 95.

[14] Ibid., p. 94.

[15] Ibid., p. 92.

[16] See the remark of Frederick Douglass, the pre-Civil War black, quoted in Chapter I (p. 23).

[17] Cf. *The Politics*, 1255a, trans. by Ernest Barker, New York and London: Oxford University Press, 1958, p. 14.

[18] For case of young infants, see the discussion below on pp. 220–3.

[19] See William and Joan McCord, *The Psychopath*, Princeton: Van Nostrand, 1964, pp. 85–7.

[20] This is true even in the extraordinary case of one whose cerebral functions have terminated irreversibly, and who can be kept alive only by the continued use of complex medical technology. The decision to end that impoverished existence of the person by pulling the plug that sustains his life is one that is made, not in the way in which this may be done in the case of an animal, but with compunction and out of respect for him as a person whose existence as a living vegetable is one that is incompatible with any dignity he has as a human being.

field of law so that, as Barker puts it, 'just as the parts in a play are created and assigned by the dramatists, so . . . *personae* in law are created and assigned by similar agencies' in the state.[2] Some writers, on this ground, have been led to the view that there is a fictitious element embodied in legal personhood. It has been supposed that just as the *dramatis persona* that appears on the stage is the fiction created by the dramatist's imagination, so the legal person that appears in court—the right-and-duty bearing entity—is the fabrication of those agencies of the state that produce the laws; and hence the 'real' individual with his biological and psychological makeup, no more makes his appearance in court than does the real person on the stage who is concealed by the mask or the stage-dress and makeup he wears.[3]

We should be on our guard, however, against supposing, because the term 'person' which occurs in the law was borrowed from the language of the theatre, that the conceptual features of the term remained unchanged in its new application. Plays are the creations of playwrights and so too are the characters they delineate, and the laws are the products of human activity and so too are the legal persons with the rights and duties the laws assign to them. But it does not follow that just as plays and the characters are in some sense fictitious, so too are the laws and the legal personages that they establish. Nor does it follow, because the real individual is hidden behind the mask he wears on the stage, that the 'real' individual who counts as a legal person when he appears in court does not make his appearance when he pleads his case in court and claims his legal rights. And nowhere is this kind of mistake more mischievous in the confusions it fosters than in the claim often casually made and never supported by any argument that, because the concept of rights in the sphere of law presupposes the existence of legal principles and statutes, the modern conception of rights in the field of morals, which appears in Locke among other writers, and which also represents a borrowing from the sphere of civil and canon law, likewise presupposes the existence of moral laws or principles by virtue of which moral persons correspondingly are invested with their moral rights.

Natural law theory comes to mind immediately when this kind of analogy is drawn; but neither in the Stoic conception of a natural law that contrasts with the positive laws of Athens or Rome, nor in the Aquinian natural law that may render null and void as law the statutes of particular states, is there any intimation of the moral rights with which Locke among others was concerned. Locke himself is not free from obscurity on this point. 'The state of nature,' he tells us, 'has a law of nature to govern it, which obliges everyone; and reason, which is that law, teaches all mankind who will but consult it, that, being all equal and independent, no one ought to harm another in his life, health, liberty and possessions.'[4] And in that state of nature in which, according to Locke, persons are bound by the laws of nature and exist in perfect equality, each has 'a power to execute that law . . . and may punish another for any evil he has done', although he goes on to say that no one has an

arbitrary power, to use a criminal, i.e. one who has offended against the laws of nature, when he has got him in his hands, according to the passionate heats or boundless extravagance of his own will; but only to retribute to him so far as calm reason and conscience dictate what is proportionate to his transgression, which is so much as may serve for reparation and restraint.[5]

But while Locke maintains that men have rights in the state of nature and implies that they do so because of the laws of nature, 'and reason which is that law', he does not attempt to show, by pursuing any analogy between the laws of nature and the laws of a state, which assign rights and duties to persons, how this is so. Neither does he attempt to show what surely is a quite different matter, namely, how these laws of nature may be identified with the requirements of reason itself. Indeed, when he explicitly argues for the natural or fundamental moral rights of persons, to property, life and liberty, he appeals not to the laws of nature (which elsewhere he takes to be ordinances of God) but to considerations of a quite different nature. He appears to regard it as intuitively self-evident that 'every man has a property in his own person' to which 'nobody has any right . . . but himself'. In the same vein he declares the 'the labour of his body and the work of his hands we may say are properly his'.[6] And by mixing his labor with anything that God has given to all men in common, he makes the result his, 'i.e. a part of him'[7] and hence that in which he has a property right.

Now by 'being given to all men in common' did Locke intend that God has conferred upon men a collective ownership of all of the things in the state of nature? One might well think not, for this would seem to preclude the acquisition of a right of private property, by the method indicated, to anything thus given to all men in common. Yet his words, if not his meaning, are clear enough.[8] In any case, what he intended is that each man is free, unless a private property right has been acquired by the appropriate means by someone else, to acquire a private property right for himself.

Much more problematic is the idea that a man's property is that which is a part of himself and therefore his. A man's aches and pains are his, and so are his life and liberty and any part of his person; but are we to say that because the possessive pronoun can be applied to all of these entities that they are his property? Even more obscure is the talk about mixing one's labor with things and thereby making them 'parts' of oneself. Labor is hardly like the sugar or cream that one mixes or puts into a pudding; and, if it were, then it would appear that one should lose one's labor and hence divest one's self of the labor that allegedly is 'part' of one by mixing it into an object one does not own, as much so as one would lose the sugar or cream one owned by mixing it, by mistake, into someone else's pudding. And what can be meant by this talk that one's labor, life, liberty are all 'parts' of one's self or person? These obscurities and confusions are only compounded by Locke when he remarks that the labor of one's servant who makes the turf he cuts one's own by the mixing of the servant's labor into the turf, as if there were some sort of transitivity in the method by which the turf became the master's property without it being the case that the servant had acquired any property right for himself on the ground, presumably, that the labor of the servant was not 'really' his.[9]

But, setting aside all of these obscurities and confusions, it is the conception of a person as a rational being who for whatever reason this may be has a right to his own person, which carries the burden of Locke's argument for the fundamental moral rights to life, liberty and property. There is no appeal to the laws of nature—the divine ordinances, commandments or laws of the deity—as indeed there should be if the analogy of moral with legal rights had been uppermost in Locke's mind. And although there remains a faint echo of natural law theory in Locke's remark, when he discusses the identity of persons, that 'person' is a 'forensic term, appropriating actions and their merits; and so belongs only to intelligent agents, capable of a law';[10] the conception of a moral right that is instanced in the natural rights of persons, involves a substantial conceptual change or advance, the extent of which Locke himself may not have fully appreciated, from the legal conception of rights that had been employed earlier in the field of law. What is importantly different, obscure and imperfect as his account of the matter is in Locke's conception of the fundamental rights of persons, is that these can be viewed as grounded, not in principles on the analogy with legal statutes, human or divine, but in the moral status of agents, however much that status may depend in its turn upon the agency of God, constrained as this may have been by reason itself.

The extent to which a philosopher may be insensible of the conceptual changes involved in his own thinking, this time a change in the opposite direction from that represented in Lockean doctrine, ironically enough is illustrated in the case of that stalwart advocate of the rights of man: Kant. For in his account of the fundamental principle of morality, the Moral Law, which is the last modern echo of natural law theory, and in which sovereign reason replaces sovereign deity, the considerations cited by Kant pertain only to what persons must do, but no more than in the doctrine of natural law one finds in Aquinas to what it is to which persons, as rational beings, have as a matter of their right.

If, as we have argued, there is the conceptual change involved in the Lockean doctrine of fundamental moral rights, then it is indeed a mistake to assimilate the modern Lockean doctrine of fundamental moral rights with earlier natural law theory. For there is no mention of moral rights in the account of natural law that one finds, for example, in the writings of Aquinas. But if the doctrine of natural law is to provide a basis for natural moral rights, the analogy of natural with civil and canon law must be preserved. And no such analogy is drawn by Locke. What plays the decisive role, in Locke's thinking, is the concept of a person as a moral agent, not divine ordinances comparable to the statutes of civil society which assign rights to legal personages. But there also is an important philosophical mistake, and no mere mistake about matters of historical fact, which is involved in the attempt to view moral rights on the analogy with legal rights, on the ground that the moral concept represents a borrowing in the field of morals from the use of the term 'right' in civil and canon law, or statutes that assign rights to members of civil and ecclesiastical bodies, namely, that there must be moral principles that establish or assign moral rights to human beings. But we need no such principles; we need nothing more than the concept of persons, whose features as the moral agents they are suffice for the possession by them of their fundamental moral rights, features which enable them to join their lives with one another as they go about their affairs.

II

But while there are radically new elements to be found in the theory of natural rights for which Locke was the chief spokesman, that theory in its own way is too much a creature of its time to serve as an acceptable model for us today. It was remarked in the preceding chapter that during the course of the moral development of an individual there is an interplay between conceptual development and appreciation or awareness of relevant matters of fact, so that as individuals become more sensitive to the interests and concerns of others there are not only changes in moral judgments, i.e. in judgments of the rightness and wrongness of acts, but changes in moral concepts.[11] A similar conceptual development has taken place because of the radical changes in the circumstances of human life, which have occurred since Locke's own time, as the result of which neither the moral judgments he expressed nor the very moral concepts he employed have remained unaffected.

In the rapidly developing mercantile society of his time, the chief danger, as Locke and those for whom he spoke saw it, lay not in the abuses by individuals of their powers as they sought to acquire and improve their estates, but in the abuses by the sovereign of the manifest power he has over his subjects. In the state of nature each man, Locke tells us, is king, 'absolute lord of his own person and possessions, equal to the greatest and subject to nobody' but so insecure for want of 'an established, settled known law, received and allowed by common consent to be the standard of right and wrong, and the common measure to decide all controversies between them', that persons are willing to limit their freedom and join in one society with one another 'for the mutual preservations of their lives, liberties and estates' which Locke proceeds forthwith to include under the general term 'property'. In sum, 'The great and chief end, therefore, of men's uniting into commonwealths, and putting themselves under government, is the preservation of their property, to which in the state of nature there are many things wanting.'[12]

There are two points that need to be emphasized. First, Locke is not averse to accepting as morally defensible what many today would consider to be substantial inequities and even injustices. That inequalities in benefits and burdens must occur, given the differences in the circumstances and aptitudes of men, is clearly recognized by

Locke; but what may be surprising to a reader of *The Second Treatise* is the extent to which this spokesman for the equal natural rights of all men is willing to accept what we should consider today to be rank injustices. He tells us,

Master and servant are names as old as history, but given to those of far different condition; for a freeman makes himself a servant to another by selling him for a certain time the service he undertakes to do in exchange for wages he is to receive; and though this commonly puts him into the family of his master, and under the ordinary discipline thereof, yet it gives the master but a temporary power over him, and no greater than what is contained in the contract between them. But there is another class of servants, which by a peculiar name we call slaves, who being captives taken in a just war, are by the right of nature subjected to the absolute dominion and arbitrary power of their master. These men having, as I say, forfeited their lives, and with them their liberties, and lost their estates—and being, in the state of slavery, not capable of any property—cannot in that state be considered as any part of civil society, the chief end whereof is the preservation of property.[13]

An apologist for Locke might put down these declarations, along with his implied approval here and elsewhere of capital punishment, to the fact that Locke is understandably a man of his own time, revealing here and elsewhere moral attitudes and convictions for which, however, there is no place in his own moral theory. He might attempt to defend capital punishment, for example, by seizing upon Locke's locution in the quoted passage above, and elsewhere too, 'forfeits his life' rather than 'forfeits his right to life', and maintain that the former applies to a person—one who has natural rights as a human being—whereas the latter applies to beings who, like Dr. Jekyll, having transformed himself into a subhuman Mr. Hyde, no longer is a human being with any moral rights at all. He might argue, in this vein, that someone totally and irreparably deprived of his liberty and estates, like someone irreparably deprived of his life when executed for the commission of a capital crime, loses his liberty and his estates just as someone executed loses his life, but not the rights that he has to these as the human being he is. He might point to the constraints employed in the administration of justice, remarking that in the case of capital punishment we have the execution of a criminal, one who has been held to account for his misdeed and found guilty in accordance with procedures designed to protect his basic rights. It is such a being, it might be said, who is the chief actor in the execution scene, the very impersonal and ceremonial character of which, as in other cases of punishment, is designed to serve notice upon him and everyone else that it is a person guilty of a crime who is subjected to this radical form of punishment, not mere hurt or the natural evil involved in the termination of his life, as in the case of an animal whose life one might extinguish without compunction. So one might argue that a Lockean could defend capital punishment on the ground that even here there is an important token of the respect paid to the criminal as a human being with the rights that he has as a person.

The issues involved in capital punishment, like those in the total deprivation of a man's liberty and possessions, as in the instance with which Locke is concerned in the passage quoted above, cannot be so easily resolved. For the claim that in the latter case the rights to liberty and property are preserved is surely unconvincing; it would be in fact to mock someone if one were to tell him that he has rights but no possible opportunity to exercise them, being stripped as he is of everything that would enable him to conduct himself as a human being, as much so as it would be to tell a person that he had legal rights but could not in any way avail himself of the legal procedures open to anyone else. Indeed, the issue of capital punishment raises even more serious problems. For however impersonally executions may be conducted, it does appear to many, at least, that it is cruel and unusual punishment. And if it is replied that capital punishment, terrible as it is, is the best possible symbol of the terrible deed for which it is meted out, then the reply might well be that in executing the criminal, society, in Moberly's words, 'appears to pay the murderer the compliment of imitation'.[14] Besides, it is hardly reassuring to the criminal to tell him that it is only his life that is being taken away from him, not his right, as if this allegedly inviolable right that he has to his life and person could remain intact and exist *in vacuo* at the conclusion of the grisly ceremony.

But even if one were in this way to try to dispel our doubts about the morality of capital punishment or the total deprivation of liberty and possessions imposed upon those who have participated in unjust wars, one must remain appalled by the practices of slavery and indenture. The indenture of a servant, Locke tells us, 'commonly puts him into the family of his master' (paragraph 85), subject to the latter's will; but this reminds us of the talk that was, or should have been, laid to rest with the Victorians about the superiority and inferiority of different classes of persons. For the indentured person subject by the terms of his contract to the beck and call of his master, is no mere employee who sells only his labor and remains on terms of moral equality with his employer by virtue of the rights he has in common with the latter; he sells himself into a bondage, temporary as it may be, that demeans his status as a person. And someone who has participated in an unjust war remains a person, perhaps to be punished for his complicity in the crimes of his leaders (although the issues here, as in the case of capital punishment, are complex and cannot be dealt with in the simple summary fashion indicated by Locke without attending, among other factors, to the inherent difficulties involved in determining complicity, crime, or jurisdiction). But such a person is hardly one who, as Locke thinks, may be enslaved and subjected to 'the absolute dominion and arbitrary power' of the victor. Slavery is the condition of one who, while in that condition, may be dealt with kindly and made comfortable in his lodging by a compassionate owner, but not as a human being who is concerned and accountable and to whom punishment might be meted out in order that he may expiate his guilt and redeem himself as a member in good standing of the moral community of persons. To punish someone, as we employ the term, without the scare quotes we employ when we talk about 'punishing' a cat or a dog that has deposited its litter on the living room rug, is not to train, hurt or condition; nor is it to threaten him with what lies in store for him should he repeat his objectionable performance. In its own way, punishment, when it is conceptually linked with the guilt of those who as moral agents are accountable, is a token of the respect we pay those upon whom it is imposed because of their status as persons with rights. What is radically offensive about slavery is not the lack of well-being occasioned in its victims but the treatment given the persons who are its moral victims as if they were mere chattel with whom no moral relations are possible.

Flawed as Locke's views were concerning slavery, capital punishment and the treatment to be given indentured servants, this, one might suppose, represents his failure to appreciate the implications of his own moral theory. In principle, this sort of thing is possible; a moral philosopher might display a moral callousness of which he himself may be unaware in the examples he uses in drawing altogether unobjectionable philosophical conclusions. And Locke does often write about the equality of men in the state of nature; and even when (in paragraph 54) he speaks about the 'just preference' that some may have over others by virtue of their age, merit, birth, alliances, etc., the idea advanced that these circumstances may warrant differences in the ways in which persons are to be treated in civil society is hardly the sort of thing involved in a demeaning servitude or slavery. Yet even here we need to be careful lest in thus making out a case for Locke we misconstrue Locke's meaning when he speaks about equality and just preference. For by the equality that applies to men in the state of nature, he does *not* intend that *de facto* equality in ability, strength, intelligence, etc., that Hobbes unwisely attributes to men in the state of nature, the consequence of which for Hobbes is the interminable warfare in which no one is able to gain and preserve the upper hand over others, and in that way alone bring violence to an end. Nor does he mean that moral equality that consists in the possession by all men of the same natural rights; for he intends, rather, something that is a consequence of this fact. What he intends is that in the situation in which there is no civil society and no common power authorized by the express or tacit consent of persons to impose measures protective of their rights and measures designed to punish, and to secure reparation from, those responsible for their violation, each man is as authorized as anyone else by the rights he has in common with everyone else to take whatever measures are needed to protect himself, and, in the event his rights are violated, to secure redress and reparation and to impose punishment upon the malefactor. And as for the just precedence of which he speaks, this is a rejection of an egalitarianism which would distribute benefits and burdens in such a way that all would have equal portions—a view that might be rejected not only on the ground that some deserve more (or less) than others because of the differences in their merit, but also on other grounds as well, among them the fact that some have special rights against others to benefits of one sort or another. The differences in the treatment of persons with which we are concerned are not those involving inequalities in the distribution of benefits and burdens, but inequities, and more particularly those which result from the social injustices to which men are prone, and to which Locke, like his contemporaries and most who have succeeded them in the intervening centuries, have been insensible or indifferent: the injustices that stem from the accidental advantages that some enjoy over others because of their superior intelligence, social and economic position, education, etc. These advantages, given the competition for goods, give rise to abuses that can only be described as injustices.

Still, a defender of Lockean doctrine may claim, all that this shows is that we are more sensible today than was Locke of the extent of social evil, that it is not limited to that tyranny with which in the main he was concerned. And is this not due, after all, to the fact that we have a better sense of what is implied by his own doctrine of equal natural rights? I shall argue that there is a fallacy involved in this defense, the failure to recognize that hand in hand with this heightened moral sensitivity to social injustice there has been an important change in our moral concepts. This in fact is the second of the points alluded to early in this section, namely, that in thinking as many do today that certain sorts of deprivation of benefits have been suffered by those who are disadvantaged by the accidents of fortune, we think that there has occurred a deprivation of certain fundamental rights persons have as human beings. And in so thinking an important change in our moral concepts has taken place. As in the case of the moral development of a child when its moral concepts change along with the change that occurs in its sensitivities to other persons, so in the case of those of us who have been increasingly concerned with the chronic social evils of modern societies, conceptual changes have occurred. To see how this is so, we need to look more closely at some of the features of Locke's concept of natural rights.

III

It is a familiar view that Locke's natural rights are really only the liberties that persons have to go about their affairs without interference from others. It might be thought, therefore, that Locke's natural rights are what Hohfeld and others have preferred to call privileges or liberties, on the ground that in cases in which a person has these so-called rights, nothing is implied with respect to anyone else other than the fact that he has no right to interfere.[15] Here is one example: the right one has to smoke a cigar as he sits in the privacy of his study; this right imposes no duty to smoke, and anyone else has no right to interfere if, mistakenly, he thinks that smoking cigars are not good for one. Another example: One has the right to take a hot bath in order to soothe one's aching back, this being something one ought in fact to do for good medical reasons (although saying that it is one's duty to do so would normally be stretching the point out of shape); but the right is nonetheless a matter with respect to which others have no right to butt in.

This, however, misrepresents Locke's thought. There is no reason to suppose that on Locke's account it is ever implied, in the event someone's life is in jeopardy, when overcome by a muscle cramp while swimming, that there is no obligation on the part of anyone else to come to his aid. And any thought that on his account of the matter it would be in order for a would-be murderer to complain to someone coming to the aid of his quarry that he had no right to interfere, and no obligation to his intended victim, is explicitly denied by him. We are, he tells us, 'the workmanship of one omnipotent and infinitely wise Maker—all the servants of one sovereign Master, sent into the world by His order, and about his business—His property . . . made to last during His, not one another's pleasure', and none of us therefore has any right to take his own life as one might smoke a cigar if it pleases one to do so. Indeed, he goes on to say, 'everyone as he is bound to preserve himself, and not to quit his station willfully, so, by the like reason, when his own preservation comes not in competition, ought he, as much as he can, to preserve the rest of mankind', this being an obligation that anyone has to anyone else.[16] Yet many a reader of Locke, for whom Locke's natural rights have seemed to be no more than liberties, have dismissed his explicit remark on this point on the ground that it does not jibe with the general line of thought he adopts for the right to property, where he does in fact emphasize the importance of noninterference from others. But it is important to set the record straight, to see how far this is so, lest we draw the corresponding conclusion, absurd as it may strike us, that on Locke's view, a spectator who discovers a burglary in progress in his neighbor's house is under no obligation to his neighbor to interfere with the burglar's endeavors. Let us turn, therefore, to Locke's text in order that we may determine how far, if at all, we can employ the model of privileges or liberties in grasping Locke's concept of natural rights.

Locke tells us that in the state of nature there is lacking adequate security in one's life, liberty and possessions, given the natural aggressions to which persons are prone. There are no fixed laws for all to recognize and there are no impartial judges and administrators that serve better the interests of justice than that which persons can do on their own in protecting their rights, in obtaining redress and reparation for the wrongs they suffer at the hands of others and, indeed, in punishing malefactors. But Locke is quite explicit on the point that the obligations of persons go far beyond non-interferences in the state of nature. He tells us that if anyone suffers the violation of his rights in the state of nature he has 'a particular right to seek reparation from him who has done it. And any other person who finds it just, may also join with him who is injured, and assist him in recovering from the offender so much as may make satisfaction for the harm he has suffered.'[17] Now by 'a particular right' he means what elsewhere he labels 'power', namely, the authority one has by virtue of the natural right which in this case has been violated. And in saying that any other person may join with the injured party, Locke does not mean that he is at liberty to do so, i.e. that it is permissible and with respect to which others are obliged not to interfere. For a trespass against anyone is 'a trespass against the whole species', hence everyone has a 'right' not only to assist the injured party but to punish the offender. Indeed, this right so-called is, strictly speaking, a requirement or obligation. The relevant passages, part of which was quoted above, are to be found in paragraphs 6 and 7.

Every one, as he is bound to preserve himself, and not to quit his station wilfully, so, by the like reason, when his own preservation comes not in competition, ought he, as much as he can, to preserve the rest of mankind, and not, unless it be to do justice to an offender, take away or impair the life, or what tends to the preservation of the life, the liberty, health, limb, or goods of another.

And that all men may be restrained from invading others' rights, and from doing hurt to one another, and the law of nature be observed, which willeth the peace and preservation of all mankind, the execution of the law of nature is in that state put into every man's hand, whereby everyone has a right to punish the transgressors of that law to such a degree as may hinder its violation. For the law of nature would, as all other laws that concern men in this world, be in vain if there were nobody that, in the state of nature, had a power to execute that law, and thereby preserve the innocent and restrain offenders. And if anyone in the state of nature may punish another for any evil he has done, every one may do so. For in that state of perfect equality, where naturally there is no superiority or jurisdiction of one over another, what any may do in prosecution of that law, every one must needs have a right to do.

Men are therefore under an obligation, not only to preserve themselves but in the case of anyone else, 'as much as he can', and by his own effort as required for the purpose, to preserve that person's life, liberty and goods. And although he goes on, in the next paragraph quoted above, to speak of the *right* that a person has to punish anyone, this in fact is an understatement of the case. For it is no mere right that he has, which he may or may not exercise, but an obligation, since punishment is called for in order that men may be restrained from invading others' rights. The law of nature—the rule of right reason—requires that transgressors be punished, and since a transgression against one is a transgression against everyone, reason requires that anyone in the state of nature, as required, will join in the punishment of an offender. And by the same token, everyone is called upon, wherever needed, to assist the person injured in securing reparation for the person whose right or rights have been violated.

In the state of nature, therefore, it is no mere *non-interference* from others that is implied by the fact that a person has his natural rights, but wherever appropriate and required, *performances*. For, truistically or analytically, it is in every person's moral interest that the rights of any person are protected and safeguarded, that transgressors are punished and that they make reparation for the damage they perpetrate; and it is therefore in satisfaction of one's own moral interest that one is obliged not only not to interfere with anyone exercising his rights but to contribute by one's own performances, wherever needed and possible to the protection and safeguarding of that person's rights.

Consider now the obligations of persons in civil society, as Locke views them. Given the insecurity that would exist if men were left to their own devices in attempting to protect their rights, they consent, tacitly or expressly, to live under the common power of a civil government to which they 'give up all the power necessary to the ends for which they unite into society' (paragraph 99), namely, the protection and safeguarding of their rights.

Political power is that power which every man having in the state of nature, has given up into the hands of the society, and therein to the governors whom the society has set over itself, with this express or tacit trust that it shall be employed for their good and the preservation of their property. Now this power, which every man has in the state of nature, and which he parts with to the society in all such cases where the society can secure him, is to use such means for the preserving of his own property as he thinks good and nature allows him, and to punish the breach of the law of nature in others so as, according to the best of his reason, may most conduce to the preservation of himself and the rest of mankind. So that the end and measure of this power, when in every man's hands in the state of nature, being the preservation of all of his society—that is, all mankind in general—it can have no other end or measure when in the hands of the magistrates but to preserve the members of that society in their lives, liberties and possessions . . . a power to make laws, and annex such penalties to them as may tend to the preservation of the whole . . . And this power hath its original only from compact and agreement, and the mutual consent of those who make up the community.[18]

Several comments are in order. First, the *sole* end of the power of which individuals divest themselves and transfer to the government is the preservation of the members of society 'in their lives, liberties and possessions'. Second, it is the power, i.e. the authority provided by their natural rights, not their natural rights, that are transferred to the government; men retain their natural rights in civil society. Third, Locke nowhere declares that men divest themselves of *all* of their power by transferring it to the government. That would in fact be absurd, since they would then have rights without any power or authority, including the authority they have, in the event governments breach their trust, to seek and obtain redress for their grievances. The power men transfer to the government is 'all the power *necessary* (italics mine) to the ends for which they unite in society' (paragraph 99); and that is the power to establish, administer and enforce laws the purpose of which is to serve the moral interests of subjects, including the interest all men have by virtue of the natural rights they have in common that the violation of anyone's right by anyone else will be rectified by reparation from and proper punishment imposed upon the transgressor. This does not mean that those who have suffered injury will be passive in the face of the transgressions of others. They retain the power to demand reparation from the transgressor, and if this is not forthcoming they have the power, in accordance with procedures established by the government, to solicit the aid of the government to whom they have transferred the power they have in the state of nature in order to secure reparation and to punish those who have injured them.

Nor does it follow from Locke's account that the right of anyone to life, liberty and possessions, does not impose obligations upon others to provide whatever succor and assistance they can offer those whose lives are being threatened by armed thugs or whose homes are being burgled. Indeed, it would have been inconsistent, not to say preposterous, for Locke to have suggested that in the face of such threatened violations of the natural rights of persons, others must do nothing and wait helplessly for the authorities to provide assistance and relief.

Neither in the state of nature nor in civil society are the natural rights which Locke ascribes to any person to be understood as mere liberties with respect to which others have only an obligation not to interfere with their enjoyment and exercise.

IV

But while, strictly speaking, Locke's natural rights should not be construed as mere liberties—for these rights call for performances, not mere abstentions, as their correlative obligations—the performances, by individuals or by governments are mainly protective measures, the purpose of which is to enable individuals to secure the goods their own endeavors make possible. Locke refers on a number of occasions to the public good served by governments and he does include under the authority entrusted to governments, through tacit or express consent of the governed, the authority to establish, administer and enforce legislation designed to facilitate the preservation, acquisition, transfer and exchange of property. But the public good served by the exercise of political power, which he tells us is 'the right of making laws with penalties of death, and consequently all less penalties, for the regulation and preserving of property, and of employing the force of the community in the execution of such laws and in the defense of the commonwealth from foreign injury' (paragraph 3), is the good achieved by individuals through their own unobstructed individual efforts. And the intent of such exercises of political authority is to provide individuals with a protective umbrella under which, freed from the interferences of others, individuals and groups of individuals with their own special interests may employ the procedures established for the regulation of property, together with the threat of the coercive power of government, with a maximum degree of liberty in pursuing their property interests. Given the natural inequalities of individuals in respect of inherited wealth, economic and social position, educational advantages and intelligence, the net effect of such legislation and enforcement is in fact to enable those who are advantaged to improve their estates in ways that are not available to the disadvantaged. But the thinking implicit in the restriction of the authority of governments to the establishment of protective measures for the unhindered endeavors of individuals to preserve and to improve their estates is that even in a society in which there is competition for the goods available to human beings, just as in the idyllic situation supposedly extant in a far-off America where a man need only clear the land and gather its produce in order to enjoy the fruits of his labor, persons have only themselves to blame because of their indolence and lack of initiative if they fail to enjoy the property to which they, like their more enterprising fellows, would be entitled by the expenditure of their labor. And if those who prosper, and supposedly because of their own superior merit, assist those in need, they do so out of sheer generosity or charity.

It is not too long ago—less than a century in fact—that courts in America, in one case after another, ruled that legislation designed to abolish child labor or to provide sweatshop employees with the right to bargain collectively so that they might work and live in ways that befit human beings, is in violation of constitutional natural rights (Lockean in conception), on the ground that such legislation constitutes unwarranted interferences with the liberties of persons to pursue their own fortunes by imposing undue restrictions in the contractual arrangements that employers can enter into with employees. And much more recently in the black ghettos in America, where individuals have been and still are deprived of a variety of opportunities to live in ways to which human beings are entitled—long after it has been generally recognized that it is the obligation of the government, in order to accord human beings their rights as persons, to take positive or affirmative action in matters of health, education and welfare—those who suffer from the discriminatory practices that have penned them within ghettos as social and moral outcasts, have often adopted an attitude towards the law and the institutions of government—which as they see them operate only to protect the lives, liberties and properties of those who are advantaged—which is the mirror-image of the one generally adopted outside the ghetto. To such unfortunates who are deprived by their race, lack of education and training, by their poverty and absence of available transportation that would enable anyone who might happen to be qualified to enjoy the superior facilities and employment opportunities that exist outside the ghetto, the law and the institutions of government, which often seem to them to serve as protective umbrellas for the endeavors of the advantaged, take on the aspects of instruments for their continued oppression. And it is with a view towards meeting the obligations correlative with the rights of human beings that positive measures in a variety of respects have been taken in recent years by government, social groups and individuals. One recent indication of the radical change that has occurred in the conception of the rights of persons from the one presented by and inherited in seventeenth- and eighteenth-century America from Locke, is the incident that occurred recently in the Watts district of Los Angeles where individuals and civic groups concerned with the human rights of those living there complained that the practice of banks operating in Watts of refusing to lend its residents funds for the improvements of their homes and the operation of their small business enterprises constituted, in their opinion, a violation of fundamental human rights. And it is indicative of the full circle that has been made in the conception of human rights, in no small measure because of the dramatic protests occurring in recent decades against various forms of social injustice that, despite muted voices defending the discriminatory practice on the ground of the right to freedom of enterprise, the injustice of the practice was conceded by many and even by some bankers themselves.

Those on whose behalf Locke wrote in advancing his doctrine of natural rights, living as they did in a society marked by sharp class distinctions, and in which brutal repressive measures were commonplace and served only to dull their own moral sensibilities, ignored the grinding poverty and misery of members of the lower classes. Given their moral myopia they thought that natural rights require, for those who are responsible and law-abiding and who have not forfeited their liberties, goods or lives through misconduct, in the main only those measures that facilitate their commerce with one another and protect them from the aggressions of others. But it has become painfully evident that in a complex and highly competitive industrial society much more is required in order to safeguard human rights than measures that protect the interests of the advantaged, measures which succeed only in enabling those favored by the accidents of birth and fortune to employ their superior abilities and opportunities to improve their estates to the neglect and even at the expense of others. We now recognize, many or most of us at least, that the obligations imposed upon governments, civic groups and individuals, in recognition of the fundamental moral rights of all persons is to seek to reduce the effects of the natural inequalities among persons, effects which if allowed to go unchecked would deprive many of the rights they have as human beings.

This, to a defender of Lockean theory, might appear to be not a matter calling for a revision of our concept of human rights, but only for the proper implementation of that doctrine. It might appear, in other words, that all we need do is to recognize the facts about modern human life, namely, that Locke's rights to life, liberty and property, which all men supposedly have, can be enjoyed only if social welfare programs of one sort or another are undertaken to even out the crippling effects of the inequalities that operate to deprive many of their rights. But the concept of a right cannot be divorced from the array of concepts in which it has its place. In particular, the concept of a right cannot be severed from the concept of a being who is responsible in ways that are appropriate to his nature as a human being in the circumstances in which he conducts his life. And here it is that Locke's moral individualism, implicit in his treatment of natural rights, is relevant, the view that persons, living as they do in a world with expanding and virtually limitless opportunities for the advancement of their fortunes, can, by their own efforts and enterprise, carve out riches for themselves by expending their labor, and have only themselves to blame if they do not avail themselves of the opportunities that lie before them. Given the circumstances in which we live today, it has become clear that much more than the efforts of individuals are required if they are to enjoy the rights that they have. For the extent to which individuals may be held accountable for their own failures to make good their aspirations has narrowed sharply as we have become increasingly aware of the crippling effects of a wide variety of factors: poverty, the dissolution of family life this often produces, the blight, including the moral blight that results from the lack of the education and training essential for the development of individuals if they are to be equipped for responsible life in a complex industrial society; physical and mental disease that may incapacitate them and in varying degrees prevent them from conducting themselves with others in responsible ways; the institutions of criminal justice and punishment that often compound the problems of enforcement and rehabilitation created by acute poverty and its attendant ills, and so on. In short, the conception we have of a person as a moral agent who, in Locke's own phrase, is concerned and accountable, has been materially altered with the change that has taken place in our understanding of the nature and circumstances of moral personhood.

We now have a much better conception of what is involved in the idea of a person as a moral agent, of the extent to which he may or may not be accountable for his actions, given the many factors that may serve to mitigate and void the charge of moral fault. And, further, nowhere has the change in moral concepts more conspicuously reflected the change in relevant matters of human fact than in the concept of a human right. For that concept is not, as the idealists put it, an abstract universal, some eternal object that is unrelated to the structure of our moral concepts and to those concerns of ours during our commerce with one another, but one to be employed by human beings in the concrete circumstances of their lives. It is for this reason that a human right—or, to use a term replete with older and now obsolete suggestions, a natural right—is no longer conceived as one with respect to which the obligations of others in governments, civic groups and as individuals consists mainly in adopting such measures as enable those fortunate enough, because of their opportunities and abilities, to engage in those ventures that will improve their estates, free from the aggressive interferences of others. The character of the obligations correlative with a right reflects, from the point of view of those who must respect it, the nature of the right itself. Our concept of a human right differs, therefore, from that of Locke since, for reasons now familiar and evident to all, the obligation a human right imposes upon others, goes far beyond the establishment of those limited measures envisaged by Locke.

V

Yet our own account of the fundamental rights of persons may well appear to be as defective as Locke's. For the right of an agent to pursue his interests might appear to require on the part of others only abstentions from interferences with his activities together with whatever protective measures are necessary in order to permit him to go about his affairs, without coercion, in pursuing and achieving his goods. But if we think of this fundamental human right, the importance of which has been emphasized in the account we have given of the moral relations between persons, as such a circumscribed right, this is due to our preoccupation with cases like those in which *we* normally are involved. *We* have been favored by the conditions of our own nurture in developing interests that go far beyond those possible for persons living on the fringes of our society whose poverty is so extreme that they must devote all their ingenuity and efforts to eke out a bare subsistence for themselves. *We* are favored by the opportunities and abilities we enjoy to cultivate the interests we have acquired in making our own way in the circumstances in which we live, joining our lives with others with whom we conduct our affairs in carrying out our plans and projects. And unless in *our* activities there are special rights and obligations which impose constraints upon our conduct and the conduct of others who are morally bound to us, the obligations of others with respect to us are, normally, the abstentions from interfering with us as we pursue our interests and realize for ourselves the goods these define. Yet even *we*, favored by fortune as we are, require on occasion, even when there are no special moral relations in which we stand to others, the help and assistance that they can give us when, because of unexpected circumstances, their positive contributions are necessary, if our lives and the integrity of our persons are to be preserved.

For even *we*, relatively favored as we are, are subject to illnesses and misfortunes; and for many of us who survive the natural hazards that threaten all of us, there are, in addition, unemployment and the infirmities of old age that may prevent us, in the absence of the assistance needed from others, from maintaining our integrity and dignity as human beings. It is only if we restrict our attention to quite special cases in which a relatively favored few are involved, that the right of a person to pursue his interests appears to require, as its correlative obligation, only abstentions on the part of others.

Rights are grounds for action; but their infringement may be required when, to consider only one type of case, persons are punished for their misdeeds. But punishment, distressing as it may be, is not abuse or degradation. In its full-blooded and most desirable form it is the means adopted in order to purge persons of their guilt so that they may resume their membership, in good standing, in the moral community. But the term 'punishment', applied as it is to a wide variety of cases in which measures of one sort or another are employed, and for quite different sorts of reasons, covers a nest of related concepts. Yet no punishment which is imposed, even on those who cannot be redeemed, and only in order to protect others, may ignore human rights. For even the preventive confinement of those likely to harm others, while it does restrict their freedom, and while it does infringe on their right as human beings to pursue their interests and achieve the goods these define, cannot or may not be imposed in such a manner as to brush aside their rights as human beings, even within the limitations imposed by their confinement, to live in ways that befit human beings. Even such persons may not be caged like wild beasts, comfortable as these may be in their restricted environment. But a confinement that serves no useful purpose, one that denies persons the right they have to acceptable and nutritious food, to clothing and shelter, and to the natural and social conditions of mental and bodily health, is a violation of their rights as human beings. One aids and abets this moral crime against persons if one acquiesces in those practices and social arrangements the known effect of which is to preclude the development, in those who must endure them as they grow into adulthood, of the interests that others in more favorable circumstances have, and the opportunities and the abilities to achieve for themselves the goods that these define. It would be incoherent to ascribe the right to pursue one's interests to such persons while conceding that in the circumstances in which they live, the only interests they can acquire because of their poverty, disease, lack of education and training, and the discrimination they suffer at the hands of those who are more fortunate, are the interests of social outcasts, who are resentful of their degradation and determined, whatever the cost to others may be, to fend for themselves and without regard for the rights of others. And if somehow and on occasion such persons manage to avoid this bitterness towards the society from which effectively they have been excluded, along with the mirror-image view they have acquired of the morality and the institutions of society, and aspire therefore to better their condition and enter the mainstream of society, they lack opportunities and abilities to make good their ambitions, for themselves and for those whom they love. In such circumstances the deficiencies in the stage setting essential to any exercise of the rights such persons have as human beings are of such a radical nature that it would be cruel mockery to tell them that they have rights, just as it would be mockery to appoint a person vice-president of a firm while making it quite clear to him that he must continue in his subservient and menial role within the establishment. A right that cannot play a role in the moral lives of persons is as empty as an office in an institutional arrangement which carries with it no distinctive duties or entitlements.

If persons have the right as moral agents to pursue their interests, a setting that is appropriate to this right is called for, one in which it is possible for persons to enjoy the moral equality guaranteed by this right, along with the implied authority it provides those who possess it to go about their affairs with a dignity secured by the understanding of all concerned that those who breach this right will be held to account by those who suffer the moral injury. This normative status of persons imposes the obligation upon all who are able to do so to contribute by means of their performances to the realization, wherever it is wanting, of the setting required for the enjoyment of the moral equality that persons are denied. For those who, given the radical inequalities that deprive them of the familiar interests of persons who are more advantaged than they are and the opportunities and abilities to pursue such interests and achieve the goods they define, the particular obligation imposed upon others is, wherever possible, to remove the barriers to the development of human interests, and to contribute, as far as possible, towards developing the capacities and skills of individuals and providing opportunities for their exercise. And for those too young to have any sense of the deprivations that lie ahead for them, just as for those yet unborn who in their own time will face similarly bleak prospects for the achievement of their normative status, unless suitable measures are now taken, the obligation imposed upon us now is to do what is required in order that the appropriate setting will be there for their proper development and for the opportunities and abilities they need if they are to conduct their lives in ways that befit human beings. The fundamental human right upon which we have focussed our attention—the right of persons to pursue their interests, and in this way achieve the goods these define—is no mere liberty which calls only for abstentions on the part of others; for given the inequities that exist in any modern society—Locke's or our own—the obligation imposed upon those who are able to do so is to make special contributions in order to enable those who are disadvantaged to achieve what is rightly theirs, the enjoyment of their rights on terms of moral equality with others.

It is not only the special rights of persons, as promisees, parents, children or whatever, which call for the various forms of special consideration that is their due as the possessors of their rights. It is also the moral equality of persons—the fact that as persons they are entitled as are all persons to their lives and their persons, and to pursue interests in ways that comport with the rights of others, thereby achieving the goods that are possible for human beings— which calls for the special consideration to be given those who are denied by the crippling circumstances in which they live the possibility of enjoying their human rights and the moral equality that is theirs. There are, therefore, special moral burdens imposed upon the advantaged, because of the human rights which the disadvantaged have in common with them.

The fact that moral equality may well call for the unequal treatment of persons has been noted by others. Gregory Vlastos, in an important essay,[19] has commented that in the case of the equal right to the protection of one's life and person, the protective measures adopted will vary, given adequate resources for this purpose, with the variations in the security levels of persons. And he has generalized the point of his comment to the rights to equal freedom, noting the necessity of programs of social welfare which, clearly, are selective in respect of their beneficiaries and which are designed to remove those deprivations of the general right to freedom occasioned by destitution, racial and other forms of discrimination, lack of education, etc. But this does not imply that we must endorse what he describes as 'the most complete of currently authoritative declarations of human rights, that passed by the Assembly of the United Nations in 1948'.[20] It is not that black children living in their ghettos have as a human right the right to be transported in buses to schools in white neighborhoods, but that doing just that may well be one of the special measures required in order to help remove the impediments to the enjoyment of human rights by blacks, and whites too, by improving the education of the former and removing the prejudice and antipathy that blinds the latter to the normative status of the former. Human rights are one sort of thing and they need to be distinguished from the sorts of things, e.g. vacations with pay, employment in factories and on farms, without which they may well be unable to enjoy their human rights. For the settings in which alone human rights can be enjoyed are one thing, the special measures that must be taken to rectify deficiencies in the settings required by these human rights are another; and distinguishable from both of these matters is the moral equality of persons constituted by their common human rights. In any case, it is not on the basis of the equal *needs* of human beings and the inequalities in the means available to satisfy them, that selective and unequal treatment of persons are called for, or that it is the equal values all are capable of enjoying that morally obliges those of us who can improve matters for those less well-off than we are in the enjoyment of these values. For it is surely doubtful that the needs of all human beings are equal or that it is merely with a view to improving the well-being of others that we are obliged to launch programs of affirmative action that are selective in respect of their beneficiaries. It is on account of the *rights* of persons as human beings that we are obliged to undertake remedial and compensatory measures in order to provide the appropriate settings in which these rights may be enjoyed. Vlastos himself puts the matter well in the questions he raises: 'Is an egalitarian expected to hold that people have a right to do or to enjoy things which (by hypothesis) *they are not capable* of doing or enjoying? What would be the point of such a right?'[21]

Neither does this moral equality of all persons call for equality in the distribution of benefits and burdens. Human interests and the goods these define vary enormously from one person to another; and there are at least formidable difficulties inherent in the idea that goods as diverse as they are can somehow be balanced and measured against one another, or that burdens of indefinitely many sorts can always be measured against one another and measured also against compensating goods of whatever sorts these may be. The radical egalitarian's image of a total pie to be cut up into equal portions for all is inherently defective. But even if *per impossible*, it were possible to employ this image, this radical egalitarian proposal is neither desirable nor possible of execution. Undesirable, because of considerations of merit or desert. Some deserve more and some deserve less than others; for independently, too, of the special moral relations that mandate the special considerations to be given to the interests of those to whom we are bound by these relations, there are those who deserve the punishment that they may well receive because of their transgressions. And impossible, because of the inequalities of persons in respect of their native endowments and in the training and education that enable some, far more than others, to pursue careers that are especially rewarding—not to mention the fact that no matter how great our efforts may be to provide equal opportunities for all, unavoidably, success in the competition for goods may well result from the sheerest accident of a chance bit of information, a casual and unexpected encounter, or whatever.

How far is it possible or desirable to go in levelling out the peaks and hollows in the actual distribution of benefits and burdens, it is impossible to set forth in any precise and *a priori* fashion. There are too many variables involved, and of quite different kinds. At what point does inequality in food, clothing, and shelter, threaten the right that any person has to his person, specifically to the pursuit of his interests? There is not only no line that can be drawn for any given time, place or person, but also no uniform procedure to be followed in deciding when deprivations are morally undesirable, for whatever reason that may be, which will hold good without regard to the character of the interests, the circumstances in which individuals may freely choose to live, and the extent to which these circumstances are tolerable, given the traits and the temperaments of the individuals involved. What may be morally undesirable or intolerable in the food, shelter and clothing of an individual in a modern urban area may take on a quite different moral complexion in the case of one who chooses to live in ways that accord with his interest in living in some rural area remote from the city life he shuns or in some wilderness in which he has some particular interest. And what is morally undesirable may be so for a number of different reasons: The inequity involved in his having to do without certain amenities which others, no more meritorious than he is, are able to afford and enjoy, the lack of which, however, is not a matter of great concern to him; the tedium or dullness of an existence he would gladly do without but which he tolerates and endures; or such a condition of poverty and disease for himself and the members of his family that he and they are deprived of the opportunities and abilities to conduct themselves with dignity and on terms of moral equality with those more advantaged persons with whom they must compete for the goods that make life itself tolerable and worthwhile.

No measures of social reform can or should take account of such differences in the temper and temperaments of individuals, just as no system of law can or should trim statutory penalties to the precise degrees in the abilities of individuals to withstand temptation before they break down when the opportunities to improve their lot only by committing offenses against others are presented. The lesson here is, rather, the moral one, not to judge others less fortunate than ourselves, in circumstances or in native endowments of character, and cast them out when they have reached the breaking point, any more than we should judge those whom we love, flawed as all of these are, when they too exceed their limits and offend against us. None of us is free from fault. And very few of us are removed from all danger of temptation; in this respect the only question that arises for all but the very few is when the price is right. There is, therefore, no simple and uniform answer to the question of what our moral stance should be towards those who are weaker, more flawed and more unfortunate than we, and suffer with particular severity from the hardships they endure. What is needed here, morally speaking, is sensitivity to their plight, disturbing as this may be, compassion, and, where possible, the help we can give them.

But when poverty and illness are combined with discriminatory practices suffered—racial, religious, and educational—the effect of which is to isolate their victims and deprive them of the opportunities available to others by confining them in their ghettos, reservations and barrios, thus denying them the education (even the ability to use the language of the society in which they live, as in the case of many blacks, who on that account alone are precluded from being employed to perform any but the most menial tasks) and the skills they need in order that they may conduct their lives with others on the basis of mutual respect, the inequalities are those inequities that deprive them of the conditions or setting in which the rights they have as human beings can be enjoyed. The problems created for such persons who, by the conditions of their existence, are denied their rights as human beings, call for those programs of action which select them as their peculiar beneficiaries and which often appear to those who must provide more than an equal portion of the resources required for remedial measures, as unfair. Indeed, such measures may compromise other interests that the advantaged have—witness the concerns of university faculties and administrators who must assume special burdens in providing opportunities for the admission of those members of disadvantaged groups whose qualifications, at best, are often marginal—and they may pose difficult and hard choices that must be made. Yet the cost of ignoring the human rights of the victims of poverty and discrimination, allowing the damage that has been done to continue and to grow unchecked, is too high a price to pay, moral and social, for the protection of the special interests of the advantaged. It is too high for anyone to pay whether he be the one who suffers the isolation, or he who witnesses this evil and, like the law-abiding German who 'minded his own business' and went about his own affairs at the sight of Jews being clubbed by Nazi hoodlums, accepts and tolerates the evil visited on others only at the cost of his own moral debasement—and guilt.

NOTES

[1] In *Natural Law and the Theory of Society*, by Otto Gierke, Translator's Introduction by Ernest Barker, p. xxiii, Beacon Press, Beacon Hill, Boston, 1957.

[2] Ibid., pp. lxx–lxxi.

[3] Ibid.

[4] *Treatise of Civil Government*, ch. II, 'Of the State of Nature'.

[5] Ibid.

[6] Ibid., ch. V, para. 27.

[7] Ibid., para. 26. It is not surprising that this notion, that a man's property is his property because it has been made a 'part' of him as much so as his own person, leads Locke to extend the term 'property' to apply to 'the lives, liberties and estates of persons'. Cf. ch. IX, para. 123.

[8] On this matter, see 'Property Acquisition' by Judith Jarvis Thomson in *The Journal of Philosophy*, Vol. LXXIII, No. 18, October 21, 1976, pp. 664–6.

[9] Cf. the passage at the end of paragraph 28 in ch. V.

[10] *Essay Concerning Human Understanding*, bk. II, ch. XXVI, para. 26.

[11] See ch. VI, pp. 202–6.

[12] *Second Treatise*, ch. IX, 'Of the Ends of Political Society and Government'. The passages are quoted from paragraphs 123–5.

[13] Ch. VII, para. 85.

[14] Op. cit., p. 2.

[15] See Hohfeld in *Fundamental Legal Conceptions*, Yale University Press, New Haven, 1923.

[16] Para. 6.

[17] Para. 10.

[18] Para. 171.

[19] 'Justice and Equality', published originally in *Social Justice*, edited by R. B. Brandt, 1962, Prentice-Hall, Inc., Englewood Cliffs. This essay is reprinted with minor excisions and the addition of a

concluding footnote in *Human Rights*, ed. by A. I. Melden, 1970, Wadsworth Publishing Co., Belmont, Ca.

[20] Ibid., p. 95.

[21] Ibid., in the concluding footnote.

Index